THE DAY WAR ENDED

THE DAY WAR ENDED

VOICES AND MEMORIES FROM

1945

WEIDENFELD & NICOLSON

CONTENTS

CHAPTER 3: 'TODAY THE GUNS ARE SILENT'

FOREWORD BY DAME VERA LYNN DBE

Vera Lynn, the 'Forces' Sweetheart', was the most popular female singer during the war both on the home front and with the forces abroad, entertaining the troops with songs such as 'We'll Meet Again' and '(There'll Be Bluebirds Over) The White Cliffs Of Dover'. Her BBC Radio programme 'Sincerely Yours' became one of the most important and widely remembered broadcasts of the war years, bringing hope to servicemen and boosting the morale of the war effort. As the singer who symbolised the spirit of the British people during the war, Vera Lynn was awarded the OBE in 1969 and made a Dame of the British Empire in 1975.

Below: 'We'll Meet Again' was to become one of the most popular songs of the war years. Helping to establish Vera Lynn as the 'Forces 'Sweetheart', it also provided the title of her first feature film, released in 1942.

Right: Churchill famously told the performers of the ENSA (Entertainments National Service Association) that 'Your job is to sing while guns are firing'. Vera Lynn, here proudly wearing her uniform, was one of ENSA's most famous members.

When the war ended I felt I was just somebody who was doing a programme that went out to the forces as well as the people at home. In 1940 I had started 'Sincerely Yours' on the BBC which was broadcast to our troops abroad. I would read out messages from loved ones and I suppose I was seen as the link between all those men fighting in Europe and their wives and girlfriends back home. At the time I didn't realise the effect it had. It was only after the war that we got the reaction from the servicemen – that we found out what it really meant to them. And so many of my songs were famous at that time – 'The White Cliffs', 'It's A Lovely Day Tomorrow', 'We'll Meet Again', 'Another Day'. Those songs were a soundtrack to many people's experiences of war.

I hadn't been to Europe during the war; I confined myself initially to Britain, touring camps and hospitals and then went to the Middle and Far East. Then, when the war ended, I started getting invitations to go all over the continent to the countries that were occupied, because they had been listening to my programmes too, unbeknownst to me. Which of course they weren't allowed to do – if they were caught listening to the BBC they were shot, so they were listening secretly. And all this didn't come out until after the war.

I knew the war was finishing before a lot of other people did. I had been invited with the comedian Tommy Trinder, who had also been entertaining the troops, and one or two other people to a reception at Windsor Castle before peace was declared. The war was tailing off a bit and we were half expecting it to end soon, and so when we got there we thought, 'Well, what's all this about?' It turned out to be a pre-victory reception; we were celebrating the approach of the declaration that war was over. So when they finally announced it I wasn't surprised.

On VE Day all the action was in London. I was in Sussex and then it was really much quieter down here than it is now. I don't recall very much about the festivities or the actual day other than listening to it on the radio, so I suppose my actual experience of the war ending was a lot less exciting than for most people. But the high point was when it got dark and we were allowed to drive with our lights on. That — after six years of driving all through the war in the blackout — was a wonderful feeling. So I was very glad that at least I was able to take part in some celebration, even if it was only my own! Driving with the lights on, having them show up the lanes, you know it was a wonderful feeling, it was brilliant — like the lights.

I do remember when the war was declared very clearly. We were in the garden, my mother and father and myself, and I think my brother was with me because it was my father's birthday. We were there having tea and saying happy birthday and all that, but at the same time we had the radio on, listening and waiting for any news to come through.

One was expecting it but it still came as a bit of a shock. Everyone was hoping it was going to be alright. But you know, we can't say we were too shocked or terribly surprised because it was in the wind really that something might happen. There was this feeling of uncertainty. You think, 'Well, what is going to happen now?' One didn't stop to think about a blitz. We didn't think about anything like that at that point. But as far as myself, personally, I did think that I was just beginning to become quite well known here in England. I'd been broadcasting for a few years and making records (with the Ambrose band) and the first thing I thought of was, 'Oh well, bang goes my career.' I thought, 'There won't be anything that I'll be able to do if there is going to be a war on. I shall be either in the Army or in a factory, doing something like that.' As it turned out a lot of women ended up making an enormous contribution to the war effort in that way.

I suppose that in another way I played my part in the war effort though I never imagined that entertainment was going to be such a vital means of keeping people's morale up. Everybody had to sign on and I did too, expecting to go into the Army or do something in one of the other services. I was ready to do whatever they wanted me to do, like everybody else. But I was told, 'No, you will be much more useful if you carry on entertaining.' I wondered what kind of entertaining we would be doing with all the theatres closed. You think of all the worst things that could possibly happen. But on the whole most of the theatres did keep going throughout the war.

My first taste of what was to come was when a newspaper ran a 'Forces' Sweetheart' competition when the first batch of boys, the British Expeditionary Force, went to France at the end of 1939. I suppose they thought they would give

Taking tea with mixed servicemen at a promotion for the YMCA, Trafalgar Square.

them something to take their mind off things by running the competition. They voted for me and I was really surprised – I couldn't believe it. I know I had been broadcasting and I had a lot of fan-mail, but that they voted me above the American singers and anyone else in this country was quite a surprise to me.

When Victory over Japan was declared it really was the end of the war. I had spent nearly four months in the East entertaining, starting from Cairo and going right the way through India to Burma, performing in hospitals, camps and at aerodromes, partly flying and partly travelling by road. But the problem with the

Sheet music for 'The Stars Will Remember'.

Far East war was that the troops out there were the forgotten 14th Army. There was so little said and printed about the activities of what was going on over there, which is why the boys felt somehow blighted. Not a lot was said about it either when it was finally over and the boys came home. That was the final ending of the war as far as I was concerned and I thought of those that were still out there, because I'd actually met them.

So when the war was over I had my daughter and retired. I felt I'd been doing a certain type of work that fitted the mood of the times – the songs and everything – and now audiences would be moving on. In fact the BBC told me that if I wanted to continue to work for them I had to change my style, to be more upbeat as it were.

I would say that I was fairly lucky to have lived through the war and not lost many of those who were close to me. I did lose a young man that I had more or less grown up with. He was a pilot in the Air Force and was killed. He was the one loss that was really close to me.

The blackout stayed with us for six years of war, and the words of 'We'll Meet Again' seem as apt to me today as when I first sang them:

> *We'll meet again, don't know where, don't know when,*
> *But I know we'll meet again some sunny day,*
> *Keep smiling through just like you always do*
> *'Till the blue skies drive the dark clouds far away.*

But I suppose my life just goes to show what an effect the war had on people. It's still an influence – it's still there. I still get fan mail every day, not only from ex-servicemen, but also from children and young people who talk about their fathers and their grandfathers, from all over the world. The war years have been my life, really. I don't feel any nostalgia for the war. Nostalgia is something that takes you back; but I've never left it.

Vera Lynn

During the war, Vera Lynn performed in factories and bomb shelters. Here she is in grander surroundings, firmly in the national spotlight during one of the many concerts held at the Royal Albert Hall to honour and remember those who had served in the war.

THE DAY WAR ENDED   13

I 'THE WAR'S TURNING POINT HAS COME'

ADOLF HITLER

The stories of the final battles of the Second World War have been told and re-told in countless books. We know that Hitler died in his Berlin bunker, after the German capital was surrounded by the Soviet army; and the image of the great mushroom cloud above Hiroshima can never be forgotten. Yet in the early months of 1945 no one knew when and how the war would end, nor that Europe would soon be divided into two armed camps once again. The likely shape of the post-war world was suggested by the Yalta conference in February: an exhausted Churchill and his dying friend Roosevelt at the court of Stalin, the 'Red Tsar'. But to ordinary people, civilians and military alike, the needs of the present were quite enough to occupy their minds.

On 12 January the Soviet army launched the Vistula-Oder operation, yet another of its gigantic offensives on a scale that dwarfed anything mounted by the western Allies. The concentration camps at Auschwitz were overrun before the Germans could destroy the evidence, but the unbelievable horror of the Nazi death camps had been known to the Soviet forces since the grisly discoveries at Majdenek in July 1944. The truth was more grotesque than the worst accusations levelled against the Nazis by Stalin's propagandists. This, and the liberation of thousands of Soviet prisoners of war, whose treatment had been far worse than that meted out to Allied soldiers in the hands of the Japanese, created a spirit of bloody vengeance that would not be satisfied until some months after the Red Flag flew from the Reichstag. German resistance against the western Allies finally began to falter, but the Soviet forces met fanatical opposition all the way to Berlin. More than two million German civilians remain unaccounted for as the refugees fled westwards, trying to stay ahead of the Soviet tank columns.

Allied troops at the bombed-out Chancellery in Berlin remember Adolf Hitler. The building was a casualty of the Battle of Berlin, much of it destroyed as the Soviet forces seized the city.

BBC NEWS REPORT, 1 MAY 1945
HITLER IS DEAD

We are interrupting our programmes to bring you a news flash.

This is London calling. Here is a news flash.

The German radio has just announced that Hitler is dead.

I repeat that: The German radio has just announced that Hitler is dead.

ELSIE BROWN

HOME FRONT

Elsie Brown of London's East End regularly listened to 'Evening Prayers' on the BBC. Her husband Stuart was fighting in Germany.

I never missed 'Evening Prayers' because my husband, Bert, was in the artillery somewhere in Germany and, it's silly I know, but I thought that 'Evening Prayers' was a way of staying in touch with him. I imagined him, wherever he was, listening too, and thinking about home. 'Course I didn't ever know if they broadcast it over there: probably they didn't.

Anyway, this night I was still warming the pot when I heard the news that Hitler was dead. At first I didn't believe it, then I thought, it's on the BBC so it must be true. I didn't know what to do. I wanted to tell someone, so I decided to run next door. My neighbour, Vi, worked the late shift on the buses and was always up till after midnight so I went round and banged on her door and when she opened it I shouted something like, 'He's dead, the old bugger's dead!' And she said, 'What old bugger, Alfie?' Alfie was an old bloke who lived at the corner of our road and really was a miserable old bugger, always shouting at the kids. So I said, 'No, not Alfie, Adolf!'

When the penny dropped Vi said, 'Here, Else, you better come in,' but I couldn't because I'd left the kids asleep, so she came back with me and brought a bottle of Guinness she'd been saving for a special occasion and we shared it. Of course we didn't know any more than we'd heard, but Vi agreed that as it was on the BBC it must be true. She said, 'Do you think it'll all be over soon now?' I think I nodded and I remember I suddenly started crying. I don't know why; I couldn't stop.

**MASS-OBSERVATION ARCHIVE, 1 MAY 1945
LONDON RESIDENT ON NEWS OF HITLER'S DEATH**

I think everyone's quite apathetic, if not extremely depressed. The only difference I have noticed tonight is that the two pubs I went to were packed, and they're usually rather quiet on Monday nights. But there's no gaiety anywhere. Partly perhaps the feeling that it isn't over. You get the idea that the war is positive but peace is negative. Anyway, everyone knows that war conditions will go on – rationing and shortages and so on – only without the war, and that may be even more depressing than war itself.

As far as I know, there was no important announcement on the nine o'clock news. All I've seen is Himmler saying he's the only sane one left, and that Goering's in a toga, and Hitler's dead. But I don't BELIEVE Hitler's dead. There was something tucked away in a small paragraph somewhere, saying they were all busy having their faces altered.

DOROTHEA VON SCHWANENFLUEGEL

HOME FRONT

Dorothea von Schwanenfluegel was a 29-year-old wife and mother living in Berlin when the Red Army took the city. The city surrendered on 2 May 1945 after a week of bitter fighting.

 When trees were not available, people were strung up on lamp-posts. They were hanging everywhere, military and civilian, men and women, ordinary citizens who had been executed by a small group of fanatics. It appeared that the Nazis did not want the people to survive because a lost war, by their rationale, was obviously the fault of all of us. We had not sacrificed enough and therefore, we had forfeited our right to live, as only the government was without guilt. The *Volkssturm* [Home Guard] was called up again, and this time all boys aged 13 and up had to report as our Army was reduced now to little more than children filling the ranks as soldiers.

The Soviets fought the German soldiers and civilians street by street until we could hear explosions and rifle fire right in our immediate vicinity. As the noise got closer, we could even hear the horrible guttural screaming of the Soviet soldiers which sounded to us like enraged animals. Shots shattered our windows and shells exploded in our garden, and suddenly the Soviets were on our street. Shaken by the battle around us and numb with fear, we watched from behind the small cellar windows facing the street as the tanks and an endless convoy of troops rolled by...

It was a terrifying sight as they sat high upon their tanks with their rifles cocked, aiming at houses as they passed. The screaming, gun-wielding women were the worst. Half of the troops had only rags and tatters around their feet while others wore SS boots that had been looted from a conquered SS barrack in Lichterfelde. Several fleeing people had told us earlier that they kept watching different boots pass by their cellar windows. At night, the Germans in our Army boots recaptured the street that the Soviets in the SS boots had taken during the day. The boots and the voices told them who was who. Now we saw them with our own eyes, and they belonged to the wild cohorts of the advancing Soviet troops.

Facing reality was ten times worse than just hearing about it. Throughout the night, we huddled together in mortal fear, not knowing what the morning might bring. Nevertheless, we noiselessly did sneak upstairs to double check that our heavy wooden window shutters were still intact and that all outside doors were barricaded. But as I peeked out, what did I see! The porter couple in the apartment block next to ours were standing in their front yard waving to the Soviets. So our suspicion that they were Communists had been right all along, but they must have been out of their minds to openly proclaim their brotherhood like that.

As could be expected, that night a horde of Soviet soldiers returned and stormed into their apartment block. Then we heard what sounded like a terrible orgy with women screaming for help, many shrieking at the same time. The racket gave me goose bumps. Some of the Soviets trampled through our garden and banged their rifle butts on our doors in an attempt to break in. Thank goodness our sturdy wooden doors withstood their efforts. Gripped in fear, we sat in stunned silence, hoping to give the impression that this was a vacant block, but we felt hopelessly delivered into the clutches of the long-feared Red Army. Our nerves were in shreds.

The next morning, we women proceeded to make ourselves look as unattractive as possible to the Soviets by smearing our faces with coal dust and covering our heads with old rags, our make-up for the Ivan. We huddled together in the central part of the basement, shaking with fear, while some peeked through the low basement windows to see what was happening on the Soviet-controlled street. We felt paralysed by the sight of these husky Mongolians, looking wild and frightening. At the ruin across the street from us the first Soviet orders were posted, including a curfew. Suddenly there was a shattering noise outside. Horrified, we watched the Soviets demolish the corner grocery store and throw its contents, shelving and furniture out into the street. Bags of flour, sugar and rice were split open and their contents spilled on the bare pavement, while Soviet soldiers stood guard with their rifles so that no one would dare to pick up any of the urgently needed food. This was just unbelievable. At night, a few desperate people tried to salvage some of the spilled food from the gutter. Hunger now became a major concern because our ration cards were worthless with no hope of any supplies.

The next day, General Wilding, the commander of the German troops in Berlin, finally surrendered the entire city to the Soviet Army. There was no radio or newspaper, so vans with loudspeakers drove through the streets ordering us to cease all resistance. Suddenly, the shooting and bombing stopped and the unreal silence meant that one ordeal was over for us and another was about to begin. Our nightmare had become a reality. The entire three hundred square miles of what was

The famous photograph of Russian soldiers raising the Soviet flag over the Reichstag in Berlin: an iconic evocation of their triumphant entry into the city in this staged photograph by Yevgeny Khaldei. More than 1,500 Nazis made their last stand here, lasting two days against the Soviet onslaught. The Reichstag fell to the Allies on 30 April 1945.

left of Berlin were now completely under the control of the Red Army. The last days of savage house-to-house fighting and street battles had been a human slaughter, with no prisoners being taken on either side. These final days were hell. Our last remaining and exhausted troops, primarily children and old men, stumbled into imprisonment. We were a city in ruins; almost no house remained intact.

BBC NEWS REPORT, 2 MAY 1945
BERLIN HAS FALLEN

Now we're breaking into our programmes for the second time today with some splendid news from Moscow. Berlin has fallen. Marshal Stalin has just announced the complete capture of the capital of Germany, the centre of German imperialism and the cradle of German aggression. The Berlin garrison laid down their arms this afternoon. More than 70,000 prisoners have been rounded up so far today.

IVAN BICHENKO

FRONT LINE

Lieutenant-General Ivan Bichenko, deputy Chief of Staff of the First Polish Army's armoured and mechanised troops, was part of the force that made the crossing of the River Oder and stormed Berlin.

The Battle of Berlin was, perhaps, the bitterest in the Great Patriotic War, with Germans concentrating all their reserves and removing troops from their Western fronts in a bid to prevent the Soviet Army from seizing the city. But, however hard they tried, they failed to hold their capital...

The Battle of Berlin was fighting non-stop, round the clock. Berlin has numerous canals, with water flowing between concrete walls. Germans put up extremely fierce fighting to retain the small bridges across these canals. The point is, it's impossible to force these canals as troops normally force rivers. The only way out was to seize one of these small bridges and send tanks and artillery to the other bank so later we could capture another such bridge, and so on. We had to concentrate a lot of military hardware and troops to crush that fierce resistance in every street, house and window that Nazis were firing from and to seize Berlin. Surprisingly, we saw just German troops in Berlin, but no residents, who had all hidden in cellars and destroyed buildings. Of course, some of them died because Berlin was razed to the ground. The Soviet troops were compelled to destroy every single building because there were resisting Germans in every such building. Everybody wanted to be the first to reach the city centre, the Reichstag, the Reichskanzlei – or the Imperial Chancellery – Hitler's den, where he still was, whether alive or dead we did not know then. The 1st Polish Army was most energetically engaged in capturing Berlin, and it was quite symbolic that Poland was involved in the final stage of fighting, the fiercest and the most bloody one in that war.

We all knew the war would soon be over, so we were happy as we seized another and yet another home in Berlin. When the seizure of Berlin was announced by radio, we took it as a big holiday. We realised that even if the Soviet troops still had to cope with some pockets of enemy resistance, the victory and the end of the Great

ВОДРУЗИМ
НАД БЕРЛИНОМ
ЗНАМЯ ПОБЕДЫ!

'Let's raise the Victory Banner over Berlin!' Soviet poster, 1945.

Patriotic War were near. Everybody wanted to be photographed in those memorable places. We found ourselves in the Imperial Chancellery and saw the floor covered in thousands of sheets of paper, whether some written orders or propaganda leaflets. The Reichstag walls were all covered in inscriptions by the victors, by those who were the first to reach it. But those who came later also added their names if they found free space. The representatives of the Nazi Command signed Germany's unconditional surrender, and we all hoped we would soon be back home to celebrate a reunion between us and our families, to celebrate the fact that we had managed to survive that horrible war. We suffered huge losses there, especially during the assault crossing of the Oder. The joyous expectation of a near victory drove the Soviet troops to Berlin, and today, almost 60 years after that great victory against Fascism was won, it is hard to imagine just how strong that all-consuming emotion was. This is my memory of the way the Great Patriotic War drew to a close.

LOTHAR LOEWE

Lothar Loewe was born 1929. As a member of the Hitler Youth, he attacked tanks in Berlin with a bazooka at the age of 16. He was taken prisoner by the Red Army but was released two weeks after the end of the war.

Why didn't we do anything to get out of Berlin? Why didn't we turn and run? We wouldn't have known where to go. I was at home in Berlin; at least I had an aunt there. We didn't have an apartment, but we didn't know where else we could go either. I didn't have any relatives in the West, and I wouldn't have been able to get there anyway. Apart from that, there was an atmosphere of doom, of the end of the world, because of the reports from the East, of the Russian advances into Germany.

We began to believe what Goebbels had said so often: If the Russians invaded, they would kill everyone, and whoever wasn't killed would be sent to the mines in Siberia, and whoever was sent there didn't come back. We would simply join ranks with the army of forced labourers there we'd heard so much about. Every civilised, organised form of life would come to an end.

It was the courage of desperation which motivated the soldiers. Berlin was defended so bitterly only because so many of the soldiers, so many of the civilians were afraid of Soviet imprisonment. They wanted to save themselves, to keep the Russians out of Berlin for as long as they could. Everything possible was done to stop them, to gain a little more time. If we were lucky, the Americans or the British would get to Berlin first. This is what any intelligent person hoped for.

To me, Bolshevism meant the end of life. And, in my opinion, that's the reason for the terribly bitter fight in Berlin, which wasn't only street to street, but house to house, room to room, and floor to floor. The Russians and the Germans suffered such horrible casualties here because every single brick was bitterly fought over for days on end.

In mid-April, my Hitler Youth unit was mobilised. The fighting was in an area of Berlin I knew like the back of my hand. At 16, I carried messages under fire. My CO was a lieutenant with a wooden leg and a medal. He spent nights with his girlfriend. Every evening he stopped the war and said, 'Come back at 8:00 tomorrow morning.' The next day, we'd go back to the front on some street or other.

We had bazookas. I had a Belgian pistol and an Italian tommy gun with no safety catch. Once it almost went off and killed a sergeant. My CO always wanted me to wear a helmet, but I didn't like them. The things were so big they slipped down onto my nose, and besides, I couldn't hear when I wore one.

It was a bad war. The nights, when the women in the occupied side streets were raped by the Russian soldiers, were awful; the screams were horrible. There were terrible scenes. But these, on the other hand, only encouraged us all the more. We were genuinely afraid the Russians would slaughter us. They didn't take prisoners. That's when I knocked out a tank with a bazooka.

Three tanks had broken through, and I shot at them along with another older soldier who had several stripes on his sleeve for knocking out tanks. I fired from a cellar door. It had quite an effect because there was a wall behind me, and the bazooka's backblast was really something. The tank flew into the air – an impressive sight to a teenager.

The Russians retreated, and then I had a horrible experience. This had all happened on one of the side streets of the Kurfurstendamm. People who lived there had put out white flags of surrender. There was this one apartment block with white bed sheets waving from the windows. And the SS came – I'll never forget this – and went into the house, and dragged all of the men out. I don't know whether these were soldiers dressed in civilian clothing, old men, or what. Anyway, they took them into the middle of the street and shot them.

I was infuriated. Of course we didn't dare do anything about it. But anywhere you went you saw military police. Even when the Russians were already in sight, you could see police a hundred yards farther on, still trying to check people. Whoever didn't have the right papers or the correct pass was strung up as a deserter, and hung with a sign saying, 'I am a traitor,' or 'I am a coward.'

I was wounded on 1 May. After I was hit, I was always afraid of being wounded again whenever the shooting started. I had never been afraid before, but now I was really scared. I'll never forget sitting in a bunker and hearing of Hitler's end. It was like a whole world collapsing. The report was that he'd been killed at the head of his troops in the heroic Battle of Berlin. Adolf Hitler's death left me with a feeling of emptiness. Nonetheless, I remember thinking that my oath was no longer valid, because it had been made to Hitler. We had sworn an oath to the Führer, but not to Doenitz, his successor. So the oath was null and void.

Now the trick was to get out of Berlin and avoid falling into the hands of the Russians. Close to dawn everything started moving. I went out into the streets. Berlin burned: oceans of flames, horrible clouds of smoke. An entire pilgrimage of people began marching out of Berlin. I spotted an SS Tiger tank unit with room in one of the tanks, so they took me along. I assumed this would be a sure thing because the tank was a heavy one. The SS men made a very determined impression; they didn't want to fall into the hands of the Russians, and neither did I. It looked as though we had a good chance of reaching German troops who were supposed to be still fighting a few miles away.

Somewhere along the way I peeked out of the hatch and saw the rest of my unit, which I had lost. I told the tank driver to stop, and I jumped out and went back to them.

Hospital trains were supposedly ready and waiting outside Berlin. The picture of white beds on a train which might roll all the way to Hamburg was very appealing to me. I hadn't washed in ten days and was bloody, wounded and dirty – a real mess. We pushed our way right across a troop-training field. And there I saw a firefight between Labour Service people and Luftwaffe soldiers. The Luftwaffe thought the Labour Service men were Russians because of their brown uniforms. And the Labour Service people thought, because they were being shot at, that the Luftwaffe men were Germans fighting on the Russian side. They could yell as much German as they wanted; they didn't believe each other, and continued to shoot at one another. This went on for about half an hour, and a few were killed. I just laid low and thought to myself that I was about to be killed in German crossfire. Finally, some experienced officer suddenly stood up and commanded everyone to hold their fire, stand up, fall in, and march. And they obeyed and said, 'Sorry about that, buddy,' to one another, and moved on as if nothing had happened! An eerie scenario.

Everything ended on 5 May, in a village south of Nauen. Thousands of soldiers had gathered there: a few generals, our unit, and many wounded. The Russians had surrounded us, and we were being shelled. At one point there was a pause in the firefight, and the Russians sent a couple of parliamentarians over to encourage us to give up. The generals were emphatic about the wounded being sent to a hospital by truck before the rest would lay down their weapons.

My commander didn't like this. He had a great deal of experience on the Eastern front. There were only about 20 of us left when he said, 'I dismiss you all from *Wehrmacht* [the German armed forces]; I dismiss you from duty. Hand over your military passes. I personally do not intend to surrender, and neither does my aide. We plan to take a half-track with a full tank of gas and break out of this dump when it gets dark. Our last chance is to take this vehicle full speed ahead cross-country at night.' His theory was not to parade out of there, but to keep it subtle. 'I won't force anyone, but whoever wants to come along may join us.'

There were ten or twelve people on the half-track with bazookas, tommy guns, hand grenades, and light machine guns. Some wore helmets, others didn't. It was a mixed crowd; a few women Air Force helpers were also with us. And we actually succeeded in breaking out. The Russians didn't shoot. I believe they weren't interested in chasing anything any more.

We drove cross-country for a while, then turned onto a highway. Suddenly, we encountered a Russian column turning in from a side road. My commander's driver

spoke Russian; he was a Volga German. He told them we were Russians, and we joined the tail end of the column as the last vehicle. The column was rolling west, that was the important thing, so we went along, happy as pie. By this time many Russians were driving German vehicles, so no one thought anything about us.

Then the column turned, and we drove on alone straight ahead. The Russians wanted to stop us, they yelled 'Stoj!' and swung red flashlights. My commander told us to keep going, and only to shoot if we were shot at. They fired into the half-track. Several of us were killed or badly wounded. We continued for about three miles, but the radiator had been hit, so we stopped and got out.

We continued on foot until we ran into a Russian company. They formed a skirmish line and came right toward us. The question was whether we should fight a last battle or not. The commander told us there was no point, and we raised our hands. There were about six of us left. The squad that took us prisoner lined us up against the wall of a shed where there were two dead civilians lying on the ground. I was sure we were going to be shot. There was a big discussion with one of the officers, and then suddenly they just came up and took our rings and

Three 14-year-old German prisoners of war, captured by the 4th Division of the 3rd US Army. These Hitler Youth were part of the Volkssturm – the Home Guard formed of men unfit for military service, the young and the old – which was mobilised during the final days of the war as a last reserve of manpower.

watches. But I also found myself with two packs of cigarettes I hadn't had before – the Russians pressed two packs of German cigarettes into my hands.

They led us to some trucks and took us to the next town, where they handed us over to a Ukrainian artillery unit. And the image of Soviet subhumans I had carried with me finally collapsed. This unit had a woman doctor with them, and the first thing they did was to see to the wounded. After that we got something to eat from these Bolshevist 'subhumans'. The average Russian sympathised with young boys like us, and there were quite a few of us in this campaign. I had neither a mess kit nor a spoon. I had nothing; I'd even thrown my pistol away. And it was this Bolshevik, this person I'd always believed to be a monster, that lent me, the Nordic German, his mess kit and spoon to eat with.

I had seen many Soviet POWs during the war. And I had also seen how they were treated. All POWs were treated better than the Russian prisoners we had. The Soviets were always beaten, really, and they never got anything to eat. They were made to look like the subhumans we imagined them to be. The idea that a German soldier would give a Russian prisoner his mess kit and spoon to eat from was simply unimaginable to me. And the fact that this Soviet gave me his, voluntarily, happily, because he felt sorry for me, shook the foundations of my image of them.

That's when I told myself that maybe the Soviets were very different from what they had told us to believe. This was my first encounter with the Soviet people, and I'll never forget it for the rest of my life.

UNKNOWN

FRONT LINE

This testimony is from an unnamed member of US General Devers's 6th Army Group, who successfully penetrated German-held positions in central Europe in 1945.

At the time I could not understand it, this resistance, this pointless resistance to our advance. The war was all over – our columns were spreading across the whole of Germany and Austria. We were irresistible. We could conquer the world; that was our glowing conviction. And the enemy had nothing. Yet he resisted and in some places with an implacable fanaticism. I know now what it was that animated the enemy although I didn't then, in 1945. The world of those children of the Hitler Youth was coming to an end. Soon there would be nothing left. No parades, no songs, no swastikas, no marching and no fighting for the Faith – for the belief in Hitler. The roof was falling in on those children's ideals. Denied the opportunity to be real soldiers, to wear a proper uniform and to fight as soldiers in a formal unit, those kids were determined to show us that they knew how to sacrifice themselves.

There was one boy whom we took prisoner. His rocket had hit my tank but had not exploded. I was livid that this snotty brat should endanger my life and I was out of that tank very quickly cuffing him about the head and shouting. When I let go of him he fell to the grass crying and saying something. I do not speak German but Abrahams my sergeant did. What that child was saying was that he should have died for the Führer. The silly bastard was sorry that he had not been killed knocking out my tank.

HEINZ BARTHEL

HOME FRONT

Heinz Barthel, eight years old at the war's end, was a schoolboy in Potsdam, near Berlin. He was on the west side of the river Elbe, where American and Soviet forces triumphantly met in April 1945.

'Quickly, quickly!' shouts a man in an American uniform (how come he speaks German?). 'The hall is needed for wounded people! Pack your things and get going!' And so began the first morning of peacetime for us, for my mother, my 18-year-old sister, and for me – an eight-year-old schoolboy from Potsdam, near Berlin.

The ballroom floor of a small village guest-house near the river Elbe on the west side had been completely covered with straw. On it people were laid out in tightly packed rows, old and young, many children. They were refugees from the eastern part of Germany, some of whom had been on the move for the four months since January 1945. They were fleeing from the ever approaching war front – fleeing from the Russians, the Red Army. The fear that drove them on was written all over their faces which bore the evidence of indescribable strains and stresses.

Their fear was a terrible mixture: from the horror stories of the Nazis – 'now these subhuman creatures are coming to take dreadful revenge!' Everyone knew those ugly Bolshevik faces – they had been portrayed almost daily in the *Volkische*

Beobachter [a Nazi-run newspaper] and these were now buried deep in our souls, especially for us children. And there were the horrors of the nights of perpetual bombing from which we had escaped. And worst, there were the reports from eye-witnesses among the refugees, some of whom had escaped from the Russians several times and in the process had lost members of their families. There were those who had had to watch as others, mostly women and children, paid with their lives for the horror that the Nazis had started among eastern Europe's peoples. And there were the German soldiers fleeing, often for good reasons, from imprisonment by the Russians: whole SS Panzer Divisions were pushing towards the West in the hope that the Americans would unite with them to drive the Russians out of Germany again.

And now today, there is no reason for fear any more. We had finally and happily arrived in the land of peace on the West side of the Elbe with the Americans.

It was the 2 or 3 May 1945 – still very early in the morning and still no end to the war, but we were, or so it seemed to us after the peaceful night, safe.

When the people who had been lying on the floor realised that the man who spoke German – in spite of being an American – had been serious with his order to empty the hall, they quickly piled together their remaining possessions, a woollen blanket for sleeping on at night and some food, mostly from the German Army's 'iron rations', choca-cola (fliers' chocolate), and the fruit bars that the very young German soldiers had slipped to us the previous day, still on the Russian side of the river, sitting in their trenches obviously waiting to go into action. And tins of preserved pork, daily rations of crisp-bread whose cardboard packs the soldiers could use as postcards.

And even before the last refugees had left the room the medical orderlies pushed in carrying stretchers and tipped their sad loads onto the straw, which was still spread out. And we knew at once that we had already seen these blood-stained groaning bodies ... that had been the previous day – these were those same very young German soldiers from the trenches on the other side of the river, no doubt members of the Hitler Youth, who had quickly been pushed into military uniforms and sent off to fight the Russians, just to gain one or two days in which the fleeing German soldiers at the front might succeed in being captured by the Americans. THAT'S why they risked their lives and now the 'leftovers' were being brought into our nightly shelter.

ADOLF HITLER, 13 APRIL 1945
SPEECH GIVEN THE DAY AFTER THE DEATH OF PRESIDENT ROOSEVELT

For one last time our mortal enemies, the Jewish Bolsheviks, are throwing their weight into the attack. They are attempting to shatter Germany and annihilate our people. You soldiers in the East already know full well the fate awaiting German women and children. The older men and children will be murdered, women and girls will be debased to barrack-room whores. The rest will go on foot to Siberia.

... Whoever fails in his duty now is a traitor to our people. The regiment or division that abandons its position will be a disgrace to the women and children who have withstood the bombing terror in our cities.

Berlin stays German! Vienna will be German again. Europe will never be Russian. ...

At this moment when fate has carried off the greatest war criminal of all times from the face of this earth, the war's turning point has come.

JANINA BAUMAN

REFUGEE

Janina Bauman (née Lewinson), a Polish Jew, was born in Warsaw in 1926. After the 1944 uprising, Janina and her family were deported to the south. They found shelter with an old woman and her son, a priest. They remained there in hiding until Soviet forces arrived.

There was a very short shelling and the Germans went away and the Russians came. On the same night I went to the shed to bring some wood, some timber for the fire... and I saw a German soldier. Not so much him as his coat. I went to my hostess... and told her, reported excitedly, 'You have a German!' She said, 'Very well. Take him some food, he must be very hungry.' I went there and he was invisible. He hid among the wood but when he smelt the food he came out and [he was] a young boy, he was my own age or even younger, frightened to death and terribly hungry. He started eating and I looked at him but I felt nothing. Not hatred, not satisfaction or pity. Nothing... This incident for me marks the end of the war.

Previous pages: Exuberant
Soviet prisoners of war hoist
aloft one of their liberators,
a soldier from the US 9th
Army, at their camp in
Eselheide, Germany.

TOM SMITH

PRISONER OF WAR

Tom Smith of the 7th Battalion King's Own Scottish Borderers, prisoner of war for seven months, had been a forced labourer at the Hermann Goering Iron & Steel Works in Germany when Allied forces began to get near.

POWs, mostly Arnhem veterans, we had been marching for five days through the Harz Mountains, in Germany.

We were starving, our guards tried their best to get potatoes which we ate raw. We had left the work camp (the Hermann Goering Iron & Steel Works) because the Americans were approaching.

Our clothes and skin were impregnated with iron ore which we had shovelled daily. We wore sabots, as our boots had worn out. We never knew what day it was – but this day was a day of great elation for us, but of great sadness for millions. I will always remember it.

We heard a bugle playing the charge very faint, but then louder. Being a Western fan, I knew it was the Yanks and, sure enough, along came a column of Sherman tanks, 'Old Glory' flying and bugle blowing.

Our guards hopped it and we were free, free; a lot of hand shaking and back slapping went on as they gave us all the food and fags they had.

The officer in charge, a major, stood on the leading tank and said, 'We are delighted to have liberated you, but, today, for us, and the whole American people, this is a sad day. We have just heard over the radio that today 12 April 1945, President Roosevelt died. Will you join me in one minute's silence?'

Four of us decided, firstly to find some food and then head west for home and beauty and off we went into no man's land.

Every village, every farm was in ruins. So we left the main road and took to the side roads, got a bit of food here and there. Gradually, we found people, white sheets hanging from the window sills. One village had dead men hanging from the lamp-posts – Russians. The villagers wanted us to stay and protect them from the hordes of slave workers from all breeds, but SS men and German Army deserters came into the towns and villages each night for food and comfort and hanged many non-Germans.

We used to sleep in barns, etc. Finally we reached Koblenz. By now we had discarded our filthy, lousy uniforms and were in civvies. I had a floral waistcoat. We were arrested as suspected SS men. We had kept our emblems and finally persuaded the officer who we were. Then off through the Ardennes and finally we hitched a lift on a barge on the Marne and got to Paris.

We had a letter from an American padre in Koblenz, which we showed at the American aerodrome, and were flown to Brize Norton in Oxfordshire where we were stripped, shorn, scrubbed, deloused and kitted out and put in hospital for two weeks. We all had malnutrition.

Then leave to James Street in Whickham. I was greeted by my wife and three sons, one whom I had never seen. I asked my wife if it was a boy or a girl. I had no letters all my POW life, seven months.

Next day there was a street party and my old friend Jimmy Frances sang 'Ain't It Glad To Be Home'.

WW2 People's War

WINSTON CHURCHILL, 17 APRIL 1945
SPEECH ON THE DEATH OF PRESIDENT ROOSEVELT

I need not dwell upon the series of great operations which have taken place in the western hemisphere, to say nothing of that other immense war proceeding on the other side of the world. Nor need I speak of the plans which we made with our great ally, Russia, at Tehran, for these have now been carried out for all the world to see. But at Yalta I noticed that the President was ailing. ... What an enviable death was his! He had brought his country through the worst of its perils and heaviest of its toils. Victory had cast its sure and steady beam upon him.

WALTER MORISON

PRISONER OF WAR

Walter Morison of the RAF was an undergraduate at Cambridge when war broke out. He was held at Stalag Luft III and Colditz prisoner of war camps.

I was a prisoner of war at the Luftwaffe's main camp, Stalag Luft III. The 'Goons', as we called the Germans, treated us well and observed the Geneva Convention, an international treaty on the treatment of POWs. But of course we wanted to go home, so escaping was popular.

Getting out was hard enough, but once out you faced a journey of several hundred miles to neutral territory: a long walk or a train ride. My friend Lorne Welch and I argued that, despite the perils, it would be better to borrow an aircraft

Walter Morison (left) and Lorne Welch, whose escape plan was devised by 'Big X', Squadron Leader Roger Bushell, who also masterminded the Great Escape. They are seen here disguised as Luftwaffe ground staff shortly after their recapture.

from the Luftwaffe and fly to Sweden. There was an airfield just down the road.

When at last we got out, dressed as Luftwaffe ground staff, we had many adventures, including the humiliation of being ordered by the rightful crew of our chosen aircraft to start it up for them and watch it fly away. In the end we were recaptured and returned to the camp where we expected the usual penalty of a couple of weeks in the cooler (solitary confinement). Not so.

We had broken the rules of escaping: don't wear German uniform, don't use violence, and don't engage in espionage or sabotage. Arguably wandering about on Luftwaffe airfields was espionage and I suppose nicking an aircraft would be sabotage. Fortunately we hadn't broken the other rule: don't use violence. Instead of a short rest in the cooler, we were threatened with Court Martial, even sentence of death. But in the end, they just sent us to Colditz.

Colditz is a small town on the banks of the river Mulde, some 25 miles from Leipzig, and has a magnificent medieval schloss, used as a prison for persistent escapers and for the *Deutschfeindlich*, or otherwise troublesome POWs. Not surprisingly they were a lively lot.

When Lorne and I arrived in 1943 it held some 300 British and Allied officers. Some unreliable reports had led to it being described in a British newspaper as 'The Nazi Hell Camp'. Untrue, but the reputation stuck. In fact it was one of the most comfortable POW camps in Germany.

Over the centuries the defences of the schloss had been developed with the object of keeping the enemy out, but now the purpose was to keep us in, which is a different problem altogether. This crew of experienced escapers joyfully set to work to exploit the weaknesses so that Colditz had an outstanding record of escape, not only out of the camp, but also in getting home.

Escaping was what maintained morale in an environment where our open space was a courtyard some 30 x 20 metres. There were plenty of other pastimes, but escaping was a serious purpose.

It was technically demanding, exciting, sometimes a little dangerous; a sport really. But as 1944 wore on it became increasingly certain that the Allies would win and there seemed less and less point in the hard work and risks of escaping. Moreover, most of the ways out had been blocked. The Goons, who had more to worry about than playing games with POWs, had published a notice 'To all Prisoners of War' and headed 'To escape from prison camps is no longer a sport'.

We learned with horror that 50 RAF officers who had escaped from Stalag Luft III had been shot (as later featured in the film *The Great Escape*). This was no longer cricket. Not, I hasten to add, that the Luftwaffe was to blame. This atrocity was perpetrated on the direct order of Hitler.

However, one major escape project continued: the glider. Believe it or not, high in the roof of the north wing, where there were two unoccupied floors, a hidden workshop had been contrived. In it Jack Best, Bill Goldfinch and Tony Rolt were building a glider, with a view to being catapulted off the roof. Impossible? Not so. It was completed, but the end came before it was launched. It was a properly designed and constructed aircraft. After the war a precise replica was built and it flew perfectly.

When the first V1 and V2 weapons were launched against London, the German papers announced a great victory, but we knew better. We had a radio and could receive BBC broadcasts. This radio was crucial to our morale and

indeed to our safety and was a closely guarded secret. At the end of March 1945 we knew that the Allied armies were only 150 miles away and advancing rapidly. Morale began to revive, but there remained the nagging doubt: how would it all end? Then on 11 April the radio reported the fighting to be close.

Soon it was all over. The great wooden doors of which for so long we had seen only the wrong side swung open and the Yanks were in the courtyard. Their tanks seemed to be dripping with Grand Marnier. 'Hey fella, take a swig of this.' Everything was a whirl, a dream.

The glider was brought out and rigged for all to see; the parts fitted together perfectly. The French, who had a sense of occasion, were called out on parade and were addressed by their senior officer: '*Les Messieurs Français, Prisonniers de Geurre pas encore.*' Did they play the Marseillaise? I forget.

WW2 People's War

Walter Morison, seecond from left, again in costume, with fellow cast members from an amateur performance of French Without Tears *at Stalag Luft III.*

CHARLIE HOBBS

Charlie Hobbs, a tail-gunner in the Royal Canadian Air Force, was held at an Air Force prisoner of war camp at Fallingbostel near Hanover. When the Allied forces began to close in the prisoners were marched out.

They weren't really taking us anywhere, they were just marching us. They'd tell us to turn left or right and the whole column would do it. If the Russians pushed one way, they'd bring us the other way. If the British pushed this way, they'd send us that way. This went on for a month. We were starving; they weren't feeding us. We stole what we could, but they had dogs on these columns, you know. We got strafed by our own fighters, too – killed many of us. So it wasn't a very happy time.

I talked to my buddy Cam, who couldn't run because he'd had part of his foot shot off. I said, 'Cam, this isn't for me. Do you think you can get away?' He said, 'No, I couldn't get out of it quick enough.' So I gave him all the food we had and waited until I got the opportunity to skip out of the column, and I took off and headed into the trees at the side of the road. I didn't stop. It took me five days, heading west, steering by the stars. Slept in the daytime, travelled at night. Eventually I was spotted by a German farmer's boys. The farmer told me to come down to the house and he gave me some milk, which I hadn't had for years. Then he said, 'I'll lead you to the British lines.' He was just a simple farmer, but I felt at least he was human.

So I walked into a British bivouac. I thought the guy was going to shoot me. I was too tired to feel much. They fed me food that I hadn't seen in years – white bread! Bacon and eggs! Lord, the camp cook really went out of his way. Then he takes me out to his ammunition carrier and opens up all the trays, and every one of the trays has nothing but French wine in it. I don't know where they carried their ammunition. He hands me this bottle – to hell with my blooming breakfast! Of course, I couldn't handle that. Just too much for me. I didn't throw up, but it might have been better if I had!

DENNIS HUTTON-FOX

PRISONER OF WAR

Dennis Hutton-Fox of the 3rd Battalion Coldstream Guards was posted to Palestine and the Western Desert. After being captured in 1942 and sent to Italy as a prisoner of war, he escaped from captivity three times before rejoining the British forces in 1944.

After my second escape I had travelled through the mountains, heading south, begging for food from remote houses or stealing when necessary, until I came across an isolated monastery called San Giorgio. I discovered it had been turned into a home for this chap Matteo and his wife and seven children. They were much more friendly than at other places I'd been to and agreed to hide me in a cave and bring me food. I stayed there for two weeks, until the night of 3 October 1943, when there was a severe earthquake. I scrambled down to the house in the dark but found myself trapped in a room surrounded by Germans. I was taken about 150 miles north to a German POW camp. I really didn't want to end up in Germany so two weeks later I managed to escape again, under fire. I had escaped three times now, and it was a dangerous business escaping. But it was even more dangerous being re-caught so I decided that I really had to avoid taking risks.

I just kept walking. I didn't recognise where I was. I hadn't any maps, and I hadn't got a compass. I didn't even know where I'd been. But one day, some months later, I saw a lonely monastery. It was an absolute miracle – I couldn't believe it: I was back at San Giorgio! I recognised that the Italian family were still living there in one wing so I lay down in some rocks and watched it for about an hour. I couldn't see any signs of Germans or any people at all, until one of the daughters, Ada, walked in and out of the kitchen two or three times and I called to her very quietly and she heard me. She was horrified, I think. Anyway she made me lie down there, and she disappeared into the house. She was gone for about three quarters of an hour, and then her father Matteo came out, and they escorted me to a cave.

I didn't know until later – fifty years later in fact – that they had been scared stiff when they saw me again there and had had a big family conference. They had recognised the high risk they had exposed their family to last time they had taken me in, and had breathed a sigh of relief to see the back of me without being punished in any way. Now to see me back on their doorstep only a few months later was really awful and they almost told me to go. But for some reason they decided to help me. I suppose this was partly because Italy had packed in and I was good insurance against them being maltreated by the British when they arrived at Ascoli.

They took me to one of the caves, quite a nice cave, and they started bringing me food again. It was November now and the weather was getting much colder.

Dennis Hutton-Fox with Matteo, his Italian host, who provided shelter in a cave and brought him food, at great personal cost.

There was no way I could keep going, I had to have somewhere to hide up for the winter. I couldn't just keep wandering over the mountains like this. And the further south I got, the thicker it was with Germans.

So I stayed. I didn't make any further effort at that time to reach our own lines. I thought I would lay up there, if they would have me, until such a time as the British overcame that part of the country, which didn't happen as quickly as I had anticipated. It worked out that I had three or four caves and I used to move from one to the other. I had a drop point, and the children Maria, Ada, Yolanda, Erenao, Carlo, Mario and Angela, would bring me food. Angela was the youngest, I suppose she was about six. She and Mario would bring me food more often than the others because they didn't seem to be at the same risk. So I grew very fond of Angela and Mario at that stage.

My favourite cave had a good vantage point. Looking across the valley on the opposite hillside, I could see the hill town of Castel Trossino. The Germans had taken it over as their headquarters and I used to sit on a rock hidden in my cave and watch their transport going up and down all the time. It was getting much colder and I felt very exposed so I built a dry stone wall across the front of my cave with an entrance at one side and a lookout on the other, and made it really quite cosy.

It was filled with leaves and I entertained myself catching snakes and skinning them and making belts for the family. I also knitted myself some boots on bits of wire. They were supposed to be socks but were so huge as I didn't know how to turn the heel and so on, but they kept my feet warm at night. I never had a fire near my cave. I would wander off, light a fire elsewhere, catch some sparrows and cook them there.

I waited at San Giorgio until our troops advanced up into Italy. One minute I was in German territory, and the next moment it was controlled by the English. They kept to the valley in their advance, and made no inroads up the mountain passes, but from where I was hiding in my cave above San Giorgio, I could see, just across the valley at Castel Trossino, the German headquarters – and suddenly it was empty! The Germans had amazingly melted away. Their trucks were no longer trundling up and down the ramp, and best of all the German sentry in the spire of the church – whom I always felt was watching my every move in my mountain hideaway – had gone.

It was time to go although I was sad to leave these good Italian friends after all they had done for me. Matteo had told me that Ascoli had fallen without any trouble at all; there had been a bit of bombing and shelling and then the Jerries had just pulled out as it wasn't a good defensive position. So Italy was now free and I was able to hitch-hike across to Rome. It was the middle of July 1944, and when I arrived in the dark, Rome seemed devastated. I stumbled around in the moonlight, not having a clue where I was, and found myself amongst some ruins. I didn't know if they were caused by bombs or not and it was only later that I discovered that I had been scrambling around the Forum.

By the KING'S Order the name of Guardsman D. Hutton-Fox, Coldstream Guards, was published in the London Gazette on 26th July, 1945. as mentioned in a Despatch for distinguished service. I am charged to record His Majesty's high appreciation.

Secretary of State for War

A rare citation for Mention in Despatches. Guardsman D Hutton-Fox was noted for his bravery and resourcefulness in escaping from German captivity.

Eventually I found my regiment and I walked into the camp exclaiming, 'I've made it, I've made it!' But no one was interested and I was amazed. Then I saw a sergeant major and he said, 'Where's your AB64?' which is a sort of Army passport. I said, 'I haven't got an AB64! If I had one I'd be a German!' They always came well-equipped – but I'd got nothing.

I went and had a jolly good meal and still no one took any notice of me. I'd been a prisoner before this. The last time I had been with my regiment was 1942 and now it was 1944. I had two years of terrible deprivations and no one seemed to ask me who I was, where I'd come from or anything. So then I went to the quartermaster and got myself kitted out with uniform, walked out of the camp back to Matteo to give him my decent boots and then returned to Rome.

I noticed that the Americans had the most wonderful recreation facilities for their troops and all the English had was a lousy old NAAFI [Navy Army and Air Force Institutes], where you eventually got a cup of tea in a dirty cracked mug and it was cold. I was pretty disgusted, so much so that when I got home I wrote a letter to *The Times*. It caused quite a stir. I had letters back from a major general and a brigadier, also from the Royal Society of St George.

They wrote back saying, they noted with keenest interest that I had said I was an English soldier – not a British soldier – and that my experiences were obviously of great interest to them and they wanted me to join the St George Society as an honorary member. I wouldn't, obviously. Well I didn't want to join anything did I? I'd joined the Army and that had been a mistake!

Eventually from Rome I was sent to Naples and I caught a boat home. We finally landed in Liverpool but because of German submarines it had taken us ages to get there. We had to go halfway across the Atlantic, almost as far as America, and then come all the way round Northern Ireland, to avoid the submarines. I remember thinking on the boat, 'Wouldn't it be terrible if, after all this, I was torpedoed!'

When I got to Liverpool I was put in a camp and given some forms to fill in. I was told I would be going on leave but would have to get medically checked first. They gave me a telegram to fill in to tell my parents that I would be home in a week and they told me to be patient and not to do anything silly. I thought this was damn silly, I was not waiting a week in that dump. So I walked out of the camp and went to the station. I didn't know wartime England at all, but got past the Military Police and eventually managed to get a slow train to Oxford. I presumed I'd be able to get a taxi home but found there were no taxis at all. So I went back into the station, put my bag down and sat there groaning. The transport officer came over.

'What's the matter soldier?'

'I think I'm dying!' I replied.

'What's the trouble?'

'Well, I've been a prisoner and I've just been shipped home and I'm ill.'

'We'd better get you to a hospital – you don't look at all well.' I was very thin of course.

So he called his driver and put me in his car. We went up the Woodstock Road and when we were nearing the hospital I said, 'Look I only live a few doors up, why don't you drop me home instead?' So he took me home. I said thank you very much and got out.

I walked up the path and knocked on the door. I hadn't seen my parents for about seven years as I'd been abroad all that time. They opened the door and there was my mother, a little white-haired old lady! It was a horrible shock for me and it was a real shock for her too because she'd been forced to consider that I might be dead. I just collapsed on the doorstep and was put to bed. That was when the nightmares and all sorts of things started.

My mother always had this conviction that her boys would come through the war, and we did. When I was reported missing they went up to London. They had friends in Cairo trying to trace what had happened to me, and she just wouldn't accept that I was dead. She would say I'd been taken prisoner but never acknowledged that I was dead. One of my brothers was in the RAF, the other in the Royal Marines and all three of us were missing at one time, but all three of us survived.

GIORGIO GEDDES DA FILICAIA

ARMED FORCES

Giorgio Geddes da Filicaia, an Italian soldier fighting with Germany on the Russian front, returned to Italy on the eve of the Italian surrender on 8 September 1943 and narrowly escaped being shot by his former allies. Under the subsequent German occupation of Italy all Italian Armed Forces personnel were declared prisoners of war. Italy's war had officially ended – but the fighting was not over.

When I heard about the armistice, I was in a state of shock. I had personally realised that the relationship between Italy and Germany had greatly deteriorated, especially after Stalingrad – when the Russian Army, immensely revived by supplies from the US, managed to change the course of the war – and with the Allied bombing of Germany. These events convinced most Italians that a German defeat was possible and that the signing of the armistice was a timely decision in order to stop, or at least reduce, the carnage in Italy. But I was not expecting such an immediate reaction on the part of the Germans with the occupation of Italy and all of the resulting tragedies.

Giorgio Geddes da Filicaia in uniform in Voroshilovgrad in the Donets basin, aged 23.

Up to one day before the armistice, I had respect for the *Wehrmacht*, who were soldiers carrying out their duties, but none for the SS, which was full of cruel extremists and fanatics who would stop at nothing to reach their goals. The occupation of Italy by the Germans, especially as it became a ruthless reprisal against all Italians, military and civilian, turned me against them.

I had just recently returned from the Russian front and was on special leave granted to me by the General Staff of the Army. During my meeting at the General Headquarters of the Italian Army, which, as I recall it, was practically invisible and, I believe, even underground, the general whom I had been ordered to meet said, 'Lieutenant Geddes, you have been chosen for a very important position. At the General Headquarters of the German Army in Italy, commanded by Field Marshal Kesserling at Riva del Garda, you will take the place of one of our senior officers because we do not trust him. We want to know everything that you can observe about the movements and orders given by that headquarters or received from all of the German troops operating in Italy.'

The atmosphere in that sort of underground headquarters was not easy to identify. The officers seemed unaware of the great events that were brewing and certainly could not have known that they would take place three days later. I realised that this would be a particularly delicate situation and that it probably indicated a high state of tension on the part of the Italian General Staff regarding our German allies. With this intuition, but not sure that I wasn't mistaken, I took my two days of leave.

Before reaching Riva del Garda, I was first to stop in Bolzano at the Italian military headquarters to receive further orders. As I was part of the RIE [Army Information Section], I was allowed to travel in civilian clothes. If I were to travel in uniform and not find a free seat, I would have to travel standing up since a military officer is not allowed to sprawl in some corridor. However, if I were to travel in civilian clothes, I could blend in with the other travellers and behave as I saw fit. I chose the second option.

Shortly after departure for Bolzano, one of the Italians on the train asked me if I had heard anything about a proclamation by Marshall Badoglio, Prime Minister of Italy and Commander-in-Chief of the military, on the radio during which he announced that Italy had signed the armistice with the Allies, thus ending the war. According to this rumour, the German Army would be withdrawing its troops from Italy in an orderly manner. I began to think that my new job with the German allies might be more or less to assist them in packing up and leaving Italy.

It was well past midnight when the train stopped in the middle of nowhere and I woke up. We were perhaps 15 kilometres from Bolzano. There was an anguished silence and I realised that I was the only person left on the train. I didn't have to wait long to be shaken out of my bewilderment since the night was shattered by an intense bombardment in the direction of Bolzano. The bombing continued, with sinister flashes and explosions, for about an hour, after which it calmed down, but the train did not move again. I decided to try to sleep and, at dawn, I awoke and looked out of the window. I was totally surrounded by German soldiers. I greeted them in German (my German was excellent, having spoken it since I was two years old). Was I military or a civilian the German officer asked me. My army case was stored next to me and lying would have been risky so I told them that I was on leave and that's why I was in civilian clothes. At that point, the officer told me that he had to deliver me to the *Wehrmacht* headquarters which was about 2 kilometres away from where the train had stopped.

My army case was carried by two *Feldgendarmerie* [German Military Police] and we walked to the headquarters, which was guarded by two German tanks. I was amazed to see the barracks already crowded at that early hour with all sorts of Italian military personnel. The other Italians told me that Marshall Badoglio had made a radio announcement on 8 September confirming that the war had come to an end. There were no newspapers or radios available in the barracks, so everyone was guessing what was going to happen next.

The question was quickly answered when a German officer walked into our barracks and said that he had to deliver a very important message to everyone and that he needed somebody, if available, to translate it into Italian. I stepped forward from the group and translated his short message word by word: 'The Italian government has signed a separate armistice with the Allied Forces, betraying Germany, which will continue the war to victory. Consequently, from today, all members of the Italian military are our prisoners of war. In the next few days, you will start your trip on foot towards Germany where you will be imprisoned in a concentration camp until the end of the war.' He told us that his words were Hitler's final decision and no one who heard the message had doubts that, although one war might have ended the day before, today had not brought any peace and all anyone could see ahead were new sacrifices. I can remember this message as though it had been engraved in my memory.

When the German officer left, two fellow officers, whom I had never seen before and who were also dressed in civilian clothing, suggested we take advantage of our appearance and obtain authorisation to leave the camp. They did not speak German and they asked me what I thought about the possibility of getting out of there. Knowing the Germans through having fought next to them over the previous two years, in my opinion there was only one possibility and that was to lie convincingly to the commander at the gates about our position as civilians and risk being shot if they were to discover the truth. We discussed this for a while and decided that walking to Germany and starving to death there or becoming the victims of Allied bombings was worse than trying to escape and being killed by a German platoon.

I told the two officers to follow me, never to open their mouths and to be ready to risk their lives. We reached the gate and I told the German officer that we were leaving the barracks because we were not Army people, but had been caught up by the news and had come there to hear what was going on. The gate officer was impressed by my German. I said that we had been verbally authorised to go on leave by a German officer and I looked into the crowd in the courtyard and pointed one guard out. He asked if I was sure and I replied affirmatively, suggesting that he go and ask him. The gate officer replied that he would and that if I was lying we would be shot on the spot. In the meantime, the officer I had indicated had disappeared in the crowd and I could not see him any more, nor could the officer at the gate. He turned to us and said, 'I believe you, you can go.'

In a split second, the three of us were out, with my two followers completely unaware of what had happened. I did not say a word about it and told them to follow me on the road going south. My target was to distance us from the barracks and hide. We had probably gone 400 metres when a German car came towards us. The car stopped and the driver asked where we were going. I told him that we were civilians and that we were going to Trent or nearby to find food. My German made him think that I was of German descent and he believed me, but he told me that we had to turn back immediately because we were needed as manpower to work for the German cause. '*Raboten*' [Russian for 'work like a slave']. I said, 'Yes sir, we will walk back and work for Germany as you have ordered.' The two officers behind me did not open their mouths but I told them in Italian that the order was to go back and work. The Germans understood my message in Italian and fortunately did not ask us to step into the car, which would have brought us back to the barracks. I will never know why they didn't take that precaution. They drove off and the moment the car disappeared, I told my companions that, if we were to have a chance to survive, we had to hide. When night fell, we approached a farm house, knocked at the door and an Italian voice reassured me that we could ask for hospitality. We were able to change into peasant outfits, thus becoming a part of the big crowd which was roaming about Italy in those days.

We left for the first small train station and we parted ways. I arrived in Florence and the next morning the doorman woke me at about 7.30 saying that there was an officer of the Fascist Army at the front door who wanted to speak to me. I learned afterwards that his name was Captain Carità, who became notorious in Italy for his cruelty and for capturing Italians who did not return to fight with the Germans. He asked me to step into the car and go to his headquarters, all the while two of his guards with their guns pointed into my back. At this point, I asked the Captain if he could first take me to the German headquarters since I was fluent in German, had just returned from the Russian front, and had been awarded a medal by General von Mackensen. I told him that I wanted to continue to fight with the Germans because of my knowledge of the German language and my experience with them in war. Evidently, this made him think that I was under the direct command of the Germans and, not wanting to interfere with higher authorities, he let me out of the car less than 100 metres later. He told me, however, that he would check on my whereabouts very soon because, if I had not joined the Army again, he would consider me a deserter. Knowing that the area was now dangerous for me, I managed to reach my family in the mountains where I had to hide for some time to avoid being drafted again. I stayed there until I was able to join the liberation units that were being formed to chase out the Germans, thus freeing Italian cities and consequently avoiding further bombings, and saving lives, art works and property.

One war had ended on 8 September with the signing of the armistice with the Allies but, on 9 September, a new one started which was as bad and perhaps worse than the previous one, since a civil war had started in Italy. The official war was, in many ways, a typical one with all of the tragedies that war produces. But it was clear who the enemy was and it was fought along more or less standard lines. The civil war was very treacherous. The Germans were fighting us with greater fury since the signing of the armistice was considered as betrayal by the Italians. Civilians and military were indistinguishable and Italians were fighting Italians.

About one year later, the war seemed to end in Florence with the arrival of the Allies. We really felt that we had been liberated and celebrated that day as though it were really over. However, we were not really free of war until D-Day because only that victory meant that there was really no more risk of a German revival.

HUBERT SCHMIDT

FRONT LINE

Hubert Schmidt of the German Army was stationed in Alborg, Denmark.

News about the war came mostly from the Danish newspapers. We had someone who could interpret some of it, and it would keep us a little abreast of what was going on. I guessed that the German High Command, being the controlling force, made sure that they would not print the real truth, but only their truth. Interpreting the news about glorious retreats by the German Army from areas in Germany gave us truth enough. It did not look good.

Visiting local stores, I met the proprietor of a small grocery store, and he sold delicious smoked eel, my favorite snacking food. He was really the only Danish civilian with whom I could converse a little in German. One other delicacy for me was the whipped cream cake sold at the bakery.

It did not come as a great surprise when on 4 May 1945, some Danish civilians were seen carrying arms. I had just returned from the HQ Paymaster, carrying about 10,000 kroner in my pocket. Passing a newspaper stand, I saw the headline and the reason for the armed civilians. It read: 'Germany has capitulated'. It was in Danish, but I knew enough to know what it said.

The war was over and Hitler was dead. At this moment, it actually was anti-climactic. The hope that we would win the war had long passed, ever since the great defeats of our troops in Russia and the invasion of the Allied troops.

When I entered the major's office, he had already received the following orders from Headquarters: 1. Do not pay the soldiers until further notice. 2. Do not hand over your arms to the Danes. 3. Prepare to march under arms to the German border. 4. Surrender only to the British High Command. 5. Do not take any Danish products across the border. That included money. We had a long walk ahead. Alborg is located as far north you can go in Denmark and it is about 300 kilometres to the German border.

I looked at my major, and tried to hand over the payroll to him. He quickly stopped me, and told me that I would have to hang on to it, and use the money in Denmark for buying food supplies for the troops. When I told my friend Joachim about the money situation, he agreed with my concern that I could become a target, having all that cash. Some enterprising bad guy might conk me over the head and take the money. I stuffed the money into my uniform pockets, and slept against a wall, while Joachim placed his bunk bed in front of mine. Our quarters were relatively primitive. All of us, except the NCOs [non-commissioned officers] and the major, slept in a large hall in bunk beds.

The next day, we packed our stuff, ready for the march to the German border. Transportation was not available and that left the question of what to carry on our march. The major and I agreed on at least one ledger, with the names of our troops and with an accounting of the money in hand and the distribution to purchase goods. We agreed that by the time we reached the German/Danish border we would have spent all the Danish money.

A long march was ahead of us. I had one advantage being the paymaster: I did not have to carry a rifle or a machine gun, just my Luger. Somehow, I thought it prudent to keep some of the papers accumulated by my former paymaster. I packed a whole bunch of ledgers in a footlocker. We decided that, between Joachim and I, we could carry the wooden box by holding onto its two handles. Only our cook had a vehicle, a truck with supplies, pulling the large cooking kettle. Carrying the box for just four hours convinced us that we could not and would not carry the box even one more mile. We handed the box over to the cook to use it and the contents for heating material. Most of us decided to dump our gas masks, but kept the container. It became my egg holder.

Instrument of Surrender

of .

All German armed forces in HOLLAND, in

northwest Germany including all islands,

and in DENMARK.

1. The German Command agrees to the surrender of all German armed
forces in HOLLAND, in northwest GERMANY including the FRISIAN
ISLANDS and HELIGOLAND and all other islands, in SCHLESWIG-
HOLSTEIN, and in DENMARK, to the C.-in-C. 21 Army Group.
This to include all naval ships in these areas.
These forces to lay down their arms and to surrender unconditionally.

2. All hostilities on land, on sea, or in the air by German forces
in the above areas to cease at 0800 hrs. British Double Summer Time
on Saturday 5 May 1945.

3. The German command to carry out at once, and without argument or
comment, all further orders that will be issued by the Allied
Powers on any subject.

4. Disobedience of orders, or failure to comply with them, will be
regarded as a breach of these surrender terms and will be dealt
with by the Allied Powers in accordance with the accepted laws
and usages of war.

5. This instrument of surrender is independent of, without prejudice
to, and will be superseded by any general instrument of surrender
imposed by or on behalf of the Allied Powers and applicable to Germany
and the German armed forces as a whole.

6. This instrument of surrender is written in English and in German.

    The English version is the authentic text.

7. The decision of the Allied Powers will be final if any doubt or
dispute arises as to the meaning or interpretation of the surrender
terms.

B. L. Montgomery
Field-Marshal

4 May 1945
1830 hrs.

On 23–24 March, Field Marshal Montgomery's troops crossed the Rhine and advanced into the north German plain. On 4 May, the German forces in Holland, north-west Germany and Denmark surrendered to Montgomery on Lüneberg Heath.

It took us six days to march the 180 drudgery miles to the German border. From what I saw, Denmark had housed a lot of German soldiers. Fortunately, the weather cooperated, keeping any precipitation away. On our last day in Denmark, just about 300 kroner remained in my possession. Shortly before the border checkpoint, a few elderly ladies were standing at the side of the road watching our procession. I thought, why give the border police the money? I walked over to one of the ladies, took the 300 kroner and handed it to her. A surprised look, then a smile. It was a nice finish to my Denmark experience. The Danish border guards required us to empty our backpacks and display everything in our possession. If they could, they probably would have body-searched us. Any Danish products were confiscated. Some German soldiers tried to bring kroner across in their gas-mask container. The border police were not fooled.

As soon as we crossed the border, British soldiers directed us to a pile of weapons where we discarded ours, including my Luger.

After one more stretch of about ten miles we arrived at our so-called POW camp; a farm, with a large barn, and a duck pond. I do not know how many German soldiers were housed in the general area, but it had to be tens of thousands. The farmer provided the straw in the barn and straw for the few tents we brought with us. As paymaster, I could pitch my tent, giving me separate quarters. My friend Joachim pitched his tent next to mine. Our major, the cook, and the NCOs all had tents as quarters. By the time we had a few days of prison behind us, it became clear that if you had to be in a prison camp, let it be a British camp.

MICHAEL LEWIS

ARMED FORCES

Michael Lewis was a British NCO and cameraman with the British Army's Film & Photographic Unit at the liberation of Bergen-Belsen concentration camp. He was one of the first to enter liberated Copenhagen on 5 May 1945.

I remember the moment we crossed the border into Denmark. It was as if we had been travelling at night for years and the sun had suddenly come out. We had been through Europe, witnessed the misery and the pain, the grief, the death, the uncertainty, houses smashed. Now here were a people who were well fed and happy. Houses were standing up and the sun was shining. The end of the war must've been near? I couldn't believe it. We had to cross a stretch of water by ferry to reach Copenhagen. On the outskirts there was rather a broad road with a grass verge and someone had given the orders for the usual break. We'd been travelling a long time and the whole column stopped alongside the grass verge, and out came the brewing-up cans and the tommy cookers, and we sat on the grass brewing up.

For what was the hurry? Life was good, it was marvellous. We sprinkled our mixture of tea, sugar and milk onto the water and began sipping our tea when, from the distance, from Copenhagen, came a group of youths and girls on bicycles. Their spokes flashed colours and when they stopped cycling they turned out to be red, white and blue streamers. They stared and stared at us and they said – they spoke English – 'Why have you stopped? Copenhagen is waiting for you.' We didn't know that Copenhagen was waiting for us, that it was still in the war frame of mind really, and we said, 'We've just stopped to have a cup of tea.' They could have hugged themselves with joy, they must've heard about the British always having tea, and now they knew and had seen us actually having a break for tea before we entered the capital as liberators. They knew that we must've been British and that the end of the war was at hand.

When we entered Copenhagen the city was filled with thousands of people, hanging from windows and doorways and squares. Unwisely, I got out of the jeep to take a picture, and the jeep immediately disappeared under waves of people, who sank the whole jeep down to its knees, nearly put its springs out of action. We could hardly get them off and I was nearly swamped and mobbed. Oh, it was lovely being a hero.

WARREN DUNN

ARMED FORCES

Warren Dunn, 20, from Santa Barbara, California, was part of the unit to liberate Dachau concentration camp in April 1945.

We heard very little about what was happening to the Jews in Europe. I don't think there was any awareness of people being incarcerated in Germany, in Poland and other areas; until I was actually in the concentration camp I had absolutely no knowledge of people being gassed and cremated.

My first experience of this was in Dachau. As a company commander I was ordered to liberate the camp which I thought might contain several hundred POWs. We arrived at six o'clock in the morning with instructions to talk to the prisoners and assure them that help was coming from medical and food service personnel. But before we got there another unit had captured some of the guards and many of the Germans who were not able to flee, and they had actually executed them – stood them up against the wall and shot them. In fact the

Young survivors at Dachau
concentration camp cheer
the US troops liberating
the camp.

company commander was court-marshalled because of that but you know, when you see this kind of thing and the people responsible, it gives rise to a tremendous amount of hate.

The first thing we saw outside the camp on railroad tracks was forty boxcars – I believe that was the count – absolutely filled with dead bodies. Then we shot the locks off the gate and went inside and saw thousands more bodies lying around the whole compound. And not having had any knowledge of what we were facing, this was unreal, totally unreal. The weather was still cold so there wasn't the stench you might have experienced had it been warmer. But there was the smell of death – I'd smelt that during combat when we'd come upon the enemy – dead soldiers and horses and all that. And the odour was there, of death, mingled with the smell of the internees because they hadn't had a bath or a shower in forever.

I guess that seeing that train load of bodies was the first revulsion – I felt the bile coming up into my throat from seeing this. I couldn't understand what in the world had gone wrong here. I was a young lieutenant of 20 years and had never ever seen anything of this sort before. I'd seen death, of course, in combat, but you know, we're fighting an enemy and you expect to find dead people when you're shooting live rounds. But to find something like this – I just couldn't believe what I was seeing – I could not believe it. There were probably 15,000 dead bodies in Dachau alone and I imagine a similar number in Buchenwald, Bergen-Belsen and other camps. With all those bodies, we found only one live person on that train.

All the time I was there, I couldn't figure it out – why are all these people here? Why are so many dead? What did they do to deserve all this? Those were my thoughts. Not having any background knowledge, I couldn't understand what the Holocaust was – what is this cruelty from one human to another? I couldn't fathom it – it was overwhelming to all of us that went in there, even to hardcore combat veterans, we'd never seen anything like this. Being a company commander I had to maintain control of my troops; my job was to lead them and tell them what to do and not go to pieces myself. I had an awfully hard time doing this – this was very different to death in combat. A lot of my guys had a terrible time with this, some of them fainted, some vomited. I felt like vomiting myself, but I couldn't let myself do that, since I was the leader of this group. And there was another difficulty: here I am, supposed to be a liberator but my orders were to keep all the inmates in the camp because if they had gotten out, they'd have died; they hadn't had enough food and could hardly walk, to say nothing of going out into the world again and fending for themselves – it would have killed them. But many of the prisoners who could speak a little broken English came and thanked me. They wanted to tell me about how they'd experienced this horror for so long and then, all of a sudden, they had been given hope that they were going to survive – that's what they wanted to tell me. I couldn't communicate too well with them, but I think they knew – I felt that they knew we were there to save them. From that standpoint, I was very elated to think that we'd saved so many lives.

MASS-OBSERVATION ARCHIVE, 30 APRIL 1945
REACTION TO THE DISCOVERY OF CONCENTRATION CAMPS

I saw the atrocity film at the new gallery today. Of course I expected it to be terrible, but it's more terrible, not because of the pile of corpses – after all they're dead – but because of the survivors. They just aren't human anymore. They don't talk together – they just go about with their eyes on the ground. I think the worst moment of all was when one of these almost skeletons tried to smile at an American soldier – you know, his face simply couldn't express a smile anymore. The audiences were deathly quiet; not even a whisper. Some of it's shown without commentary, and I have never heard such a hush as there was all over the cinema.

LESLIE SPIRO

CONCENTRATION CAMP

Leslie Spiro, a Jew from Hungary, was sent to Auschwitz-Birkenau in 1945. He was one of the few surviving members of his family.

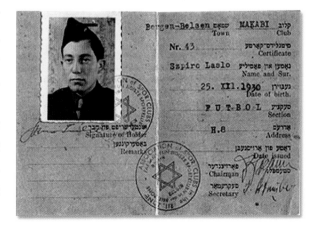

Leslie Spiro's ID card from Bergen-Belsen Displaced Persons camp. After liberation he spent 18 months looking for people he had known before the Holocaust.

At the beginning of January, 1945, the Russian Army was closing in on the camp. The Germans transported the prisoners to the west, first killing those who were sick or unable to make the journey. I was placed in a cattle car headed for Mauthausen concentration camp. It was very cold and I didn't have warm clothes. My feet were frozen so badly from the cold that I could not walk. Fortunately for me, when I arrived at the camp, a French Jew carried me and hid me in a makeshift hospital. When they took off my shoes, parts of my toes

Far right: The Spiro family before the war: father Adolf, mother Helen, Leslie and sister Katalin. Leslie and Katalin survived the camps; their parents did not.
Right: Leslie and Katalin.

on my left foot came off. Since the Germans were killing those with physical problems, I was very lucky. I spent a long time on my back and was cared for and fed by my new-found friend. He put some stuff on my feet, axle grease or something like that and wrapped them up with paper and he looked after me for days. He shouldn't have. It was dangerous for him.

The Germans left the camp a few days before liberation, realising that the Americans would soon be arriving. Liberation was on 5 May. I still remember that day, a lot of emotions. When the gate first opened, there was this Jewish boy from New York. He didn't speak much Yiddish. I remember he sat down on a big stone, took off his helmet and cried. But many of us died from malnutrition and starvation even in the care of the Americans. They were giving us this Army food and nobody was used to it. We were not used to eating much more than bread and plain soup. I did not see the French man who had saved my life. I was never able to track him down.

LEO LOWY

CONCENTRATION CAMP

Leo Lowy was born in 1928 in Carpathia, then part of Czechoslovakia, in the city of Berehovo. In 1943, under pro-Nazi Hungarian rule, he and his twin sister were transported along with other local Jews to Auschwitz-Birkenau concentration camp.

About 1940–41, things escalated suddenly. I remember that panic set in when we heard about an uncle and aunt and their family who were taken from their home and deported to Poland for not having the proper documents. News filtered out that they were executed. At first we couldn't believe that something that inhumane could have happened.

In 1943 some prominent Jews from our town were taken to the synagogue and held there for ransom. Everyone gave as much money as they could, but the men were never released. Soon afterwards, everyone in our town was rounded up. The Hungarians took my family and me to a brick factory. Then we were transported to Auschwitz by train, with a hundred or more people crowded into a cattle car. There was little food and no facilities. They slammed the door shut, and we rolled along for days. We arrived in Auschwitz in the middle of the night but they didn't open the doors until the morning. We had to listen to people screaming and dogs barking. The cries and the stench of that car is something I will never forget.

We were lined up along the tracks and soldiers went up and down the rows, looking for people with physical abnormalities and for twins. One of our neighbours called out that she had twins and pointed to Miriam and me, saying that we were also twins.

Miriam and I were taken to a hospital in Birkenau. We were told that everything would be all right and that we would be reunited with our parents later. Something didn't seem right, though, and I was scared. I asked some people what was happening there and they pointed to the chimneys. I never told my sister Miriam. I

Hungarian Jews from the Berehovo Ghetto on arrival at Auschwitz-Birkenau concentration camp.

kept it a secret from her because I wanted to protect her. From that day on, I never took my eyes off those chimneys.

We were taken to a separate place and visited by Dr Mengele, whom the inmates called 'Dr Death'. For about nine months, Mengele and many other

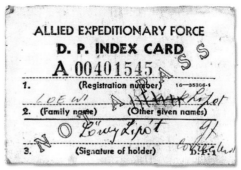

doctors examined my sister and me, sometimes alone and sometimes together. They injected us with fluids and took blood samples from us. I was only about 14 at the time.

Day after day, they measured different parts of our bodies. They checked our hands, our bone structure and our eyes for colour comparisons. They also took samples of our hair. It was very scary because the rooms we were taken to did not look like laboratories. They were grey and dingy.

As twins we were treated a little more humanely, because Mengele needed us for his medical experiments. One day, when I was doing some work with three men, we ran into two drunken German soldiers, who hauled us into a vacant room. The soldiers started beating the men with canes and made them jump out of a window. There must have been an angel watching over me because, when my turn came, I just blurted out the words, 'Dr Mengele' and 'twin'. The soldiers just froze and let me go. Being one of Dr Mengele's experimental subjects saved me.

There were some twins in our group who were so identical that we couldn't tell them apart. There were also people with physical deformities and one family, seven of whom were dwarfs. I had the misfortune of having the same blood type as one of the German soldiers. One day they took me and laid me on a table and put a tube in me and another tube in the soldier. They transferred my blood to him, which was very scary.

As they were doing these experiments, I was just grateful that it wasn't worse than I expected. I often felt dizzy. I don't know if it was the fear or the drugs and dyes that they had injected. The doctors never explained what they were doing. We were drained physically and emotionally. We lost a lot of weight, not only because of the diet but also because of our fear of what the next step would be.

In January of 1945, we were marched a couple of miles from Birkenau to Auschwitz in the heavy snow and bitter cold. I was able to escape and hid in a basement. I waited until morning, when everything was quiet and all the screaming had stopped. When I came out of my hiding place, the camp had been deserted. Slowly, some other prisoners began to emerge. A couple of hundred of us gathered. A few days later we were liberated by the Russians.

Later I learned that my twin sister Miriam had, by some miracle, met up with our three other sisters on the death march from Auschwitz. They were liberated by the Americans about four months later. Miriam survived; unfortunately, my three other sisters were so weak that they died within a week of liberation. If it wasn't for the fact that Miriam and I were twins, we would not have survived.

Everyone else in my family – my parents, aunts, uncles and cousins – were all gassed in Auschwitz. All the other children from my hometown were gassed on the day of our arrival in Auschwitz. None survived.

BBC BROADCAST, 19 APRIL 1945
RICHARD DIMBLEBY DESCRIBES BERGEN-BELSEN CONCENTRATION CAMP

I have seen many terrible sights in the last five years, but nothing, NOTHING approaching the dreadful interior of this hut at Belsen. The dead and dying lay close together. I picked my way over corpse after corpse in the gloom ... the convulsive movements of dying people too weak to raise themselves from the floor ...

JANUSZ KORZENIEWSKI

CONCENTRATION CAMP

Janusz Korzeniewski, a member of the Polish Resistance from 1941 until 1943, was imprisoned in Pawiak prison in Warsaw and Auschwitz-Birkenau and Mauthausen concentration camps between 1943 and 1945.

In the last days I suppose the Germans wanted to camouflage the evidence so they killed so many that there were heaps of people lying everywhere. The end happened on 5 May at 5 pm. A few days before the end the SS men left the camp and the guards were replaced by an army of old people, over 60s. They gave the impression that they didn't really care about what was happening. Rumours passed from mouth to mouth that food was getting scarcer – although we were working less because all the power stations had been destroyed. We were getting less and less food and for the last three or four days we didn't get any at all. On 5 May at 5 pm American men in a tank appeared at the gate. It was such a contrast in this big war which had lasted so long. There was a small man dressed in a grey uniform and he said 'Now you are free, this is the end of the war for you!' There was a big silence for a moment and then everybody exploded with joy, everybody was singing and shouting in his own language and there were many nationalities. The majority were Polish, but there were Russian, Spanish, French, Dutch and even a few English acting as interpreters. This is how the war ended for us. Up until the very end I had hoped that my father was alive but he disappeared somewhere during the war, nobody knows where.

These experiences I had in concentration camps are never very far away from me. Soon after our liberation three or four lorries full of food came into the camp intended for distribution among the prisoners. As they stopped, the prisoners rushed to the lorries and the food disappeared in a matter of minutes in spite of the protestations of the American Army. During this time one of the internal *Kapos* [prisoners chosen by the SS to head work gangs], who was quite cruel and killed quite a lot of people, didn't manage to get away from the concentration camp because Polish people put their guns outside to make sure that criminals didn't escape. Most of them did but this *Kapo* didn't. He was so unaware of the changes in the camp, he thought the Americans could manage the prisoners. He drew attention to himself and in a moment the prisoners abandoned this food and they rushed towards him. There was a sharp shriek. I stood about 20 yards away. When the crowds dispersed only the shreds of this man were scattered on the ground. They tore – or cut with their knives – everything apart and threw it on the ground.

LUCIEN HUT

HOME FRONT

Lucien Hut, born in 1931, lived through the German occupation of Rotterdam.

I don't remember the actual day the war ended. But I vividly remember when American B-17s started flying over, very low, dropping crates of canned goods, sometimes in fields, sometimes in streets, but without parachutes. They just dropped them. And the English prepared special low fat, high nutrition cookies for us. We had to be very careful what type of food we started to eat. Our bodies couldn't tolerate too much fat, sugar or anything heavy. Thus, American soldiers were warned not to give chocolate, or candy, to children. It could cause them to get deathly ill or even die.

Distribution of the cookies was a problem so they were loaded in trucks and sprayed on the streets with mechanisms for spraying salt. People were so malnourished and ill that every second was a survival second.

On my own body I counted over 100 ulcerated sores. Also, almost everyone was covered with lice, so the Americans set up special DDT stations in the streets. I shall never forget going through one of those.

Such great numbers of people died that mass graves were established. There may have been some funerals, but basically people were just 'placed'. They were carried to the graves in *rouwwagen*, black wagons with four corner posts, pulled by one or two horses. Coffins were unavailable so bodies were wrapped in black blankets. One time I saw a wagon in which one of the blankets had come open and a man's head just dropped out.

Leen arrived home first, probably a month after the war was over. He came in an American truck and wore an American uniform. About a week later, my dad and Jan arrived together in a Canadian truck with Canadian soldiers, wearing Canadian uniforms. The whole truck was piled with food. They unloaded 'tons' of it into our house. I don't know how long my father and brother had served with the Canadians, probably about eight or nine months, but when the war was over they came home and brought that truck with people and food.

It seems to me that the most lasting impressions in life are those you receive as a young child. They stick with you. And strange as it is, the older I get, the closer I feel to the war years. My experiences as a young child have never left me, such as that of walking with the young girl who was shot right through the shoulder, the time the Germans blew out the woman's brains in front of my grandmother's house and on and on. These were daily occurrences.

So, in general, the war is still always with me. It was embedded deep within and it will stay that way forever, I suppose.

Lucien Hut in Rotterdam. Food shortages in Holland had reached such critical levels in April 1945 that the German occupying forces agreed to hold their fire while Canadian bombers dropped 11,000 tonnes of food. Twenty thousand Dutch civilians died of starvation.

HÉLÈNE DELATTRE

Hélène Delattre was a 29-year-old housewife living in Beuvry in the north of France when war broke out.

Before the hostilities started, we had the '*drôle de guerre*' (the 'phoney war') which lasted several months when neither side moved from their frontiers. The French Army seemed a bit asleep, it did not remain vigilant, this was the impression that one felt... Especially in the night of 9–10 May, when suddenly the German attack struck us like lightning. Breaking all international laws, they crossed neutral countries such as Belgium, Netherlands, Luxemburg, and bypassed the 'Maginot Line' which was supposed to protect us.

In just a few days the enemy completed their invasion. There was no opposition to them. Our Army hardly fired a gun. The Germans arrived in impeccable order, with shining unused guns and dressed in new and clean uniforms. They took immediately all administrative positions, mayoralties, schools, post offices; all mail was stopped. They did not steal or plunder, they had plenty of money and bought what they wanted, but shops rapidly sold out of all the essential goods: coffee, flour, butter, wool to knit, etc...

And then the government declared the end of war for us. France was now under the control of Marshal Pétain, this man that had been the hero of 'Verdun' in the First World War... and one heard from England a so-called de Gaulle telling us to continue the war. Many thought he was a holy fool... 'What does he know of our condition?' And gradually France divided into two rival camps, some for Pétain, others for de Gaulle and in many families one no longer dared to say what one thought, and there were denunciations to the local German authorities which brought terrible reprisals...

Thereafter, our great fear was from the bombing by English and American planes that aimed especially at railways, but many civilians were killed, by miracle none from our family.

So then we waited until 1945 in order that this World War would finally end and the Germans returned to their homeland, sad and confused, having lost the arrogance that accompanied their triumphant arrival.

DAVID PARKER

Lance-Corporal David Parker, of B Company, 6th Durham Light Infantry, joined the Forces at the age of 14. He was captured in France in January 1940.

I had been at this camp [in Danzig] for nearly two years when, with the Russians approaching, the Germans moved us out on 19 February 1945. We were rounded up at our work-place, returned to camp and within half an hour were off to the big camp. In all the rush we were not able to say goodbye to Franz who had been such a good friend giving us news. That same day we set off to march across the north of Europe. We crossed the Oder at Wollen by boat and continued marching across Germany.

The names of the towns we passed through were: Stolp, Koslin, Cammin, Wollin, Swinemunde, Anklam, Neubrandenburg, Neustrelitz, Gustow, Wismar, Schwerin, Laurinburg, Perleburg, Stendal and Wittenberg.

In Stolp we were marched into a school for the night and across the road we found a party of girls in pyjamas and had a good chat to them. The next morning the place was absolutely quiet and we were told by a Pole that the girls had been told that they could take a bath there but when they were in the water they were all electrocuted, killing the lot. In one place we went into a barn for the night and

David Parker, standing at far right, as a prisoner of war in Stalag XXB.

found a number of Air Force POWs who were in a very bad way with terrible guards. They were on German rations of a small cup of soup each and a loaf between seven. We gave them some of our Red Cross parcel contents but they marched off before us and we later found their haversacks by the roadside with the gifts still inside. The guards had made them throw it all away.

It was on the march from Danzig that Lance-Corporal Harry Nichols learned that he had been awarded the Victoria Cross. He had been with us in the French campaign and had been badly wounded. We were told to parade in a hut and as we stood there Lance-Corporal Nichols was asked for but he had not arrived. We thought something was wrong. A German general arrived and still no Harry. At last he did arrive with guards prodding him with their rifles. When he saw the general he just casually strolled up to him and the general put out his hand to shake hands but Harry kept his in his pockets. The general said, 'If you will not shake hands with me as a German, will you shake hands with me as a soldier?' Harry's hands remained in his pockets and the general then told him that he had been awarded the highest award for gallantry that a soldier can be given.

In our party we had disguised two Russians with battledress and Scots hats. They spoke virtually no English. Every morning two prisoners had to clear out the officer's room before we marched off and one terrible day he chose these two and started giving them instructions which they did not understand at all. A sergeant quickly stepped in and said it was no good speaking to them as they were Welshmen. When the officer replied that Welshmen speak English he was told that these two did not and would need an interpreter but the day was saved when the officer lost patience and chose two different men. Later these men were handed over to some Russian troops and that was the last we heard of them.

When we reached Wittenberg we stayed for a week. We had picked up Red Cross parcels in some of the towns on our way but were short of bread so went into the town to trade some cigarettes and on the fourth day we managed it. We were set to loading bricks on to waggons beside the railway where a train stood which was loaded with people wearing what looked like blue and white striped pyjamas. All day long we heard firing going on, on the far side of the train on what we thought was a rifle range. Local people told us that the Allies were very close and as we left we realised that we were billetted in a potato loading and were allowed to walk on the platform where the potatoes were unloaded at harvest time. From there we saw dead bodies being loaded on to the truck and it appeared that the Germans had been shooting the people in the pyjamas.

A shell came flying over the town and hit the big Singer factory which had been making arms. The German officer in charge would let us march out of Wittenberg only after we promised that we would wait outside the town until the Allies came along, but the first American tank which crossed the Elbe was so far ahead of their troops that they had to retreat and the Germans blew up the bridge. We heard later that it was some time before the Americans could take the town. We returned to a small village near the railway where a German woman came and asked the guards if some of the POWs could do some work for her. The guard took out six men who had been captured near the Maginot Line very early in the war. The guard left the woman to return the men to the group after

One of David Parker's letters to his father from Stalag XXB: 'Dear Dad, I often think that we will be having a good talk when we meet again having gone through being prisoners of war in different wars.'

finishing the work but as they were walking along the road they met an SS tank. They were told to march and when they reached us they stopped but the tank commander shot at them and told them to march on. We called our guard who went to say the men were his prisoners but the SS fired at him and told him to go. They marched on for ten minutes to a place which was hidden by trees, when we heard firing which killed all but the oldest of the men. He died that night and we buried them all in the local churchyard.

We were marched out of the town and retraced our route north, back to a village about seven miles outside Schwerin. Here a British plane flew overhead and waved to us one evening. Next morning when making a fire to heat water, I saw a tank coming up the road and asked an American prisoner where the Germans had got a tank like that from. He looked and went mad saying, 'By God. It's one of ours'. The whole camp went mad and the guards marched off. Some tried to run away and were shot for their trouble. The last time I heard 'Heil Hitler' was when the Germans were told to march off up the road carrying a white flag and they came to our camp where we rounded them up. One was a high-ranking German officer and he was taken away after someone took his watch, the same as had been done to us in 1940. His aide tried to go with him but was prevented from doing so by an American officer. The German gave the Nazi salute before turning away and was kicked in the back by one of the ex-prisoners and finished up face down in the mud. We must have rounded up about 3,000 or more Germans who slept in the fields with us guarding them.

When the time came to leave, we were taken in an Army truck to Luneburg Barracks where we were de-loused, medically examined and re-kitted. For two days we waited at Luneburg airport for a plane to take us home. While we were there a plane landed and out stepped Monty, who came over and said the war was ceasing and that he had signed the German surrender. We flew to Brussels where we changed aircraft for the last plane to fly out to Wing in Buckinghamshire. As we flew over England we saw all the bonfires burning below as a sign of our victory. It was VE Day. We were taken to London which we expected to see as flattened as the German cities were. The Germans had told us that London had been destroyed. We were surprised to find so much of it untouched, though the centre was in ruins.

Everywhere we went on our way home we were greeted with hugs and kisses, making a lump in the throat. Even the military police carried our bags. When I got back home, the first person to greet me was Mary, the five-year-old daughter I had never seen, shouting 'Dad, Dad'. Peggy had been in the cinema with Mary

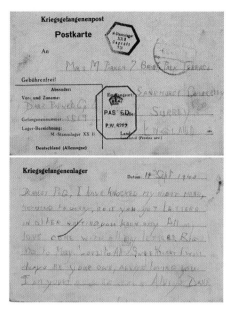

A postcard to David's wife Peg from Stalag XXB.

when a message came up on the screen for her to return home. There she found a message that I would be home soon. From being a little girl, Mary had been shown pictures of her Dad and had been told that she would see me 'one sunny day'. Now that day had come and as I got off the bus she crossed the road and rushed to greet me as though she had known me all my life. I was home again.

MASS-OBSERVATION ARCHIVE, 5 MAY 1945
LONDON SHOPKEEPER ON THE GERMAN SURRENDER AT LÜNEBERG HEATH

You're interested in what people think about war news, aren't you? Well, I've done a lot of counting up for you. There have been 55 people in this shop today so far, and every single one of them has mentioned the weather and not a single one of them has mentioned the news!

WINIFRED BASHAM

HOME FRONT

Winifred Basham and her husband Percy, a teacher, were raising their family under continuous threat of air raids by German bombers in Ipswich. Winifred kept a diary.

SATURDAY 3 MARCH – There was a warning round about 5 am and it seems the doodlebugs have started again after all these weeks. It is sickening. I kept listening for the siren all the evening.

SUNDAY 4 MARCH – I thought Percy had been dreaming when he said there had been a warning in the night, but we heard later that the Germans have begun piloted raids again and that they dropped bombs in Seymour Road – 8 killed. Uncle Charlie lives there. And I heard nothing whatever!

After an uneventful day during which it rained so we couldn't go out the siren went at 7.44. The cuckoo [air raid siren] was on from 7.55 to 8.45. Two Jerries came over and we were treated to the usual firework display. All-clear at 8.58. Who says the war is nearly over!

THURSDAY 8 MARCH – Percy was very late home to tea and brought a large lump of ice cream which the children had never had before.

MONDAY 19 MARCH – We had warnings from 3.22 to 3.57 am, 5.40 to 5.52,

8.08 to 8.17 and 9.08 to 9.24. During the last there was a crash from 9.10 to 9.15 and a doodlebug came over in the clouds. I was afraid it was going on like that all day but all was quiet actually.

SATURDAY 24 MARCH – There was a warning from 2.58 to 3.11 am and a doodlebug came over the town but not near here. At 7.02 the sirens went again and the crash was on from 7.07 to 7.15 when another came over. All-clear at 7.19. There was another warning from 7.44 to 7.57. This was rather depressing but when we heard the news that Monty and the 21st Army are across the Rhine we felt better.

MONDAY 26 MARCH – Just as I was getting tea ready we heard a plane diving steeply and the next minute there was a terrific crump. A Mustang had come down in flames the other side of Henley Road. The American pilot was killed.

THURSDAY 29 MARCH – I was quite startled to hear an all-clear at 6.02 am as I was finishing the baby. Goodness knows when the warning went. Since then the siren has been going all morning. I think they must have slung everything they had left at us, though actually we only heard one doodlebug. We seem to be doing as we like in Germany.

FRIDAY 30 MARCH – Mrs Scase was full of tales of yesterday's raids – doodlebugs 20 at a time and so on. Anyhow the sirens haven't sounded for 24 hours so whether Jerry has withdrawn from Holland we don't know, as there is a security silence over Monty's movements. But all sorts of places such as Heidelberg and Mannheim have fallen to us today.

SATURDAY 31 MARCH – The war still seems to be going well but the security silence still holds though they did say today that Monty is 70 miles east of the Rhine. Danzig where the war began has fallen to us today.

SUNDAY 1 APRIL – The clocks go on for double summertime tonight. Mornings are going to be hard for a time.

WEDNESDAY 11 APRIL – It was rather alarming to be awakened in the small

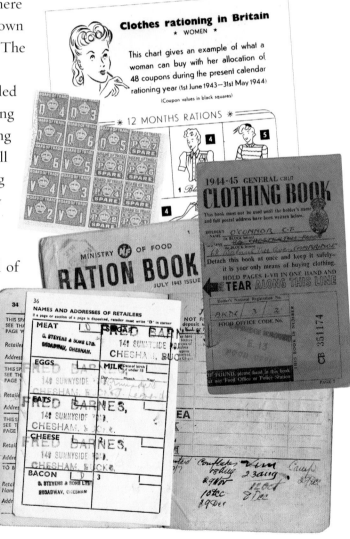

Rationing: part of daily life on the home front, continued long after the war ended.

As news services reported the Allied forces' increasing penetration of German defences, those at home waited in anticipation of the Victory announcement.

hours by the Claydon Cow sounding an all-clear, but as nothing apparently happened I suppose somebody pressed the switch by accident.

WEDNESDAY 18 APRIL – Magdeburg has fallen to us today and the Americans are in Leipzig and Nuremberg.

FRIDAY 20 APRIL – Nuremberg has fallen today and we have nearly reached Hamburg and Bremen.

SATURDAY 21 APRIL – We have taken Bologna and the Red Army is said to be in the outskirts of Berlin.

WEDNESDAY 25 APRIL – The Russians have completely encircled Berlin and in Italy we have taken Moderna, Ferrara and Spezia and are across the Po in strength.

FRIDAY 27 APRIL – The Russians have met the American armies. In Italy there has been a patriot rising and they have captured Genoa, Milan and Turin, and dozens of other places. They are also reported to have caught Mussolini. General Dittmar has also surrendered to us.

Things really do seem to be getting on though the Russians are being awkward at the San Francisco Conference.

WEDNESDAY 2 MAY – The German armies in Italy and Southern Austria have surrendered. The air-raid warning system came to an official end today – no more sirens!! Evacuees have been told they may return to London.

THURSDAY 3 MAY – Berlin has fallen. We have taken Hamburg without firing a shot. In fact the Germans seem so scared of the Russians that they are only too anxious to surrender to us. Rangoon has fallen.

FRIDAY 4 MAY– All the Germans in W. Germany, Holland and Denmark have agreed to surrender to us at 8.00 tomorrow. In the South we have taken Salzburg.

SATURDAY 5 MAY – Percy had to continue with his course this morning which seemed rather hard. This afternoon we had a haircutting after which he proceeded to take down our air-raid shelter. It's lovely to be able to move in the dining room again. More Germans in Austria and Czechoslovakia have surrendered today. Norway is about all they have left now.

SUNDAY 6 MAY – Percy spent the morning taking down the blackout in the hall which has been wire-netted since the early days of the war.

The wireless says VE Day will probably be early this week.

WW2 People's War

Following pages: Liberated Russian slave workers dance on the roof of the Goebbels house in Wurzburg, Germany.

DAILY EXPRESS

No. 14,015 | SATURDAY MAY 5 1945 | FOUNDED BY LORD BEAVERBROOK | Coast dim-out 10.14 p.m. to 5.56 a.m. | One Penny

MONTY ANNOUNCES BIG SURRENDER

Holland, Denmark, N.-W. Germany out

Only Norway, pockets and Czechoslovakia left

FIRING STOPS AT 8 O'CLOCK THIS MORNING ON VAST FRONT

ALL German forces in north-west Germany, Holland, and Denmark have capitulated to Field-Marshal Montgomery, it was announced by Allied Supreme Headquarters last night. The surrender comes into force at eight o'clock this morning. All the Greater Reich, except Norway, central Czechoslovakia, and a few pockets has gone.

The announcement said: "Field-Marshal Montgomery has reported to the Supreme Allied Commander that all enemy forces in Holland, north-west Germany and Denmark, including Heligoland and the Frisian Islands, have surrendered to the 21st Army Group. The capitulation becomes effective at 08.00 hours D.B.S.T. tomorrow. This is a battlefield surrender, involving the forces now facing the 21st Army Group on their northern and western flanks."

The number of troops involved is not yet fully estimated, but there are reported to be 110,000 soldiers and marines in Denmark and up to 200,000 men in Holland.

In north-west Germany are well over half a million, most of whom had already given themselves up.

Greater Germany is now a series of fragments scattered over Europe. The biggest area is Norway. A S.H.A.E.F. message said last night:—

"It is possible that the Germans may try an ineffectual stand in Norway, merely to gain a few more days; but it now seems to be merely a matter of choice between outright unconditional surrender or swift and complete annihilation."

There is a pocket north of Berlin, hemmed in by the Americans and Russians. In the south, the so-called Redoubt has been chopped into isolated pieces. General Patch's Seventh Army has driven through the Brenner Pass and linked up with General Mark Clark's Fifth Army in Italy. Salzburg and Innsbruck were entered. The Third Army came within five miles of Linz.

ALL FIGHTING STOPPED

In Czechoslovakia the Russians and General Patton are still moving forward. Apart from these areas only the "suicide" Channel ports and the Channel Islands remain of Hitler's Empire.

Late-night despatches said that the surrender in the north followed negotiations that had been in progress since Thursday between Montgomery and the German commander in Denmark.

Yesterday there was not a single report of any shots being fired by ground troops on the Western Front.

R.A.F. planes were harrying the fleeing Germans who still tried a Dunkirk evacuation from Schleswig-Holstein, but the British Army was advancing rapidly and unopposed to the liberation of Denmark.

As Montgomery's forces closed up to the border, great masses of jubilant Danes assembled along the frontier to give them a riotous welcome.

The Germans, bewildered and confused, were jamming the roads ahead of our troops. Tired, hungry Wehrmacht troops were streaming northward, either on foot or bicycles.

The Danish Freedom Council issued this communiqué —"Allied troops at this hour are crossing the Danish border. Parts of Denmark are already liberated. The Danish people must give Allied troops all possible help.

A proclamation heralding the surrender of the German forces holding out in the pockets around the naval bases of Emden and Wilhelmshaven was broadcast by the German radio station situated in this area last night.

'TO PREVENT LOSS OF LIFE'

It was signed by Rear-Admiral Bayer, German commander in the Weser-Ems sector, and Johl, described as a Government Deputy. It said:—

"Men and women of the Weser-Ems region. For weeks now the enemy, with greatly superior naval and land power, has been assaulting our area in the hope of ripping up our front and overcoming our forces.

"He has had to pay dearly for every gain of ground, but now he has compressed us into a small area.

"For this reason the German authorities have taken measures to prevent loss of life, and destruction. These measures can only be effective if we all act together and abide by them.

"Calm order and discipline are essential to ensure their being carried out, and are also the only hope for our Fatherland.

"For six years we have stood together and carried on the fight in a decent and honourable way, and we do not propose to fall victims to disorder now."

Women in surrender convoy

From JAMES WELLARD

WITH THE NINTH ARMY, Friday. — Today marked the high point in the Wehrmacht's collapse.

Thousands of German soldiers in varying stages of drunkenness and accompanied by their women, arrived in a long convoy of assorted carts to surrender.

It is estimated that 50,000 of them are wandering along the eastern bank of the Elbe across to the Ninth Army without discipline or even a pretence of military order.

They have stripped the countryside of food, have broken into Wehrmacht liquor warehouses, and are carousing in an almost orgiastic manner as the Russians close in behind.

Rowing over

Generals are abandoning their formations and requisitioning rowboats to cross the Elbe and give themselves up.

Where the American troops have crossed the river to make contact with the Russians, the German soldiers are trying to bribe our men with Luegers, cameras, and wrist-watches to take them prisoner.

Scores of Wehrmacht men mounted on bicycles pursue our trucks down the road with a full kit, yelling to be taken aboard.

They grab the trucks and try to climb on, abandoning their bicycles.

Immediately the slave workers rush on to the road, try to get the bicycle and join the columns.

The confusion is reaching uncontrollable proportions and American facilities are almost breaking under the strain of handling hundreds of thousands of panic-stricken German soldiers and civilians.

Some American divisions are trying to pass on their prisoners to neighbouring forces but nobody wants them.

Something almost resembling a civil war has broken out on both sides of the Elbe.

On the Russian side all German order, discipline, and administration have broken down entirely. What is going on can only be likened to the Dark Ages.

Fantastic chaos

Even on the American side in the rear areas the chaos, though more localised, is fantastic.

We have German burgomasters complaining about the raids on their towns by S.S. men who are still holding out in the mountains and forests.

These S.S. and Werewolf bands descend on little towns and villages, strip the place of food and make away before American troops can be called.

Somebody inside unoccupied Germany is still fighting a terror war. Enemy planes with special sabotage crews are landing on our airfields. Sometimes the saboteurs surrender; sometimes they are shot dead; sometimes they escape.

Germany which when we hit the concentration camps resembled a charnel house, now resembles a lunatic asylum.

The final stage of dissolution and chaos has been reached as German turns on German and rends the country apart.

Two more lists

The United Nations War Crimes Commission, it was announced last night, has compiled and transmitted to the authorities charged with the duty of arresting war criminals two additional lists.

Haw-Haw's deputy says—

Don't fawn on the victors

EDWARD RODERICK DIETZE, Lord Haw-Haw's deputy, yesterday gave some advice to Germans on "behaviour towards the Anglo-Americans." He said over Wilhelmshaven radio:—

I feel obliged to say a personal word to you. Many of you will know me, and some of you will remember that I used to broadcast in English, trying to make my British listeners understand the points of view and the German cause.

I would like to recommend you urgently to face the enemy with dignity and self-consciousness, and not to show any submissiveness.

Doomed

Attempts to flatter the enemy or to make concessions which are contrary to human dignity are doomed to failure.

Anglo-Americans would only answer with hard treatment, kicks and smacks in the face. This is my long experience in intercourse with Anglo-Americans.

Dignity and self-consciousness are the things to which the German people are fully entitled.

We have fought heroically for years in the interests of Europe and of the culture of the whole world, and the Germans had to bear terrible sufferings, particularly by enemy air actions and by the Bolshevist terror.

The German people has the right to look everybody in the face with a free conscience. Only if we behave in this way may we expect to be treated correctly by the Western Powers.

Big Ben—from Hamburg

Big Ben gave the time signal on Hamburg radio last night.

And this is . . . ?

From the nine o'clock home service last night the B.B.C. announcer's name will not be broadcast. It is stated that this war-time emergency measure started in 1940 for security purposes is no longer necessary.

Air ban lifted

The South African Government were the first to ease a wartime control in a proclamation issued yesterday lifting restrictions on civil flying.

The proclamation, which applies to South Africa and South-West Africa, repeals that of 1939 dealing with the suspension of the Civil Air Board.

WOMEN OF GERMANY WEEP

THEIR WORLD HAS BROKEN in pieces around them and they weep. German prisoners behind them are about to be marched off to the cages. . . . British troops, driving on to their Russian link-up, had entered Wittenberge, which lies beyond Hamburg to the east.

GERMANS: WE LAY DOWN OUR ARMS

FOR the first time the German High Command communiqué yesterday used the phrase when referring to German troops that "they laid down their arms."

This concerned "the majority of our troops in the Mecklenburg area, who, after heavy fighting, succeeded in gaining the west bank of the Elbe and behind the Schwerin-Wismar Line."

There these troops "reached territory under Anglo-Saxon control."

The communiqué, broadcast from Copenhagen several hours later than usual, made the belated admission that the "fight for the German capital is ended."

It also admitted the occupation of Hamburg and Neumuenster by the British and said that the "enemy" had entered Fiume.

NO COMMUNICATIONS

German troops in Lombardy were "cut off from communications." The communiqué reported that there was no fighting in Courland, Denmark, or Holland. It added:—

"In eastern Jutland our divisions disengaged themselves, according to orders, on to the Emden-Lake Gluckstadt line up to the Kieler Forde."

Reviewing the fighting south of the Danube, the communiqué indicated that the Allies were either in or on the outskirts of the great Austrian city of Linz, saying: "The Americans pushed on to Linz further to the south, to land across the River Inn eastwards."

South-east of Moravska Ostrava the Russians gained fresh ground against the German flanks.

Britain to stop paying prisoners

Express Political Correspondent

WHEN the fighting in Europe ends the Allies will have more than 3,000,000 German prisoners of war in their hands while all the Allied prisoners will have been released.

Under the convention, a detaining Power is supposed to pay the Service pay of a war-prisoner and to reclaim the money from the prisoners own Government.

Conditions are such that it will be impossible to collect money from the Germans for some time, and the major Allies are to consider what shall be done.

It is probable that once fighting has ceased, the automatic payment of German prisoners in Allied hands will cease, although some payment for special work done such as farming may be given.

It is likely that the whole conditions of German war-prisoners will be reviewed, as the Russians are expected to ask for many thousands to repair damage in Russia.

Spanish fishermen looted France

PARIS, Friday.—France is complaining to Spain that Spanish fishing-boats which supplied the Germans in the Atlantic coast pockets carried off looted furniture and works of art from German-held territory there. Spain is being asked to ensure that this is restored.—B.U.P.

12 generals on secret flight

Twelve German generals who had travelled overnight by train from Windermere arrived at Bovingdon airfield, Herts, yesterday morning for an unknown destination.

They went by train to Boxmoor and were taken by a United States Air Transport Command truck to the airfield.

CAPTURED Vs TO BE TURNED AGAINST JAPS

All secrets in our hands: Experts going to Germany

By GUY EDEN

SOME of Germany's secret weapons may be used by the Allies in the all-out assault on Japan which will be launched the moment the war in Europe ends.

Not all of the weapons have been used against the Western Allies—because the places in which they were being made were overrun before effective supplies could be manufactured.

Allied technical experts will probe the secrets of the secret weapons, and all those worth using will be put into production in Allied arsenals.

The specifications of some of the weapons will be put into secret archives as being of historic, but not practical interest.

Others will be handed over at once to arms manufacturers to see if they can be improved or adapted to the special conditions of the Far Eastern war.

Some of the weapons—rockets and V1's, for example—may form part of the fixed defences of the Allied countries which will have the task of ensuring that Germany does not again become an aggressor nation.

Under an arrangement between the major Allies all discoveries made will be "pooled" and made available to all the Big Powers.

Among the secret weapons so far discovered, none appears to have been of overwhelming importance, although some might have done great damage if used in large numbers.

U-boats complete

The Daily Express Air Correspondent writes:—

All Germany's military and scientific secrets are believed by now to have fallen into the hands of the Allies.

Many of the secrets that Germany was preparing for us might have revolutionised the employment of future war weapons and even the strategy and tactics of our military leaders and scientists.

Of great importance are the long-range U-boats that were found on their cradles at Danzig, Stettin, and Bremen—submarines that had never put to sea. They included equipment never before used by the enemy.

Rocket discoveries are complete. They are believed to include plans for launching long-range V weapons capable of reaching targets more than 1,000 miles away.

Front page letter

To the Editor of the Daily Express.

Sir,—

Let Mr Churchill, Marshal Stalin, and General Eisenhower broadcast VE to the world from Berlin. What more fitting end could there be to the war?

And let Admiral Doenitz or Himmler, or whosoever speaks for Germany, surrender at the microphone in words that all the world can hear.

Let their words be recorded so that no future generation of Germans can have any illusions.

H. L. McNALLY.

London, May 4, 1945.

LATEST

2 MORE GERMAN ARMIES GIVE IN

Remnants of German Ninth and Twelfth Armies surrendered to U.S. Ninth Army yesterday, says S.H.A.E.F. despatch.

Bremen and Europa to be broken up

Express Shipping Reporter

BRITISH shipowners do not want the Europa (49,746 tons) nor the Bremen (49,746 tons), captured intact at Bremen, for although they were the pride of the German Merchant Marine and popular Atlantic greyhounds before the war, they were heavy losers commercially.

They were "show" ships with no cargo space to make them pay and were subsidised heavily by the German Government.

It is expected that they will be used for the repatriation of the American armies and then broken up.

Five more enemy liners have been found in Hamburg and Bremen, it was disclosed yesterday. None has suffered from R.A.F. bombs. They include the Japanese liner Asama Maru, 22,000-ton flagship of the Nippon Yuen Kaisha, Japan's greatest shipping combine. She was forced into hiding in Bremen in 1942.

Rundstedt: Air power beat us

WITH U.S. SEVENTH ARMY, Friday.—The biggest single reason why Germany lost the war was the Allies' tremendous air superiority, said Field-Marshal von Rundstedt today.

He answered questions in the coldest military manner imaginable.

The German war machine, he said, was paralysed from the air. —B.U.P.

2 'THIS IS YOUR VICTORY!'

WINSTON CHURCHILL

The end of the war in Europe was marked by spontaneous public rejoicing across the continent. The dark underside to the celebrations was a long anticipated retribution against those who had collaborated with the Nazis. Flowers were thrown, hidden champagne unearthed, and heads were shaved and scores settled. Millions of displaced people trekked east and west across central Europe, some seeking home, others sanctuary from the Allies or from the Soviet forces.

There was a brief period of genuine warmth and friendship between the Soviet frontline troops and the Allies, before Stalin's men intervened and the iron curtain descended. At least a million men from the USSR had survived capture and imprisonment in German hands, but their hopes of liberty were soon curtailed: to surrender, they learned, was equated with high treason. Soon they were behind the same barbed wire, only guarded now by Stalin's paramilitaries instead of the SS. Millions of German servicemen spent the summer of 1945 behind wire too. Those held by the western Allies were processed with speed and only a handful of the most irremediably evil were brought to the rough justice of Nuremberg. Those held by the Soviet Union endured thorough interrogation or random execution, depending on where they were held; many would be held in Soviet prison camps for up to ten years before finally being released.

For British and Commonwealth troops in Burma, or Americans on Okinawa or the Philippines, the end of hostilities in Europe was of rather academic interest. The soldiers knew from bitter experience, and senior officers concluded from statistical analysis, that an amphibious assault on the Japanese home islands was likely to cost half-a-million Allied lives and perhaps five times as many Japanese deaths. Japan, like Nazi Germany, showed no sign of negotiating for peace even with the end in sight.

Victory is declared, Tuesday 8 May 1945: Londoners in Piccadilly Circus celebrate the end of six years of total war in Europe.

BBC NEWS REPORT, 7 MAY 1945
VICTORY IN EUROPE

This is the BBC Home Service. We are interrupting programmes to make the following announcement. It is understood that in accordance with the arrangements between the three great powers a special announcement will be broadcast by the Prime Minister at three o'clock tomorrow, Tuesday afternoon, 8 May. In view of this fact, tomorrow Tuesday will be treated as Victory in Europe day, and will be regarded as a holiday. The day following, Wednesday 9, will also be a holiday.

His Majesty the King will broadcast to the peoples of the British Empire and Commmonwealth tomorrow, Tuesday, at 9 pm British double summertime.

NELLA LAST

HOME FRONT

Nella Last, a housewife in Barrow-in-Furness, and her friend Steve Howson were eagerly awaiting the announcement of the war's end, recorded in her diary on Monday 7 May.

Steve pooh-poohed the idea that VE Day would come tonight. I said, 'It *might* have been announced in a programme,' and I put the wireless on at five minutes to nine o'clock. We agreed that, if Stuart Hibberd said, 'The King will speak in approximately one minute's time,' we *would* have missed an announcement – and smiled at each other when it proceeded normally. Then, when he said so unemotionally that tomorrow was to be the VE Day, and that Churchill was to speak at three o'clock, we just gazed at each other, and Steve said, '*What* a flop! What a *flop!*' We could none of us believe our hearing. It was as if a body of psychologists had been consulted and been told, 'Now sort out the events and announcements for us. We want to tell them, of course, but with no dramatic announcement, no build-up. We want to let them know the European war is over, but not to emphasize it. You know, it's only the first half: we *must* keep that in people's minds, not let them maffick and forget what's ahead.' We felt no pulse quicken, *no* sense of thankfulness or uplift, of any kind. Personally, I've felt more thrilled on many occasions by news on the air. At intervals, Steve chanted, 'But what a flop,' as if fresh angles had struck him. I'd heard people say, 'I'll kneel down and pray if it's in the streets when I hear it,' 'I know I'll cry my eyes out,' 'I'll rush for that bottle I've kept – open it and get tight for the first time in my life,' and so on. I rose placidly and put on the kettle and went through to prepare the salad. I looked on my shelf and said, 'Well, dash it, *we must celebrate somehow* – I'll open this tin of pears,' and I did.

**MASS-OBSERVATION ARCHIVE, 10 JUNE 1945
RAF OFFICER IN REGENT STREET**

It was obvious for a week, a month, or more that V Day was on the way. I could not get thrilled or excited to save my life. After the news in the past few weeks, I feel that I will never show undue enthusiasm again. My brain is past comprehending such titanic moves that have and are going on around me.

TONY BENN

ARMED FORCES

Pilot Officer Anthony Wedgwood Benn, stationed in Egypt, was on leave in Palestine and staying in a Jewish Kibbutz near the Sea of Galilee.

On the morning of Monday 7 May we got up at about seven and went in for breakfast, which consisted of laban, bread and tea. Laban is a large dish of thick sour milk and lumps of cream cheese which I found hard to stomach but gallantly ate. After breakfast we set off through the fields, joined a dusty rough road and walked across into Syria. We joined the road to Tiberias and got a lift in. We hired a rowing boat and rowed out into the Sea of Galilee, trying to pick out Capernaum on the side of the lake further up. Coming in, we entered a little Arab restaurant for refreshment and, as we walked towards the place, a Jew hurried up with a smile and said, 'The war is finished!'

    We didn't know whether to believe it or not so we smiled back. It seemed to be confirmed by a special edition of the paper. So we solemnly celebrated with an

Anthony Wedgwood Benn.

orange squash and an ice cream each – hardly believing it could be true, hardly thinking of it, it seemed so remote. Returning later to Shaar Hagolan, via another settlement, we found them preparing for a festival to celebrate peace.

It was nearly ten o'clock and we understood that the King was to speak, so we asked to listen to the wireless. As you know, he didn't, but in consequence we missed the gathering on the lawn when the leader of the settlement gave an address of welcome in Hebrew to the 'three English officers'. Think of the wonderful opportunity for replying with a speech – what we missed! I was disappointed.

Outside on the grass an effigy of the swastika was burned and the settlement crowded into the eating hall, where a little wine and lots of biscuits and nuts were laid along tables.

I asked for an orange squash and was given one, however one old boy emptied half a cupful of wine into it, and I drank it up – it was practically communion wine – rather an appropriate beverage to celebrate peace.

Then the national dances began – Germans, Czechs, Poles, Turks, Yugoslavs, all did their national dances. Then there was a pause and an announcement in Hebrew. Everyone looked at us and it was explained that the RAF officers would do an English national dance. Hurriedly deciding to do the boomps-a-daisy, two of us took the floor – it was an instantaneous success and everybody joined in.

That is how I celebrated the peace.

EDNA STAFFORD

ARMED FORCES

Edna Stafford (née Hodgson) of the RAF Allied Expeditionary Air Force, was at Reims in May 1945 when German and Allied representatives signed the peace treaty.

Towards the end of April 1945 and the first few days of May 1945, German Officers could be seen visiting 'the Little Red School' in Reims. American MPs [Military Police] and the RAF SPs [Service Police] guarded all doors and entrances and one could not pass in or out without a careful scrutiny of one's pass. There was an air of excitement about the place and word was passed around that some very high-ranking officers were expected at the school.

In the early hours of the morning, the German Army Chief of Staff, General

Jodl, had surrendered to General Montgomery and other officers, such as General Bedell Smith, who was deputy to General Eisenhower, and his Chief of Staff. What had taken place in the early hours of the morning of 7 May 1945 was to be read about later in the newspapers in some detail.

In the afternoon, however, General Jodl arrived, together with Admiral Doenitz and, I understand, Admiral Friedeburg. There was also a Russian officer looking very smart in his mauve uniform with polished belt and buttons, and gold braided epaulettes on his shoulders. As each officer came into the building so they were saluted by the Military Police and this was acknowledged.

General Eisenhower and Air Chief Marshal Tedder [Deputy Supreme Commander to Eisenhower] were also around but it was not until later that they met up with General Jodl and Admiral Friedeburg. General Jodl was dressed in his impressive uniform which was accentuated by the wearing of highly polished black knee-length boots. He was the German Chief of Staff throughout the war and months later he was convicted as a war criminal at the Nuremburg trials and hanged.

After a few hours they began to leave the building and to avoid the crowds of interested civilians waiting outside, their respective cars drew up in the square at the rear of the school. Overlooking this square was a balcony and again we had a good view of what was taking place. General Eisenhower and ACM Tedder both were driven away and within a few minutes the Russian officer left. Then a car with drawn blinds drew up and we could see the German officers, with brief cases under their arms, being hustled into the car and, with a wail of sirens from their escorts, they vanished out of sight.

It was a lovely sunny day and after they had all gone we stood on the balcony talking about the day's events and whom we had seen. It was a day I shall never forget. When reading about the events of the previous twelve hours, it gave me a strange feeling to have been there at some part and to have witnessed some of the comings and goings. Signals were flashed to all parts of the world as the following day, 8 May, was to be formally known as VE Day, with Mr Churchill making his speech from London and General de Gaulle to the French nation. Of course, His Majesty King George VI had spoken to the British Commonwealth.

All that remained now was to try and get things sorted out which would be a problem in itself, but more particularly to have the war with the Japanese ended as quickly as possible. It was not over for the soldiers in the East who were still suffering. The 8th of May was another lovely day, symbolic of peace, so it seemed, and as the hour of 3 pm drew near for his speech, groups of people, both indoors and out, gathered round any available wireless set. We were gathered in one of the offices and suddenly everyone became quiet. Our office overlooked the railway bridge and local streets, and I recall looking round at people close to me, catching

Daily Mirror

MAY 8

Tuesday, May 8, 1945

No. 12,911   ONE PENNY

Registered at G.P.O. as a Newspaper.

VE-DAY!

PUBLIC HOLIDAY TODAY AND TOMORROW—OFFICIAL

Czechs flown from Britain to save Prague

Soon after a Czech Spitfire squadron left Britain for Czechoslovakia yesterday large formations carrying Czechoslovak ground troops also took off for home—and the battle for the liberation of Prague. The commander, before leaving, said, "This is the greatest day of my life."

IN a final burst of fiendishness, S.S. troops in Prague last night were firing the last shots of the war on helpless Czech civilians.

S.S. men went through the streets driving people out of their homes as other S.S. troops waited to mow them down with machine-guns.

So bad has been the conduct of the German troops that the Wehrmacht commander of the area broadcast a warning to his men to respect international law.

"Some breaches," he actually admitted, had occurred.

But earlier he had announced that he did not recognise what he described as the "armistice."

"German troops will continue to fight until they have secured a free passage out of the country," he added.

According to refugees who have reached Pilsen the S.S. men, knowing that they will be executed when caught, have abandoned all normal conduct.

Another Prague broadcast reached Czechoslovak circles in London yesterday. It was an S O S from the Czechs pleading for speedy Allied help and asking "send us aircraft."

It spoke of heavy fighting in the streets, said the Germans were throwing hand grenades at houses showing Czechoslovak flags and reported the bombing by German planes of broadcasting house and other public buildings.

Meanwhile Patton's famous Fourth Armoured Division is speeding towards the capital and last night was reported to be fifteen miles south of the city.

SPAIN BREAKS WITH GERMANY

Spain has severed diplomatic relations with Germany, it is officially announced in Madrid.

War winners may broadcast today

The Prime Minister will broadcast at 3 p.m. today.

It is probable that later in the afternoon General Eisenhower, Field-Marshal Montgomery and Field-Marshal Alexander will also speak over the radio to the Allied world.

At 9 p.m. the King will broadcast.

Goebbels and his family are found, poisoned

DISCOVERY has been made in Berlin of the bodies of Dr. Goebbels, his wife, and their six children.

They were found by the Russians. All had taken poison and this was the cause of death.

Hitler's body has not been discovered and neither has the body of Goering.

There is now some speculation as to whether, after all, the Fuehrer and Goering may not have fled to a place of hiding.

It is pointed out, however, that their bodies may have been burned and the ashes lost in the wreckage of the burning Chancellery, or some other of Berlin's destroyed buildings.

★On top of the world

In the heart of London an Allied soldier — he climbed the Eros statue at London's Piccadilly—gets just as high as he can to celebrate the lifting of the shadow from Europe.

Celebrations delay due to a 'technicality'

By BILL GREIG

THIS IS VE-DAY. AFTER FIVE YEARS, EIGHT MONTHS AND FOUR DAYS OF THE BLOODIEST WAR IN HISTORY BRITAIN AND HER ALLIES HAVE GAINED VICTORY IN EUROPE.

Capitulation of Germany to the Allies was announced by Doenitz yesterday—but a mere technicality in the arrangements made with Russia and America delayed the British people's celebration.

One result of the delay is that Britain's workers get two clear days' holiday—today and tomorrow. This Cabinet decision was disclosed last night.

Spend VE in camp, CO's say

"Daily Mirror" Reporter

COMMANDING officers of Army and RAF camps all over Britain told their men yesterday: "Spend VE-Day how you will, but PLEASE spend it in camp."

Thanksgiving services, concerts and later "closing time" for the canteen and sergeants' and officers' mess bars were some of the arrangements to persuade the men to stay in camp.

At an operational station near London the *Daily Mirror* was told by the Station Commander: "I have a lot of Australian air-crews here and they don't think VE day means the war is over as far as they are concerned. They've volunteered to forgo celebrations to do any odd job that comes up.

German prisoners of war have erected victory flag-poles at Catterick camp in North Yorkshire

Originally it was intended that the first day's holiday would not begin until the Prime Minister had spoken.

The announcement late last night will be VE-Day was the final act in a bewildering day following the German surrender.

The people thronged out into the streets all over the country. In London there were thousands in Whitehall outside Downing-street patiently waiting for the word, little aware of the drama taking place inside No 10

There was chaos and bewilderment where there should have been celebration.

Here is the story of what happened in No. 10. When the news of the German surrender arrived the Prime Minister was ready to broadcast at 4 p.m. Hurried telephone calls were made to Marshal Stalin and President Truman so that the announcement could be made simultaneously.

Then it was that the trouble started. It was found that arrangements already made did not allow for the war ending so suddenly.

Mr. Churchill put his broad-

Continued on Back Page

the eyes of one or two, and it seemed as if the same expression of thankfulness and pleasure could be read in each, in a silent sort of way. Glancing out of the open window even the buildings seemed to reflect the atmosphere.

The Daily Mirror's *Victory Day edition.*

Of course, as soon as Mr Churchill had announced to the world that the war in Europe had ended, whistles, sirens and anything that could make a noise was sounded. People in the street kissed and hugged each other but the most poignant noise, I thought, was the sound of the last All Clear. It seemed to go on and on, and I thought about all the All Clear sirens I had previously heard when air raids had finished, and people emerged from underground shelters, or even houses to take stock of the damage done.

That night there were celebrations of all descriptions taking place and really I think very few people actually slept. All of a sudden the place seemed transformed as the French people put on their very attractive and colourful national costumes, and danced in groups on street corners. People formed themselves into processions and went down every street. They must have had some good hiding places for their costumes and dresses. As the summer evening wore on, torches were lit and bands began to play and, wherever we went, we were immediately swept along with the crowd. Sometimes one felt choked at the emotion shown.

The following morning I was up at 6.30 am and, together with two or three friends, we were on the road to Paris. Again it was a lovely morning and as we were driving along, at a fairly high speed, the wind whipped the colour into our faces and we reached Paris feeling that it was great to be alive. Paris looked remarkably quiet at 9.30 am but of course there were obvious signs of the celebrations carried out the previous night. Streamers and decorations were strewn across the roads and flags flew at every window and shop windows were decorated with red, white and blue. Bottles were lying in the roadway, some cafes had overturned chairs, all telling a tale of their own – but who cared? We made our way back to Versailles at lunchtime, returning to Paris and arranging to meet up with each other later in the evening.

My boyfriend at that time was a Welsh guardsman and, as we walked along one of the side streets off the main boulevard, we noticed a café. As we approached, the proprietor was standing just inside and he had obviously seen us coming as he had a champagne bottle in his hand with a napkin over his arm. We were shown to a table for two set in a secluded corner, and the quietness of the place, broken only by the strains of a violin, made such a contrast to the noise and din going on outside. After a couple of hours, during which time our glasses were refilled time and time again, we decided we had better depart. Again it occurred to me that the French must have had some good hiding places for their wines and spirits during the occupation.

WW2 People's War

ALBERT RICKETTS

ARMED FORCES

Flight Lieutenant Albert Ricketts, 2nd Tactical Air Force, was attached to Montgomery's HQ at Lüneberg Heath. Originally trained as a bomber pilot flying Lockhead Venturas, by the end of the war he was transporting high-ranking RAF and Army staff as directed.

The war had reached the point where the Germans could not hold out much longer and it came as no surprise when we learned that they had surrendered to General Montgomery on 4 May. It transpired that one of our aircraft was detailed to fly into the unoccupied part of Germany with the instruction that if they were shot at they were to 'get the hell out of it'.

Obviously they succeeded because after they had surrendered to Monty, I was instructed to fly the Surrender Team of General Admiral Von Freideberg and Colonel Pollack to make the total surrender to General Eisenhower at Reims, which was his HQ.

On 5 May I took off with the Germans on board together with two British officers, Lieutenant-Colonel James and Major Lawrence, to fly to Reims airfield. Unfortunately, as we got closer to Reims the cloud base became lower and lower until eventually I was forced to fly above the cloud. As my radio was not performing I had no alternative but to return to our main base at Brussels. This meant that the German party together with their British escorts had to complete the journey by road. Whilst arrangements were being made to obtain a vehicle, it was deemed as not sensible to take the Germans into the main buildings.

We therefore, whilst waiting, resorted to walking with them up and down the tarmac outside. It was left to me to walk with the Admiral and he asked in broken English if the clouds were 'too deep'. With the weather as it was and the inability to mend the radio we were even prevented from following the party to Reims and flying them back to their base. We were therefore denied seeing the euphoria of handing the Germans over to the supreme commander. Knowing how the Americans would have and indeed treated such an occasion, it was not inconceivable that I would have featured in the cinema news of the day.

I flew back to my own base the following day. On 7 May news came through that the final surrender had taken place. It was decided that the following day (8 May) would be celebrated as VE Day and that everyone would stand down. That is, everybody except me who was detailed to fly to Canadian Army HQ to pick up Major-General Templar who greeted me with the words 'we must be the only silly b******s working today'. I found myself warming to a person with his understanding. On the evening we decided to have our own fireworks but the only thing we had was a Very pistol and some Very cartridges. The cartridges were fired away from the back of the building which was in the opposite direction to the aircraft. Unfortunately the person using the pistol fired one cartridge straight up into the air and the wind carried the burning cartridge over onto one of our Auster aircraft, setting it on fire so that it ended up completely wrecked. Somehow or other we managed to cover up this unfortunate accident.

WW2 People's War

BBC NEWS REPORT, 7 MAY 1945
THOMAS CADETT WITNESSES THE SURRENDER AT REIMS

Whatever sense of drama was there – and it was – it was because we carried it in our own hearts. Remembering that this meant liberation, freedom from suffering and spared lives for countless thousands in tortured Europe, it was not the ceremony that mattered, but the thing itself.

JOAN STYAN

Nine-year-old Joan Styan lived with her mother in London throughout the Blitz.

My mother said to me: 'Let's go to the West End, Joan, and join in the celebrations.' So we jumped on a train from our nearby Clapham Junction station to Victoria and were astounded to see such huge, swirling crowds. We tried desperately to make our way to Buckingham Palace and staggered shoulder to shoulder with the crowds. What an incredible sight. A wave of humanity confronted us. Impassioned emotions would never be as high again. London was aflame with human exhilaration. Bonfires blazed continuously over London and the sky was alight with the glow of victory. No more suffering and hardship; peace had finally descended upon us and everybody was at one with each other regardless of race, creed and status. Survival and freedom were all that mattered. We had waited so very long for this and in our wildest dreams had never envisaged a night like this.

The vast crowds outside
Buckingham Palace cheered
the King and Queen and
their daughters. Later the
two princesses slipped away
to join the crowd themselves.

Mum and I finally reached Buckingham Palace with much effort and laughter and joined in the masses converging on the palace and celebrating outside. They sang their hearts out with many of the war songs – particularly the Vera Lynn favourites – and London was deafened once again, not from the bombs and artillery fire but from the depths of human feeling in utter, utter relief that their beloved city of London which had endured so much was free. Dear old London; this was its finest hour. Fireworks streaked through the sky instead of searchlights and bombers.

London was submerged in jubilation and screams of relief from humanity. People climbed on anything they could, statues, buildings, cars, etc., and every lamppost was scaled. Noisy dustbin lids were banged and the hysterical crowds were totally beyond any order. Nothing mattered, only freedom. The ultimate heights of pent-up human emotion were as they had never been and will probably never be again.

WW2 People's War

QUEEN ELIZABETH II

ARMED FORCES

Princess Elizabeth was 19 years old when the war ended. As Second Lieutenant Elizabeth Windsor, she had served in the ATS (Auxiliary Territorial Service) during the war.

I remember the thrill and relief after the previous day's waiting for the Prime Minister's announcement of the end of the war in Europe. My parents went out on the balcony in response to the huge crowds outside. I think we went on the balcony nearly every hour, six times, and then when the excitement of the floodlights being switched on got through to us, my sister and I realised that we couldn't see what the crowds were enjoying. My mother had put her tiara on for the occasion, so we asked my parents if we could go out and see for ourselves. I remember that we were terrified of being recognised, so I pulled my uniform cap well down over my eyes. A grenadier officer amongst our party of about 16 people said he refused to be seen in the company of another officer improperly dressed, so I had to put my cap on normally.

We cheered the King and Queen on the balcony and then walked miles through the streets. I remember lines of unknown people linking arms and walking down Whitehall, all of us just swept along on a tide of happiness and relief. I remember the amazement of my cousin [Viscount Lascelles], just back from four and a half years in a POW camp, walking freely with his family in the

friendly throng. And I also remember when someone exchanged hats with a Dutch sailor, the poor man coming along with us in order to get his cap back. After crossing Green Park we stood outside and shouted, 'We want the King,' and we were successful in seeing my parents on the balcony, having cheated slightly because we sent a message into the house to say we were waiting outside. I think it was one of the most memorable nights of my life.

**MASS-OBSERVATION ARCHIVE, 9 MAY 1945
OVERHEARD CONVERSATION DISCUSSING THE ROYAL PROCESSION**

– Didn't she look lovely. I had a grand look at her and the princesses.

– I thought the King looked very fit.

– They looked lovely. You'd never think they were real – they looked like an oil painting.

– Did you see the colour of the Queen's dress? That's the shade I wanted our Martha to have for her wedding.

EDITH PARGETER

HOME FRONT

Edith Pargeter (also known as the author Ellis Peters) was presented with the Medal of the Most Excellent Order of the British Empire for Meritorious Service (BEM) by King George VI on 8 May 1945.

The BEM, awarded to Edith Pargeter by the King on VE Day.

I was then a Petty Officer Wren in the Signals Office of Commander-in-Chief Western Approaches, Liverpool, and in the Birthday Honours of 1944 someone had recommended me for a BEM. Recipients were expected to apply to attend on any one of the future dates fixed for presentation of medals, and because of work pressure I delayed applying rather a long time and finally applied for 8 May 1945.

I travelled down to London with a Wren friend who was one of my two guests – my brother came down to join us the next morning – and we two spent the night in Wrens' quarters in town. And that evening the announcement came out of the blue that the morrow was to be, officially, the close of the European war. We were a little afraid that in the general celebrations the presentation might be cancelled, but no, it went ahead as planned.

So at ten o'clock on VE Day I was in Buckingham Palace, second in line after one Wren officer, receiving my BEM from King George VI, whom I hugely admired for his enormous moral courage. Afterwards my brother had to catch a train back to Shropshire. My friend and I spent the rest of the day rushing about London, dancing in the streets and embracing anything in a uniform. I am never likely to forget any detail of that day.

KING GEORGE VI

HOME FRONT

King George VI lunched with Winston Churchill at Buckingham Palace on the day war ended, and noted the occasion in his diary.

We congratulated each other on the end of the European war. The day we have been longing for had arrived at last and we can look back with thankfulness to God that our tribulation is over. No more fear of being bombed at home and no more living in air raid shelters. But there is still Japan to be defeated and the restoration of our country to be dealt with, which will give us many headaches and hard work in the coming years.

MASS-OBSERVATION ARCHIVE, 9 MAY 1945
COMMENT ON CHURCHILL'S VE DAY SPEECH, LONDON

Oh we saw Churchill too, he came out on the balcony of the Ministry of Health and he made a lovely speech. ... It was floodlit too and the lights were full on him and his little grandson ... he's a lovely little fellow with flaming red hair. I bet he's not half proud of his old granddad.

Triumphant Prime Minister Winston Churchill joins the royal family on the Palace balcony.

WINSTON CHURCHILL (JR)

HOME FRONT

A young Winston Churchill watched his grandfather, the Prime Minister, greet the crowds from Buckingham Palace.

I was literally brought up in a bomb shelter in London. My father, Randolph, was in the army and my mother and I had no real home. But I do remember being taken by my nanny, Mrs Martin, to Buckingham Palace in the afternoon, clutching a tiny Union Jack.

A large crowd can easily seem intimidating to a child, but the British on VE Day afternoon were simply happy and excited and glad to be alive. At about 5.30 there was a momentary hush as the French windows were opened and my grandfather stepped onto the balcony with the royal family. The King was bareheaded and in uniform, the Queen and Princess Margaret were in blue and

Princess Elizabeth was in ATS uniform.

I don't remember being the least surprised to see my grandfather in such company. Every small boy believes his grandfather to be the most important person in the world.

MARY SAWYER

HOME FRONT

Mary Sawyer, 26, worked at the Exchange Telegram Company in London during the war.

On VE day my younger sister Rosie and I went over the West End to celebrate. We were just shuffled along with everyone else. We went to Trafalgar Square, Leicester Square, we tried to get to Buckingham Palace, but we couldn't get as far as that, there were so many people. You were just crammed full and you just had to walk. Everybody was cheering, singing and dancing. But they weren't drunk. They were just celebrating – half of the time the pubs didn't even have any drink. They sold out, they couldn't get any more. There were bands out on balconies and groups playing music, everywhere you looked there were people singing and dancing. Everybody had red, white and blue in their hair. Everybody thought the world of Churchill – we wanted the Labour Party in, but we wanted Churchill in there as well. Everybody thought he was a great man.

SIR HENRY CHANNON

HOME FRONT

Sir Henry 'Chips' Channon was Member of Parliament for Southend-on-Sea, 1935–58. In his famous diaries he recorded the feverish atmosphere at Westminster following the German surrender.

8 MAY: VE DAY AT LAST – Early this morning, I was awakened by the rain – intense Wagnerian rain, which lasted for a long time; the noise brought back, as nothing else could, that September night of 1939. ...

Before lunch I walked through the Ritz, which was beflagged and decorated:

Overleaf: The view from Buckingham Palace as the crowds cheer.

everyone kissed me, Mrs Keppel, Duchess of Rutland and Violet Trefusis all seized me alternately. ... The streets were almost empty, as there is a bus strike, and taxis refused to go out – there were a few singing people, that's all.

Henry 'Chips' Channon.

At the House, Questions lasted interminably, and there was an atmosphere of expectancy in the crowded Chamber. Every seat was occupied; the Ambassadors were all present, peers queued up. At three o'clock in the Whip's Room, I heard the PM make the official announcement over the wireless that the war in Europe was at an end. I then returned to the Chamber, but owing to the ovation Winston was having in the streets, he was delayed, and for a few embarrassed minutes we had nothing to do. Members, amused, asked desultory questions, keeping their eyes on the door behind the Speaker's chair. The Serjeant-at-Arms was in Court Dress, the Speaker wore his robes with gold braid, etc. (I have never seen this done before – though I suppose it was done at the Coronation.) At last Winston, smiling and bent, appeared and had a tremendous reception. Everyone (except the recently elected cad for Chelmsford [the socialist MP, Wing Commander ER Millington]) rose and cheered and waved handkerchiefs and Order Papers ... Winston smiled and half bowed – as he often does, and turning toward the Speaker, read out the same short announcement of the surrender of Germany, which he had already given over the wireless. The House was profoundly moved, and gave him another great cheer; but his reception, even at a supreme moment like today, did not equal Mr Chamberlain's great ovation after Munich. Then Winston, in a lower voice, added his personal thanks and praise for the House of Commons and the Democratic System: some Members wept, and the PM moved that we repair to St Margaret's to offer thanks to Almighty God using the identical phraseology employed by Lloyd George in 1918.

HAROLD NICOLSON

HOME FRONT

Harold Nicolson, a junior Minister in Churchill's government and Governor of the BBC, noted the Victory celebrations in his diary.

I enter the House. The place is packed and I sit on the step below the cross bench. I see a stir at the door and Winston comes in – a little shy – a little flushed – but smiling boyishly. The House jumps to its feet, and there is one long roar of applause. He bows and smiles in acknowledgement. I glance up at the Gallery where Clemmy (Churchill) should be. There is Mrs Neville Chamberlain there instead. And thereupon Winston begins. He repeats the short statement he had just made on the wireless ending up with 'Advance Britannia' and then he lays his manuscript aside and with more gesture and emphasis than is customary to him, he thanks the House for its support throughout these years. He then proposes that we adjourn to the Church of St Margaret's, Westminster. The Speaker then leaves his seat and the mace is fetched before him. He is in Court Robes with gold facings to his gown and his Chaplain and the Sergeant-at-Arms are also in full dress.

Harold Nicolson.

We file out by St Stephen's entrance and the police have kept a lane through the crowd. The crowd are friendly, recognising some of the Members. I was with Nancy Astor, who is, I feel, a trifle hurt that she does not get more cheering. We then have a service and very memorable it is. The supreme moment is when the Chaplain reads out the names of those Members who have lost their lives. It is a sad thing to hear. My eyes fill with tears. I hope that Nancy does not notice. 'Men are so emotional,' she says.

We all go to the smoking-room, Winston comes with us. Passing through Central Hall, he is given an ovation by the crowd. A tiny little boy, greatly daring, dashes up and asks for an autograph. Winston solemnly takes out his glasses and signs. He then pats the delighted little boy on the head and grins his grin.

BBC BROADCAST, 8 MAY 1945
RICHARD DIMBLEBY, LIVE FROM WHITEHALL

Oh what wonderful luck. At this moment... at this moment, how wonderful, Mr Churchill has come out onto the Ministry of Health balcony. Now Mr Churchill is on the balcony of the Ministry of Health, he's wearing his boiler suit, the famous boiler suit that he's made so wonderful, and he has the audacity, shall I say, to put on his head his famous black hat. [Crowd erupts.] Nobody could say that it goes with the boiler suit but you heard what a cheer it raised from the crowd. He stands now in the floodlight and he's giving the victory sign with all his might from the floodlit balcony...

ELIZABETH LAYTON NEL

Elizabeth Layton Nel was a civilian personal secretary to Winston Churchill between 1941 and 1945.

Churchill's inspirational address to the jubilant crowds. His popularity as wartime leader did not extend into peacetime – Churchill would suffer a landslide election defeat within months.

I have always been lucky through my life and it happened that I was the young woman on duty on the night of 7 May which was the day on which really it was known that the unconditional surrender had been signed – that was the day when it was known for certain that the European war was over. The next two days were proclaimed to be holidays to celebrate the end of the war. And that evening I went into the study at the annexe where he was sitting. I went in at a call to go for

dictation and he said, 'Oh, hello Miss Layton. Well, the war's over. You've played your part.' And I can never forget him saying that to me and I felt so grateful to him.

And then it happened that the next night, the Tuesday night, I was also on duty – I was a very lucky young woman – and after dinner arrangements were made for him to go to the balcony – I can't think, was it the Ministry of Health building above Whitehall – to speak to the crowds. And so the private secretary said, 'You can come along too, if you want to.' It was quite a walk to get there but I went along and got on to the balcony and there were a few other people from the office. I got well out of the way, of course, and he came and there was an absolute seething mass of people – Whitehall was absolutely full of people. As far as you could see into Parliament Square it was just a sea of people. And as soon as he appeared on the balcony there were roars of appreciation, cheers and roars, the sound seemed to come up like something solid almost, this roar of cheers.

WINSTON CHURCHILL, 8 MAY 1945
SPEECH FROM THE MINISTRY OF HEALTH, WHITEHALL

God bless you all. This is your victory! [The crowd roars back, 'No – it is yours!] It is the victory of the cause of freedom in every land. In all our long history we have never seen a greater day than this. Everyone, man or woman, has done their best. Everyone has tried. Neither the long years, nor the dangers, nor the fierce attacks of the enemy, have in any way weakened the independent resolve of the British nation.

SHEILA GAYLOR

HOME FRONT

Sheila Gaylor was 14 years old and living in London at the end of the war.

Peace was declared in Europe and the country could celebrate. Mr Churchill ordered the next two days were to be a national holiday – many street parties were arranged, bunting was hung up from house to house, and Union Jack flags draped from windows, but there was no street party in my part of Kenton Lane, a rather wide road where people tended to 'keep themselves to themselves'. There didn't appear to be the same sense of neighbourliness as in the smaller roads. We didn't hang bunting or flags from our windows, and I don't recall seeing, and certainly never attended, one of these famous street parties.

My father decided that we would go up to London and join in the national celebrations in the capital. We travelled to Trafalgar Square on a crowded underground train, arriving at the top of the escalator to join the ecstatic crowd in the street, moving en masse in a swaying sea around Nelson's column, filling the entire square, waving their flags, dancing and cheering continuously. We were part of this excited throng and surged down Whitehall, shouting and singing, holding hands with strangers. We stood on the pavement amongst the cheering, euphoric crowds at the end of this famous street, shouting in unison 'We want Winnie, we want Winnie.' Everyone was hoping – and expecting – Mr Winston Churchill to appear on the balcony of the Ministry of Health building. When he eventually came out and stood before us, waving his cigar and giving us his V-for-Victory sign the crowd roared and cheered. A sailor climbed up a lamppost near me, throwing his uniform hat into the air in exuberant jubilation. The spirit of celebration and the excitement of the crowd were irrepressible and indescribable, so ecstatic and yet so meaningful.

We moved on to the Thames Embankment, irresistibly caught up in the surge of the crowd, where we waited until it grew dark enough for the anticipated firework display to begin on the River. It was a wonderful spectacle, with various set pieces and an abundance of colour erupting from the boats and then cascading down from the sky into the water – a sight I had never seen before – but with none of the frighteningly loud bangs that we hear nowadays during most of November and December. We had all had more than enough loud bangs to last us for the rest of our lives, and it was sparkle, joy and colour we needed.

At the end of the fireworks display the crowd streamed on as a huge wave to Buckingham Palace, and my father and I eventually found ourselves standing among this solid mass of humanity that covered the space around the base of the Victoria Memorial, where the flowerbeds now display their seasonal blooms. There were no neatly laid out flowerbeds in 1945. Suddenly the lights came on in all the rooms of the Palace; the blackout curtains had been taken down and it was an extraordinary sight to see the light streaming out from the windows when every building had been in darkness at night for so many years. Thousands upon thousands of thankful people shouted out 'We want the King, we want the King.' Time and time again King George and Queen Elizabeth appeared on the floodlit balcony together with the two Princesses, and everyone roared and cheered even more heartily. I don't know how many hours we spent celebrating in London that night, or at what time we arrived home in the small hours of the morning, but we were part of the throng on this memorable occasion. I shall always remember this experience, and am so glad that my father took me up to London on Victory Night.

I had not understood much of the progress of the war, and certainly did not appreciate the unspeakable horror and suffering that it brought to countless people. I didn't know anyone who had been killed or injured in the bombing, killed in action in the Forces, or who was a prisoner-of-war. My few relatives were all too old to be called up. Participating in the VE Day celebrations may have helped me to understand a little of the reasons for the elation and general rejoicing of all those who had lived through these six long years of war.

But this was a night of celebration, a night never to be forgotten, a night of joy.

WW2 People's War

MARIE AGAZARIAN

ARMED FORCES

Marie Agazarian, an Anglo-French civilian, served with the Voluntary Aid Detachment and then as a pilot with ATA (Air Transport Auxiliary) during the final years of the war.

We drove up to London on VE Day. We were flying a lot of British prisoners of war back. While the prisoners were waiting for their transport an ATA aircraft would be going round. They'd say, 'Come on, jump on.' So they'd jump on. The extraordinary thing was that they would get off the plane and they'd say, every one of them, 'Can we telephone?' 'Yes,' we'd say, 'there's a telephone here, you can telephone home.' And to a man, they'd walk in, they'd walk up to the telephone, and they'd walk away again. And I never saw one of them telephone. We got the message eventually. We'd say, 'Look, would you like to come back with us? We've got plenty of room in the house.' Each one of us would take as many as we had spare rooms in the house. We had three double rooms so we'd all bunk up and we'd give rooms to these people. And they'd come back and stay with us. We'd come back in the evening perhaps and they would have made a pudding out of broken biscuits. A week, ten days later, they'd ring home and they'd go.

It really was a slice of the most wonderful time of one's life. It's rather strange because it was over the background of the horror of the war – and it was awful. You looked every day to see who'd been killed, and even in the ATA we had the notices, the daily routine, and you'd look down to see who'd lost their lives, pilots and everybody. And you lived with it – I lost two brothers who I adored, and a

lot of other people I adored too. And it really was awful but my job was the most wonderful job in the world. It's the only job where you'd be sitting in a cinema on your days off and you'd say 'Ah, flying tomorrow'. I just loved it.

On VE Day we had three prisoners of war with us, and there was an RAF boyfriend of mine too. We drove up to London in the car, this old thing with four different sized tyres. It was wonderful, the crowds were masses, but it was a friendly crowd, they don't have them like that now. We drove into Piccadilly Circus and I remember people were rocking the cars. Ours had a slide-back roof, and we were sitting on the roof, with my poor boyfriend driving, I had my feet on his shoulders and we were waltzing on top. We said, 'Don't rock it, it'll fall over.' So they stopped. We went to Shepherd's Market, an RAF pub, and there were three chaps with DSOs [Distinguished Service Order] and DFCs [Distinguished Flying Cross], which was really something then. And I remember we sat on the pavement and one of these chaps and I changed coats, so he had my ATA coat, which of course he couldn't put on, I had his on with all these decorations and we opened tins of K rations, which were the prisoner of war rations they had in a little tin in case they were shot down. We ate these on the pavement. Somebody took a movie of it which he gave me. I played it once or twice I think and I can't find it now. It's really historic.

We went everywhere, to all the places where the RAF went – the Sweevee Club, the 400 – they made us honorary members for life, we just danced and it was wonderful, the whole of London...

ODELL JOHNSON

ARMED FORCES

Odell Johnson of the 733rd Squadron, 2nd Air Division, US Army Air Force, was to be shipped back to the US to train on B29s to continue the war in the Pacific.

We shipped out on 8 May, which happened to be VE Day. This was all planned much in advance. We formed up early in the morning at Old Buckenham, and marched the two miles down to Attleborough where we caught a troop train down to Southampton to board a Hermitage to go back home to the USA.

On the troop train, as we passed through villages and towns and – especially when we got to London – at every crossroad we came across, the streets were full of humanity. It just was wall-to-wall: people had suffered so much during the war and were now just letting it all out. So we witnessed great excitement everywhere.

And at this time, we were passing through London, through the tenement areas, where there were these five- and six-storey buildings, fire escapes on the back. And, as we did, up on the fourth or fifth floor, stood this elderly woman in the fire escape. She was probably 35 – in her hands, she had a pair of red, white and blue bloomers that would have fitted the biggest elephant you ever saw!

She stood there, waving at us Yanks going home on VE Day and wishing us well. So that is a memory I remember very much of my time over here and of going home.

WW2 People's War

SUZANNE SAMSON

REFUGEE

Suzanne Samson, born in 1924 in Berlin, fled to Italy in 1935 to escape the Nazi regime. When the Jews were expelled from Italy in 1939 she emigrated to London and worked in a factory.

The day of the end of the war was really quite something spectacular. In my memory it was just too wonderful for words. The relief, as if a huge, huge stone had been taken off your back. And then this tremendous joy of everybody going dancing to Buckingham Palace. The Pall Mall was dense with people, thousands and thousands and thousands of people out dancing in the street from Trafalgar Square all the way up to Buckingham Palace. And it was a most wonderful feeling. Everybody was your friend, people were wonderful, the world was lovely, Hitler was defeated, and this tremendous sense of freedom and relief and joy that people expressed. It was... it was a wonderful day.

MASS-OBSERVATION ARCHIVE, 11 MAY 1945
TWO WOMEN OVERHEARD DISCUSSING VE DAY

– Well, I didn't join in – I felt too sad. I went up and said a little prayer, and then I couldn't stop crying, and I didn't feel like going out among all the people.
– There was a lot felt like that, only you didn't hear about them. I felt just the same. I just stayed at home and did all my washing and gave the place a good spring clean.

RON GOLDSTEIN

Ron Goldstein, British soldier of the 4th Queen's Own Hussars, was one of five brothers all of whom served in the war. He was stationed near Venice in Italy as fighting drew to a close.

There we were, in this field in the middle of nowhere, when someone on another tank called out, 'They're going mad back home, get the BBC on your set or you'll miss all the fun.'

I tuned in my 19 set to the Home Forces station and, for the benefit of those outside the tank, hung all the earphones over the side of the hull. The crackle of the headphones soon drew a small crowd around the tank and we all listened in amazement to an unknown announcer describing the scene in Trafalgar Square.

I remember quite clearly that my emotions at the time were mixed. On the one hand it was good to feel that perhaps some of my loved ones back home were taking part in the scenes that were now taking place, on the other hand I, and in hindsight, I'm sure most of my comrades, felt somehow cheated that we, who had 'risked life and limb' and had been away from home for so many years were not there in England to share in the triumph.

WW2 People's War

SAM BEAZLEY

Sam Beazley served in Algeria and Italy as part of the British Army's Ambulance Company. In May 1945 he was stationed in northern Italy and celebrated the news of VE Day in Venice.

I started right at the bottom of Italy and I went right up the country; it took about a year or so. So by May 1945 we had finished up just outside Venice. As soon as the armistice was declared we all went in to Venice and had some fun; it was simply extraordinary. The Italians we met there were delighted – well they said they were anyway. Everybody had to say that they were delighted. But we hardly ever saw the Italians during our time there – they had either fled or were busy getting their olive groves in order. But it finally finished when we got to the top of Italy and the Germans surrendered. We happened to be in a field outside Venice, it was spring and so we decided to have an evening out in the town, which was extraordinary. There was a famous telegram from an American, which he sent back to his officer in America, 'Streets full of water, please advise.' All our boys, the British soldiers, piled into different gondolas and got drunk – basically that's what happened.

On the Grand Canal there are all the big palaces. Most of them were opened by the owners – they just flung the doors open and we went in and had drinks. I went in to a huge palace where there was a band of about six musicians and they finally left the palace and took to the streets. It was quite a long way to Piazza San Marco from where we were and we followed the band dancing around through the streets. Suddenly we arrived in the Piazza and St Mark's Cathedral was all under wraps to protect it. It had scaffolding, which went all the way up to the top. So without a moment's hesitation I flew up the scaffolding to the top, came down and went on dancing in the square again. Finally

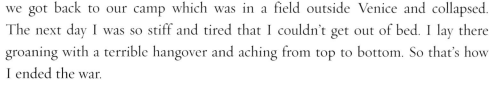

we got back to our camp which was in a field outside Venice and collapsed. The next day I was so stiff and tired that I couldn't get out of bed. I lay there groaning with a terrible hangover and aching from top to bottom. So that's how I ended the war.

It was about another three or four months before I got back to England. When I was in Venice I was having such a good time that I decided to stay in the Army another six months.

I looked after war correspondents in Vienna. They had a lovely house, and they had a good time too. We used to go to this beautiful officers' club called the Kinski Palais. It was the first time really that I had gone to hear any music properly. The Russians were rather good – they got in to Vienna three months before we did and got all the arts going again immediately. I went to the theatre because I had been an actor before the war. So we had a lovely time – but the Austrians weren't having such a good time, they were very hungry. The Viennese were very poor. One would go to hear an orchestra play, suddenly there would be a crash and the violinist would just faint, through hunger. Rough times really. Not for us, the conquering heroes; we had a wonderful time.

PATRICIA DAVIES

Patricia Davies (née Trehearne), aged 23, from Purley in Surrey, worked in Naval Intelligence in London.

From 1941 I worked in Naval Intelligence at the Admiralty where, in a deep dungeon underground, our section (NID 12) scrutinised all the enemy intercepts from Bletchley Park – Naval, Army, Air Force, Diplomatic and enemy agents' messages. The 'traffic', as it was called, came in fast and furious and we produced three reports a day informing the Board of the Admiralty of our findings and carefully disguising the wording so that they could not be traced to source. Other interested parties were informed on a 'need to know' basis. The head of section, Commander Ewen Montagu, was also involved in deception of which the most famous example is 'The Man Who Never Was' – in 1943 a dead body dressed as a marine officer was placed in the sea near Huelva in Spain. The marine was carrying letters from Lord Mountbatten and General Nye which indicated that our landings in Sicily were taking place in the north-west of the island and Corsica and Sardinia, and that further landings were to take place in Greece. The Germans swallowed the bait, moved troops accordingly and thus our Sicily operation was achieved with fewer casualties, one of which, incidentally, might have been Paddy, as he landed in Sicily three days before our troops arrived. It may seem macabre but I was always rather proud that my handwriting was on the body. I addressed the envelope of General Nye's letter to General Alexander!

Paddy and I met on a blind date, courtesy of a busybody who was staying in the same hotel as his mother and thought he did not have any girlfriends and therefore should meet a 'nice' girl she knew who was working in the Admiralty. The busybody made Paddy's mother's life a misery by constantly asking, 'Has he telephoned that girl yet?' One day he did telephone, I tried to choke him off but Paddy persisted and we arranged to meet in the Front Hall of Admiralty House, he would be blowing his nose with a red handkerchief and then take me to lunch. The night before the date Paddy had been sent to Portsmouth to watch some torpedo trials and so had a struggle to get to the Admiralty – unshaven. He took me to Martínez, a Spanish restaurant where I apparently chose the most expensive sherry on the wine list; the lunch was not a great success. About a month later I was asked to a charity dance in a large party. Paddy was also at the dance but his host's table was teetotal. He looked across the room and saw me sitting at a table where champagne flowed and everyone was roaring with laughter. Always quick to seize an opportunity, he leapt to his feet, crossed the room, asked me to dance, and could I please get him a glass of champagne? We saw more and more of each other over the next few months – by VE Day we were in love.

VE Day came and there was the most indescribable sensation of joy and relief. I went to work but there was little to do, the decrypts had dried up and we all just milled around laughing and planning our evenings. Everywhere the streets were crowded with happy joyous people, you could hardly move in Whitehall. Paddy had an invitation for us to dine with friends of his at their flat in Sloane Street and it was decided that we would all make our way to Buckingham Palace – that was easier said than done. We were soon parted from our friends by the mass of people and did not see them again that night.

It was a lovely fine spring evening, which added to the gaiety and happiness. Duke or dustman, general or private, we were all as one. I remember glancing

The fruit of a VE Day proposal: Patricia Trehearne and Paddy Davies on their wedding day.

into one of the mews near Eaton Square where there seemed to be a street party and seeing a stiff-necked Guards officer with his arms round a char-lady dancing merrily over the cobbles. We fought our way to Buckingham Palace and cheered when Winston Churchill and the royal family came out on the balcony. Finally we pushed along into Trafalgar Square and then, as it was getting darker, into Pall Mall where the flares outside the clubs were lit for the first time since 1939. The glow of the flares was sheer magic. It was then that Paddy, caught up in the euphoria of that magical moment, asked me to marry him. That, of course, demanded a celebration drink so we made our way to the Berkeley Hotel in Piccadilly where Paddy asked for champagne. The barman said, 'Don't you know there's a war on? We don't have any champagne.' There was a man whom I knew slightly sitting alone at the bar who heard all this. He immediately called a waiter saying, 'My father has some champagne in store here so please send up some bottles.' A perfect ending to a wonderful VE Day.

The couple with Patricia's sister, Anne, watching the celebrations on the first anniversary of VE Day in 1946.

FREDDY DYKE

HOME FRONT

Freddy Dyke, of Coleshill, Warwickshire, was in the NPS (National Pigeon Service) Special Section of the Royal Signals.

At long last the very day that everyone had hoped and waited for had now dawned, as it was officially announced that all hostilities against the 'Jerries' were now at an end, and the Forces of the Nazi Third Reich had accepted complete unconditional surrender. Hitler and a number of his supporting staff were dead, or were prisoners of the Allies, and the German Chancellery in Berlin was in ruins. The cease fire on all fronts was to become effective right away, so this news we received with the greatest elation after nearly six years of struggle against the enemy that had proved to be resilient, tough and determined in the European and Middle East theatres, in the air, and on the high seas. So now the war was finally over and the declaration of peace was on 8 May 1945, giving all of us servicemen and women a chance to celebrate, and thankfully reflect on the fact that we had survived during the darkest days that the citizens of our country have ever had to endure.

The country went wild with drinking, dancing and street parties that made Jubilee Day look pale by comparison, and now the whole idea was to celebrate, forget any troubles and get 'P****D UP'. The partying continued all night long provided you could stand up after consuming so much ale or spirits. I have to admit like so many others the next day was sheer agony as the sickness and the aches and pains told its own story. Yet it was all worth while, as it was just a case of temporarily suffering when we had just survived nearly six years of Blood, Toil, Sweat and Tears, so who cared? When we finally surfaced for a little fresh air 'Winnie' had to remind us all that the war was not yet over and a lot of serious fighting had yet to take place in the Far East, against the brutal Japanese, before the final ceasefire which would allow us to return to our normal lifestyle and families that we so urgently wanted.

He said we had earned our victory in Europe and we should take a few days in which to enjoy this victory, but we must still bear in mind the final objective was to rid the world of these brutal oppressors and restore peace once and for all. So now we had a short time in which to rejoice after all that we had suffered, and then back to the real job of finishing off the bloody Japs when the entire forces of the Allied nations could yield one master stroke in the final blow to defeat the enemy.

WW2 People's War

Oh my God the English upper classes do take their pleasures sadly.
We were at the Mayfair most of the time, and it was pretty gloomy,
and then that frightful moan from the King! It was only the real working
classes that thoroughly enjoyed themselves. I hear there were the wildest
goings on in places like Shoreditch and Battersea, and they roasted a pig
whole in Bermondsey or somewhere down there.

FRANCES PARTRIDGE

HOME FRONT

*Frances Partridge and her husband Ralph, both pacifists, opened their home in Wiltshire to
friends and refugees during the war.*

5 MAY – Waiting, waiting for the end. The last two nights
I have started awake with the first dimming of consciousness
into sleep, to find myself lying with a wildly pounding heart,
as if listening for something. The church bells pealing for
victory? Anyway all I heard was the sound of Saxon clearing
his throat in his bedroom, forced along the tunnel of the
passage.

Before lunchtime we heard that all the German armies in the North had
surrendered. Holland and Denmark are free.

7 MAY – All day long we were kept on the hop by the wireless telling us that the
Germans has signed unconditional surrender but that the announcement had not
yet come through – we could expect it any minute. If the war is over then it is
over, and I am bewildered to explain this fever of anticipation. The voices of the
BBC announcers betray increasing irritation, and everyone is on tenterhooks
waiting for the inevitable.

Then at eight this evening the telephone rang, and it was an Inkpen
neighbour asking if Burgo was going to school tomorrow or not. (We have been
sharing transport.) 'It's just come through – tomorrow will be V-day. Churchill
will announce the end of the war in Europe at 3 pm. It's all very flat,' she went on.

'We've just been drinking a little weak gin.' So here it was at last. Nothing could have been more prosaic that this way of receiving the news, yet on returning to the music room I found all my restlessness had gone in a moment. Oddly enough, the news of peace actually brought a *sense* of peace, very refreshing like a good drink of water to a thirsty person. R. and I sat through our evening quietly, enjoying the relief from tension. Before we went up to bed we went out onto the veranda and looked up at the sky in which a few stars twinkled mistily, and I thought of the night nearly six years ago when the war began, and how I had done the same, wondering what was in store for us all, and gazed on by those same impersonal eyes.

8 MAY – At three o'clock Churchill delivered the promised announcement. Afterwards we drove to Newbury to fetch the other Inkpen children from school. Every cottage had a few flags hung out, and in most of them a dummy-like figure of an old person could be seen at an upper window, hoisted out of bed probably to see what little fun there was to see. Near Newbury we had a narrow escape from a drunken lorry-driver veering from side to side of the road – he made the V-sign as we passed. Bicyclists were hurrying into Newbury dressed in their best; little girls wore satin blouses and red, white and blue bows in their hair.

10 MAY – I feel happier and more conscious of peace even than I expected. I am very much aware this morning of something that has just gone: – a background to our daily existence as solid as one of the scenes in Burgo's toy theatre – a background coloured by the obscenity of violence, and my own disgust at it. The fields, Downs and woods *look* peaceful now, seen with eyes that know the murder and destruction have stopped. ...

I have been reading Flaubert's *Letters*, and have just reached the Franco-Prussian war. How his reactions remind me of ours! First, horror at the bestiality of human beings. As the Germans invade he develops a more conventional desire to defend his country, followed by the most frightful agitation and despair, such as only literary men can indulge in. *No-one*, he feels sure, can hate the war so much as he does; he resigns from the Home Guard, returns to his views about the beastliness of human beings, is physically sick every day from sheer disgust, and dislikes his fellow Frenchmen almost as much as the Prussians. As for 'evacuees' they are the worst feature of the whole war.

News of VE day in London: Janetta writes: 'I've found the crowds very depressing indeed, and the flags and decorations pathetic although often very pretty. Some bonfires were wonderful, bringing back the old ecstasies of staring into a fire, but also having that appalling smell of burning debris, too terrifyingly nostalgic of blitzes. And I so loathe the look of masses of boiling people with scarlet dripping faces, wearing tiny paper hats with 'Ike's Babe' or 'Victory' written on them.'

Julia : 'We walked to Buckingham Palace, and there found a spectacular scene – all the fountains, balustrades, not to mention trees, were crowded with these little pink penguins in their droves, all facing the Palace, which was brilliantly illuminated with beautiful golden light, and draped with red velvet over the balcony. It was charmingly pretty. Everyone was fainting by the roadside, or rather sitting down holding their stockinged feet in their hands and groaning. A few faint upper-class cries of "Taxi – taxi!" came wailing through the air from voices right down on the pavement; whilst cockney tones, slightly more robust, could be heard saying, "I'm f*****g well all in now".' Of her own reaction to peace she goes on: 'It's something to do with the war having gone on just *too* long, one was at last crushed, and personally I no longer feel human any more; I mean the dynamic principle has given way and one feels like a sheet of old newspaper or pressed dried grass.'

This evening we drove to Shalbourne to give Olive a present of bacon. I remembered how after the First War some pacifists had been turned on by the merry-making crowds, for instance how Cambridge undergraduates had pushed down Harry Norton's garden wall; and wondered if our village neighbours, and 'old retainers' like Olive, might say to themselves, 'Well, *they* did nothing to help. *They've* no cause to rejoice.' But the warm way Olive and her family welcomed us and exchanged handshakes and kisses did nothing to confirm my fears.

After all, surely it's only logical that pacifists – of all people – should rejoice in the return to Peace?

ALBERT MORROW

ARMED FORCES

Albert Morrow, a Canadian Naval Officer, commanded MTB (Motor Torpedo Boat) 726 in British coastal waters between 1943 and 1945.

We were limping back after being in action over in Ostend harbour, to get some repairs in to Great Yarmouth. As we approached, a signal came over the WT down below which was relayed up to me. I said, 'Read it again.' And it was this:

To all ships in the North Atlantic, English Channel, North Sea: hostilities have ceased, splice the main brace.

So I said, 'You better bring that up to me.' I turned to the coxswain and I said, 'How's the rum, sir?'

And he said, 'Lots of rum, sir.'

So I said, 'Splice the main brace.' The tradition of course is that the men give sips to the officers and so when we'd finished the first slice of the main brace, I said, 'How's the rum holding out?'

And he said, 'Lots of rum, sir.'

I said, 'Splice it again.'

So as we were approaching the entrance to the harbour of Great Yarmouth I say, 'Coxswain, where do you make the entrance?' because the heavy seas were sweeping across the mouth and you always had to aim upward coming in because of the narrow entrance of Great Yarmouth harbour.

He says, 'Well I make it about Green 10.'

And the other lookout says, 'Well I think it's about Red 20, sir.'

So we approached it and as we were coming down I had to gun it. If we had missed we would have sunk right outside. What an end to the war!

The next day was the real VE day, so I left Number 1 in charge and hightailed it into London with a clean shirt on top and bottles of liquor out of stock and I was the most popular man in London, because they ran out on VE Day. So I had lots of friends. There's always some humour and that was the end of it.

KATHLEEN LYDON

ARMED FORCES

Kathleen Lydon (née Miller) was a WAAF (Women's Auxiliary Air Force) Flight Sergeant. As a flight mechanic she served in Bomber Command and Control Command. On VE Day she was attached to the Flying Training Command in Leconfield.

I was told I was to be a flight mechanic on aeroengines. When you're young courage is something you can easily muster up especially if someone says you can't do it. It was a very practical thing to do, engines are very complicated until you get to know them! But it was all very, very interesting, I wouldn't have missed it. In the services there was such comradeship and community and at least we were out in the open air rather than stuck inside.

On VE day I was still working, still doing the repairs out in the hangar. We each worked on one plane and on that day I was working in the engine bay of a Wellington bomber. Before that day I don't think any of us were really expecting the news. We were so busy, engines would come and go and I was a drum major in the Wings for Victory parades on Sundays – I don't think we stopped and thought about it. There was little celebration, as we knew that so many people were not going to come back. Even though the war was over, people still didn't know what the future held.

RUTH IVE

HOME FRONT

Ruth Ive worked for the department of Postal and Telegraph censorship, part of the Ministry of Information, during the war. As a censor for transatlantic communication, she was responsible for monitoring calls between Prime Minister Churchill and President Roosevelt.

I remember VE Day vividly. I remember absolutely everything I did on that particular day; it was such an incredible experience for us all. I had been a censor, a monitor, on the transatlantic radio link and this, believe it or not, was the only verbatim telephone system there was during the war. Nobody in private life could just phone up their friends in America or mainland Europe and so, to enable the Prime Minister Winston Churchill and the President of the US, FD Roosevelt, to speak to each other, they rigged up a radio link. The link was thought to be vulnerable for if the Germans could break our codes they could learn of our military plans. So they decided that every call should be censored and monitored and I was one of the censors.

We were a very small band working in a little bombed-out building in St Martins le Grande because all the radio calls were handled by the GPO and AT&T in Washington, so we were a sort of adjunct of the Post Office. I had been working with this team for three and half years. We had started in January 1942, very soon after America had entered the war. Then the volume of calls was enormous. There were very few of us doing it, all of us bound to secrecy under the

Official Secrets Act, and facing a terrible end if we didn't. Off to the tower immediately!

It was because we had to take the calls down in shorthand that I got the job for I had studied verbatim shorthand at commercial school. When I left school in September 1939 I certainly didn't expect that my shorthand would prove so significant! Shorthand dogged me all through the war. When I was recruited I was interviewed by a crusty old Admiral and other military men and they said to me, 'What can you do?' 'Can you speak French?' 'No'. 'Can you speak German?' 'No'. 'Can you drive a car?' Well, I could a bit... Then they said, 'Well girl you must be able to do something!' so I said 'I can do shorthand.' And that got me through the war because I became the official shorthand reader for all the troops mail. People wrote in shorthand in those days. It took me hours to get it back to English. From that I went up the ladder. You were thrust into extraordinary circumstances at an extraordinary time. I was by no means alone. Young people who had a skill or a flair for something got landed in jobs where the responsibility was huge.

When I first got the censorship job in 1942 I don't think I slept for the first three months. I was so worried that something would go wrong. It took that long before I settled down and treated it as an everyday job and felt comfortable with the boundaries. It was all done very expertly and efficiently. It wasn't amateur by any means. The War Cabinet agreed a list of rules, with the equivalent for the Americans, stating that, if possible, they would signal each other beforehand if they wanted to speak. Then they would set out the subject matter that was to be discussed in numbered paragraphs and they would refer to the numbers, never the subject matter. That was the theory. The PM had a  hand in drawing up these regulations and he was very good. He had a sarcastic wit. You were never quite sure what he was going to say next. The first time I heard him talking I could hardly believe it was me listening to him!

All the transatlantic calls were taken down in shorthand and then transcribed into English so the team were mostly journalists who came from all over England. There were only eight of us, mostly men over army age, older than I was, but we were all from very mixed backgrounds. Because I did verbatim shorthand I became the chief censor at 23, and I really did have to take some terrible decisions on the calls, to assess if they were a security risk. By May 1945, I was the senior censor and I really had done quite a lot of top-secret work. We knew (I knew, at any rate) that the treaty was going to be signed, that it was coming, and as far as I can remember, I did an all-night duty. I jolly well wanted to hear about the peace treaty first hand.

On that day I didn't go home as I should have done at nine o'clock, but I stayed in the office. We thought 'nobody will ever phone anybody in America', but believe it or not they did. At half past ten in the morning, there was a very routine call from one civil servant to another in the US and they said 'this will be the last call'. I remember sitting down at the desk and doing it. I took it all down in shorthand, transcribed it and that was within half an hour of the peace treaty being signed. But it was not only me who was listening to the call, for the Germans had a station in Munich by then. I had no idea that they had broken our code but every call that the Prime Minister made to the President was on Hitler's desk within two hours. I never knew at the time.

And so, at eleven o' clock the peace treaty was signed and I remember sitting there with the headphones on. We listened to the calls with big post office headphones, and I remember thinking, 'I can't believe it, we've survived.' We congratulated each other; there were about 6 of us standing round. I took my headphones off and I said 'I will never do another shorthand for the rest of my life!' It was all very low key. I remember saying, 'I'm going home thank you very much, there's no more work to do, the Germans can hear all they like, the war's over.'

I got on the underground at St Paul's station and it was very noisy when I changed at Oxford Street to get on the Stanmore line. Anyway, it didn't take me long to get home to St John's Wood where I was living with my mother. When I got back my mum said 'Isn't it marvellous, we've actually survived!' and I must say it was a great relief. I was engaged to be married and I hadn't seen my fiancée for three and a half years and I was wondering how he was going to get home. He was in Greece, with no telephone or anything, but I knew he'd surface eventually.

I remember getting something to eat in the kitchen and the telephone bell and it was a good friend of mine, Ernest, who I've known practically all my life. He had by chance got some leave from the Army and we decided we'd go back into town and take the underground to Trafalgar Square to go and walk down the Mall. Arm in arm we joined the crowds and we went down the Mall towards the Palace and it was absolutely wonderful. We all linked arms and joined in choruses and it was really emotional, it really was. We waited, for I wanted to see Mr Churchill. We waited and waited and he didn't come out. I was rather peeved by that. I won't say it was dangerous but there were so many people and it was very spirited because I don't think any of us could believe that we came through. However, for all of us, the jollity was tinged with sadness. The camps had been liberated and their horrors revealed, and the men in the Army, they'd had a hell of a life. At home we had been bombed out twice, once during the Blitz and once with a V2. We had been through some awful experiences but mostly I have to say, I was tired. I'd been working with the Prime Minister for three and a half years and Mr Churchill never liked to go to bed. He made countless telephone calls to America, he was addicted to the telephone, he called up everybody, and he chased up information. He wanted to know everything and he talked ceaselessly to our Ambassador at the Embassy at two or three in the morning. It was nothing for Mr Churchill but absolutely awful for me. It was reassuring, though, in 1942 when we really had our backs to the wall. He always exuded confidence. I wasn't quite so sure about the President.

I remember saying to Ernest, 'I'm awfully tired'. I think I'd been up half the night and he said he wanted to go home too. We waited in the crowds for an hour but nobody came, so we went home. I felt such relief that we had won for we'd always thought it was a very close run thing. Personally, the sense of relief was enormous but there was still a sense of strain and worry for we didn't know what was going to come next. Nobody thought it would be easy and the fact is that food rationing got worse, not better, but it was a day I'll never, ever forget - I kept my word, I never did any shorthand afterwards!

PRESIDENT HARRY S TRUMAN, 8 MAY 1945
VE DAY BROADCAST TO THE AMERICAN PEOPLE, WASHINGTON

This is a solemn but glorious hour. The Allied Armies, through sacrifice and devotion and with God's help, have wrung from Germany a final and unconditional surrender. The western world has been freed of the evil forces which for five years and longer have imprisoned the bodies and broken the lives of millions upon millions of free-born men. They have violated their churches, destroyed their homes, corrupted their children, and murdered their loved ones. Our Armies of Liberation have restored freedom to these suffering peoples, whose spirit the oppressors could never enslave.

MARY POLIZZI

HOME FRONT

Mary Polizzi celebrated VE Day as a young girl in New York.

I was a little girl. I remember in school they gave us tags, and we had drills all the time. And there were so many blackouts. There were people who would come around to make sure everyone had their lights turned off. I remember there were Italian soldiers who were prisoners of war, and they came to Sunday mass with us at Sacred Heart Church. And I thought it was so wonderful that the government allowed the prisoners to come. The government knew they were Catholic, and it was important for them to go. One of the soldiers said to me, 'I am so happy to be in America. It is beautiful.' He was a prisoner, and he didn't want to leave. I didn't know much about the war. No one in my family had to go, but I saw the newspapers, and I learned about what was done to people. It made me cry. I saw the mangled Jewish people that they put in this ditch. They were dead and all the people who buried them did was pour a little dirt over them. It was terrible. But when the war was over, oh! We were so happy! We never really had parties in my neighbourhood, but when VE Day came, there were block parties everywhere. And everybody did something to salute the soldiers. God, I'm proud to be an American. Thank God nothing like that would ever happen here, the torturing of people. It makes me cry when I think of the people who never made it back. I'm so thankful I was born here. God bless America.

MILTON LIPSON

ARMED FORCES

Milton Lipson was a Secret Service agent periodically assigned to protect Presidents Franklin D Roosevelt and Harry S Truman.

On VE Day, I was assigned to the New York Secret Service office – doing advance work for expected Presidential trips. We actually knew a few days before VE Day that the war was ending. Word went out on the office grapevine. So, when it was announced in our office that VE Day had actually come, it was no surprise. President Roosevelt, whom we always called The Boss, had died only the previous month. Our main reaction to VE Day was that The Boss had known it was coming when he died. He'd gotten information from Allen Dulles, later the CIA director, that the Germans were dealing. It would have been terrific if The Boss had lived to see VE Day. But at least he had the satisfaction of knowing it was coming.

ELSIE OWENS

HOME FRONT

Elsie Owens lived in Harlem, New York, and worked at a factory in downtown Manhattan.

The factory where I worked, on 8th Street, made polo shirts. I didn't find out about the surrender until I left work that day. People came running up to me in the street – hollering that the Germans had surrendered. The emotion was so overwhelming that I began crying. I was thinking about my brother Jesse, who was in the Army in Europe. To get home, I had to reach 127th Street and Lenox Avenue. I got on the subway, but it was so mobbed with cheering, shouting people that I had to get off at 34th Street. So I joined the crowds at 34th Street and celebrated for a while before going home.

JOSEPH HELLER

ARMED FORCES

Joseph Heller flew 60 missions as a B-25 bombardier in the US Army Air Force during the war.

VE Day was pretty banal for me. I was back from overseas, stationed at San Angelo Army Base in Texas. We knew VE Day was coming, but didn't know what day it was going to be. Finally, we heard the announcement over the radio. The day came and went. I don't remember any great celebration. Most of the men were mostly concerned about the point system that determined when we would be discharged. Everybody was asking: 'How many points do you have?' I was actually discharged the next month, on 11 June.

PATSY GIACCHI

FRONT LINE

Patsy, from a farming family in Hackensack, New Jersey, was drafted into the Army when he turned 18 and served in the 94th Quartermaster Railhead Company in Normandy. He was one of the lucky ones to be sent home at the end of the war in Europe.

When the war ended, I was in Germany, in a town called Ulm. Out of the clear blue sky over the loudspeaker they say, 'The war has ended! The war has ended!' Here I am in a foxhole talking to one of my buddies. 'What did they say?'

'Pat! The war has ended!' You'd see there were some of them out there going crazy. Guys were shooting each other by mistake! GIs, yes, they were shooting themselves, from the excitement. They tried to tell everybody, 'Calm down! Be careful!'

And I was in a foxhole down there. 'The war is over! The war is over!' I was crying in the foxhole from joy, I couldn't believe it. The following morning they called formation outside, they said, 'The following names, please step forward.' Finally, 'Pfc. Patsy Giacchi!' I step forward.

'Okay,' the captain says, 'you guys are all going home.'

Boom. One guy passes out from the excitement. I couldn't believe it. I think I was 21 years old then.

Now I'm on a liberty ship coming home. All of a sudden, after about a week, they said, 'Here it is, boys.' We come around a big bend, and they say, 'You guys want to see it? Go up on the top deck, you can see it.'

What is it? We're hitting Newport News, Virginia. And you look, as you come in, the United States! And there's a big sign that says, 'Welcome home, boys! Well done!' I'm on the deck there, I'm crying, I can't believe it.

All of a sudden you start to line up. I said, 'Pat, be careful now, Pat be careful, you made it through the whole war. Don't get killed, don't fall off the ship or get hurt.'

Then they call your name; you step down. When I got off, I kissed the ground. I cried.

They said, 'When your name is called, step up, salute the officer who's giving you your discharge papers, make a turn, go back, you're discharged from the Army.'

'Pfc. Patsy J. Giacchi.'

'Pfc. Patsy J. Giacchi!'

A guy goes, 'Hey, that's you!'

'Oh, yeah! Yeah!' I go up there, nervous. They give me that paper. I walk back. 'You don't go back and sit down! Get the hell out of here, you're discharged!'

I see an officer go by, I salute him. He says, 'You're not a soldier any more.'

'I'm sorry, Sir.'

'That's okay.'

I'm the only guy that's coming toward Hackensack. They told me where to get the next bus to go from Fort Monmouth to Newark. I'm on the bus a couple of hours, and then the driver says, 'Newark, Penn Station!'

Penn Station! I remember that from when I was a kid! Penn Station in Newark. I got off the bus. I went to a telephone booth. There were many guys there. My time came. I took out my wallet. Now I didn't know my phone number, because when I left it was three years ago. So I opened up my wallet to look for my phone number. I had my mustering out pay. They gave me 300 dollars when I got discharged, plus I had another 200 dollars. That's 1945. That's a lot of money. I'm nervous. All of a sudden, 'Hello. Who am I speaking to?'

'You're speaking to Nellie.' Nellie's one of my sisters.

'Nellie, please, now don't get excited. This is your brother Patsy.'

'Who?'

'Patsy!'

'Who?'

'Patsy!'

Boom. She dropped the phone. She passed out.

Jane picks up the phone, my older sister, and she says, 'Who's this?'

'Jane, please, it's your brother Patsy. Please, don't get excited. I'm in Newark, New Jersey.'

'Oh my GOD! We'll send somebody.'

'No, no, no. I'm coming home. I'll take care of it. I'm coming home.'

'Patsy, please be careful. Oh my GOD!'

I left my wallet there. I had some change in my pocket, and a couple of bills.

I got on the bus. I took the bus from Newark to Hackensack. Then from Hackensack on Main Street I took a taxicab to West Street, where I lived.

As I'm coming around the corner, they've got a big sign for me in front of my house, 'Welcome home, Patsy!' All my Italian neighbors are waiting for me. I get out of the cab, and they're grabbing me, my mother's trying to grab me, my father – no, my father's dead – my mother was trying to grab me, my sisters were there. The neighbours were there. Across the street the DeLorenzos. 'Ohhh, Patsy, it's good to see you,' and everything else. Who's pulling me here, who's pulling me there.

After about two hours, some of the neighbours disperse, we go inside, we start talking. Then Jane says, 'Gee, Patty, have you got any pictures?'

'I've got one or two pictures. ... JANE! My wallet! I left it in Newark.'

'Oh my God! How much was in it?'

'Five hundred!'

'Five HUNDRED?!!!' Then it was like five thousand.

We call up Newark. They say, 'Would you please come down?'

We get down to Newark. I go where I made the telephone call from. Behind the counter, there's a couple of cops there, security or something else. They said, 'Soldier, we get this every day. You're going to have to give us some real good detail. Everybody tells us black wallet, brown wallet, something like that. Tell us if you can what's in your wallet.'

'Well,' I said, 'I've got a couple of this, a couple of that.' 'Keep going.' The other guy's writing it down.

I said, 'Okay. I've got it! Okay, now look.' I was always excited. 'Take your time now,' he says. 'Okay. You'll see a picture of my girlfriend, an Italian girl with long black hair. She's got a dress on' – I bought her this dress – 'and the dress has got an emblem of a little parrot.'

That did the trick. They gave me the wallet, with the money in it and everything else.

'Sir,' I said, 'who returned this for me?'

He said, 'A little old lady. She said, 'Some poor bugger left his wallet here with all his money. Please see that he gets it.'

I said, 'Can I give her a reward?'

He said, 'She doesn't want a reward. Just take care of yourself, she said.'

US troops return home from the war in Europe. Their war had ended – but many were sent to the Far East.

GENERAL DWIGHT D EISENHOWER, 8 MAY 1945
SUPREME COMMANDER OF AMERICAN FORCES ADDRESSES HIS TROOPS

The crusade on which we embarked in the early summer of 1944 has reached its glorious conclusion. ... Full victory in Europe has been attained. Working and fighting together in single and indestructible partnership you have achieved a perfection in the unification of air, ground and naval power that will stand as a model in our time. ... To every subordinate that has been in this command of almost 5 million Allies I owe a debt of gratitude that can never be repaid. The only repayment that can be made to them is the deep appreciation and lasting gratitude of all the free citizens of the United Nations.

ARTHUR BARRACLOUGH

PRISONER OF WAR

Arthur Barraclough, aged 25, was in the 1st Battalion York and Lancaster Regiment. He and an Australian companion escaped from the Markt Pongau prisoner of war camp near St Johann in Austria and travelled to Bruck.

There was a farm nearby and I had to go and ask them if they would give us a bit of something to eat, which they did. I made a sort of veiled threat 'You know the Americans are coming and if we tell them you have fed us it will be to your advantage.' We had a meal and we considered that perhaps by now the area was clear of Germans. We came down once again, but once more a German officer saw us. We met each other. There was no point in running away and what he had to say was quite unexpected, totally unexpected. He said, 'I have been on the Russian front, I was wounded. I have been in hospital. I was discharged as unfit for further military service and I am now wanting to make my way to the Americans. But, if you can help me, I will help you. I will help you to get to the Americans if you will help me.' We gladly acceded to this suggestion.

The three of us – the German, my Australian friend and myself – travelled by train from Zell am See bound for Innsbruck, but stopped after Kitzbühel in the middle of nowhere. We then continued on foot and reached Worgl where we were met by an approaching American armoured vehicle.

The vehicle stopped and the driver said, 'Who the blazes...?' He was obviously confused that here was an Australian – with his big slouch hat – me in English uniform, and in the middle of us was this German. We told him quickly who we were and that we were hoping to get away and that the German, having paid for the tickets, had got us to here. I did my best to ensure they didn't shoot him there, but he was taken away, presumably for interrogation, and our ways parted there.

The American said, 'Do you know what day it is?' and quite frankly I was not at all sure, but I said, 'Well, I think it is Wednesday,' and he said, 'Do you know anything else?' and I said 'No, what should I know?'

He said, 'It's VE Day!' and that was the day we met them.

We were then taken by the Americans to Innsbruck where the place seemed to be teeming with American soldiers, and we stayed in a house which they had taken over as a billet. The dear old lady who presumably lived in the house, realising I could speak German, asked me, 'Would you be so kind as to ask these people, I know I can't stop them from sleeping here and living here but would you ask them not to kick the furniture about.' We were told by the Americans that we should report in and go through the proper channels for returning POWs. But they did also point out that there were quite a number of German vehicles which had been left, deserted, and that many of them were quite roadworthy. We took the hint and found an Opel car in German livery. The Americans gave it a quick inspection. One of the chaps, who must have been a mechanic said, 'The brakes need adjusting, but I will see to them for you.' They checked the oil, they filled it up with petrol, they gave me a map and then we started after once again loading our stomachs with some food. We set off, then, from Innsbruck in this car, making our way home.

HARRY FREE

FRONT LINE

Harry Free, a miner from South Kirby in Yorkshire, was a member of the Army's 43rd Reconnaissance unit patrolling Germany and Belgium at the end of hostilities.

Seeing the concentration camps for the first time was a terrible shock. I couldn't believe that people could treat human beings like that. The guards at these camps were the dregs of Germans. I felt sorry for the state of the inmates – I couldn't really take it in, seeing all the bodies and the people like skeletons. As a recce unit, again all we could do was continue to advance leaving the infantry to deal with the situation.

My attitude to the German people didn't change – I just carried on doing my job. Perhaps it's more difficult to associate yourself with foreign people – if the concentration camp inmates had been English prisoners of war being treated like that, or if I'd actually had to go in there and deal with the situation, maybe I'd have felt differently, more vengeful.

There was no drinking of alcohol when you were on a recce apart from the usual rum ration – which was in fact only available when the weather was cold. I was detailed to collect the rum rations from HQ so I developed quite a liking for it! During action, we rarely drank apart from that – again there was no time – except when we were in France and we had all that Calvados.

When the war ended, there was much more drinking. Some soldiers got hold of illegally distilled Schnapps from the Germans. It was lethal – rumoured to make you go blind. We were warned against drinking it and we didn't in our troop, though I know some infantrymen did.

My memories of VE Day were that it was just like any other day for us. It was 'spit and polish'! On VE day we were in civvy billets patrolling near Celle, maintaining a curfew. If we saw anyone out after curfew we took them back to base. VE day was a routine day for us. It was different for others as they were waiting to be told they could go home, but as a regular I had to complete my seven years which would be in 1947. We heard the celebrations in London on the radio – I remember feeling envious because all we were doing was patrolling.

I felt glad it was over, but there were rumours of a 'werewolf movement', an underground German movement which we were apprehensive about, and we were still resented by some people. The ordinary Germans weren't cowed by defeat and I remember seeing a torch-lit parade in Wuppertal with Germans singing and marching. It was an impressive sight.

WW2 People's War

LORD CARRINGTON

FRONT LINE

Peter Alexander Rupert Carington, 6th Baron Carrington, was a major in the Grenadier Guards and was awarded the Military Cross in 1945. He fought in Germany.

VE day was, for those of us in the Army in Germany, something of anticlimax. The fighting had ended a month or so previously and we had already got used to a rather safer and more peaceful life. My battalion had ended the war north of

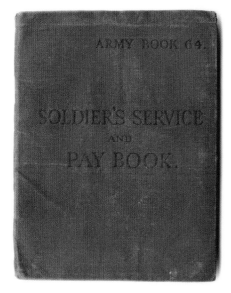

Hamburg. Shortly afterwards, we were told we were to lose our tanks and revert to infantry. This took the form of a great parade called 'Farewell to Armour', in the presence of Field Marshal Montgomery. The Sherman tanks with which we were equipped were markedly inferior to their German counterparts and there was some ambivalence in being parted from them. Nevertheless, in an armoured battalion in war, a squadron leader has a great deal of latitude. We ran our own affairs with little interference from battalion headquarters.

This changed very rapidly as we were forcefully reminded of the rigorous discipline expected of an infantry battalion in what was then the household brigade. The adjutant, subsequently a notable general of repute, made this abundantly clear.

At the same time, we were ordered to move to the Rhine and my company took over a moated schloss in the village of Vilich on the opposite side of the river to Bonn – not far away from Bad Godesberg, where the curtain rose on the Munich Agreement.

In addition to our peacetime activities, I was put in charge of a camp of several thousand forced labourers from Yugoslavia. During the war they were united in their dislike of their German overseers. In peacetime, since half were Serbs and the other half Croats, they were united in their dislike of each other. This gave me a good introduction to the Yugoslav problem with which I became involved 50 years or so later.

The aftermath of war was all around us. The devastation of Cologne, not as bad as Hamburg, but dreadful, the scores of refugees wandering homeless and penniless along the roads. The deprivation suffered by the Germans themselves, with whom we were forbidden to 'fraternise'. But the weather was glorious, the sun shone and the orchard of the schloss was a restful place to sleep after a VE Day lunch and we were glad to be alive.

Left: Every British soldier was issued with Army Book 64. This 20-page booklet was their 'passport', containing all personal identification information. Failure to produce the document when requested was a punishable offence.
Below: The Military Cross, awarded for gallantry in the field.

Overleaf: After the battle. Occupying Soviet soldiers patrol the ruined city of Berlin in July 1945. For those in defeated areas of Europe VE Day was an altogether more sombre affair.

LORD WEIDENFELD

HOME FRONT

George Weidenfeld had come to London from Vienna in 1938. As a linguist he worked for the BBC World Service.

I spent the morning of 8 May 1945 in my office at 200 Oxford Street, that by now legendary building which belonged to the Peter Robinson store and served as headquarters for the BBC World Service. I say legendary because it housed – performing the most diverse duties in supervising broadcasts in both English and every conceivable vernacular of the then British Commonwealth as well as radio newsreel and what is now the BBC World Service in English – such names as George Orwell, William Amson, Peter Quennell, Edmund Blunden, Cecil Day Lewis. The canteen in the lower ground floor was open 24 hours a day. That morning the buzz of excitement and thrill of experiencing a climactic point of one's existence was palpable. Nightshift workers lingered on endlessly. My own morning commentary, a five-minute piece in radio newsreel, was recorded at twelve o'clock noon. I was thirsting for coffee and sat at a table next to a ravishing editor of the Far East service whom I had always admired from a distance. The electricity of the event, the sense of finality after years of skating on ice, doggedly, on the whole confidently, but never quite certainly, had a dizzying effect on both of us. We decided to go out and find some lunch before eventually parting to our abodes, both in south-west London. Oxford Street, Marble Arch, Park Lane were teeming with liberated humanity. No taxis or buses in sight. And as we walked all the way to Hyde Park Corner, empathy and mutual attraction grew exponentially. VE Day brought – and kept – us together for three years.

EDWARD PALMER

FRONT LINE

Edward Palmer served with the British Expeditionary Force and the Bedfordshire Yeomanry in France. On VE day he was stationed in Brunswick, Germany.

My Colonel and I went to Hamburg on the day of the surrender. We wanted to liberate some really good binoculars from the U boats. To be in Hamburg that day and witness the desolation was incredible. Occasionally you saw faces peering out from a cellar, though they would disappear rapidly if they were spotted. Otherwise you didn't see a soul. To be honest, it was good to see how much they'd suffered after all that we had. At that time one had no sympathy for them at all. To see the U boat pens and all the docks completely destroyed and boats on their sides was a satisfactory end to the war from our point of view. Though it sounds rather grim, we then celebrated VE Day.

We got rather drunk. I remember the following morning my Colonel appeared for breakfast with a great bit of sticking plaster over his nose. I said 'What on Earth happened to you?' He said, 'Well I was taking my boots off to get into bed and I fell over and hit my head against the stone floor.' That was the sort of party we had that night.

EDMUND DE ROTHSCHILD CBE

ARMED FORCES

Edmund de Rothschild was serving in Italy as a major in charge of 604 ('P' Battery), one of three batteries of the 200 Field Regiment, Royal Artillery, part of the Jewish Infantry Brigade Group.

Nearing Udine, on the last day of the war in Europe, an aeroplane circled overhead and I had a strong sense that I was going to be killed. I dived for cover, the first time I had done so in Italy, but the plane flew off – and that night I dreamt that my father was standing by my bed.

Udine, which the New Zealanders had liberated, was teeming with unruly Serb irregulars, all armed, and the problem arose of how to get them to surrender their weapons. I do not know who came up with the solution, but it was arranged that Field Marshal Alexander should take the salute at a march-past on a dais in one of the town squares – for which I turned out part of the guard of honour, with a 25-pounder on each side of the dais. This square, it so happened, led into another square, with a narrow exit. As the Serbs went singing and cheering past they found that they were unable to get out of the second square without handing over their weapons.

For two days my trucks were then used to return Uzbek soldiers to the Russian zone. The frontier was a humped-back bridge with a Union Jack flying on one side, the Hammer and Sickle on the other. All day long, as the Uzbeks crossed over, tearing off their medals, one could hear the sound of gunfire; later we learnt that the Uzbeks had all been shot as they reached the other side. When a train arrived from Yugoslavia carrying Russians who had fought on the Tito front, it was my duty to provide them with food. I met the Russian colonel who was in charge of the train, and, seeing a desperately sick woman, suggested that she be taken off the train and sent to hospital. Twice I asked him, and twice he refused.

The mood in 'P' Battery at the end of the war was muted; so many of my men's relatives and friends had disappeared into concentration camps or been killed. And so rather than organise a celebration I asked the rabbi attached to the brigade to conduct a short service of thanksgiving for our deliverance, which was attended by many non-Jews as well.

ARTHUR FARRAND RADLEY MBE

FRONT LINE

Major Arthur Farrand Radley was fighting alongside partisan groups in north-east Italy as a member of SOE (Special Operations Executive).

How had I ever got into this? Three years in Malta on half rations and daily blitzing before volunteering for SOE at the call of people who were 'not musclebound'. I was originally selected for the Resistance in Austria but the only British officer in that area was caught. One operation with the SOE in France and now here I was with this Leftish outfit in Italy. They were less interested in winning the war for the gallant Allies than in settling their own scores with the Fascists. But so long as they fought Germans that was all right by us at the time. They had had a hard winter doing just that.

Now the intention was to plan for the last stage of the war in Italy. ... The Nino Nannetti [partisan] group intended to occupy a set area and to mop up any demoralised Germans before 'liberating' the area from Fascist aggression. It needs little imagination to understand what that meant.

All that was needed was a signal from base and this came when it was clear that Kesselring was ready to negotiate. Our partisans did what they said they would do and more than 8,000 Germans surrendered to them in a moving ceremony in the main square of Montaner, a small village. The local band played 'Bandiera Rossa', the 'Red Flag' and more than a thousand vehicles were handed over and left in a vast column strung right along the main road, a real prize and legitimate booty for all that had been suffered.

Back in Vittorio Veneto it was an odd situation. Our war was over but the war in Europe was not yet. The New Zealanders were ordered to dash along the motorway and take Venice. They crossed the main A road to the north-west and saw a lot of chaps wearing the wrong uniform. These were the German 91st Light Infantry Division (Hermann Goering) also with orders to get the hell out of it all. What was there to do? Simple. Salute mutually and carry on. When the Kiwis got to Venice they found our 'Nino Nannetti' boys in full possession, so much so that when I got there myself I was met by our own gondola and escorted to our own Palazzo on the Grand Canal; the Volpi.

And what of VE Day itself? As I said before, 8 May was an irrelevance to us in Italy; we had already won OUR WAR. But VE Day did call for a celebration and we radioed our base asking for provender to fuel a Partisan Victory Banquet. They sent us a plane-load of corned beef.

To the partisans the war didn't end with VE Day. It was just the beginning of their war against the Fascists. When I left Italy it had been sunny; just as I crossed over the border it started to rain. I thought of Manchester, where I had been born and knew that the war really was over and that I was home.

PIERRE CLOSTERMANN DSO, DFC*

FRONT LINE

Pierre Clostermann, France's most highly decorated citizen, volunteered as a fighter pilot with the Free French Air Force in Britain. He was stationed in Fassberg, Germany in May 1945.

Soon ... came the armistice, like a door closing. Eight days of bewilderment – an indefinable mixture of gladness and regret. Noisy jollifications, followed by long periods of calm, and, especially, a thick unaccustomed silence, which hung heavy on the airfield, on the tarpaulin-covered planes, on the empty runways. The snapping of the nervous tension was dreadful, as painful as a surgical operation.

That evening in the mess was like some extraordinary vigil over a corpse. The pilots were slumped in their chairs – no one spoke a word, or sang, or anything. Round about eleven o'clock Bay switched on the wireless. The BBC were giving a running commentary on the scene in the streets of London and Paris, where the population was really letting itself go. All eyes turned towards the set, and in them you could read a kind of hatred.

It was so unmistakable, and yet so surprising, that I glanced enquiringly at Ken. I heard a crash of broken glass – someone had hurled a bottle at the set, at all the noise, at all those people shamelessly parading their sense of relief and deliverance before us.

One by one the pilots got up and eventually only Ken and I and the sleepy barman were left in the silent mess. From the smashed wireless still came a feeble whispering noise.

I again looked at Ken. No need of words, we both understood. Half an hour passed, an hour perhaps. And then, suddenly, I swear I felt they were all there, round us in the shadow and the cigarette smoke, like kids who have been unjustly punished.

Mackenzie ... Jimmy Kelly ... Mouse Manson ... young Kidd ... Bone ... Shepherd ... Brooker ... Gordon ... dark uniforms too, with tarnished gold stripes ... Mouchotte ... Mézilles ... Béraud ... Pierrot Degail – all those who had set off one fine morning in their Spitfires or their Tempests and who hadn't come back.

'Well, Pierre, that's that. They won't need us any more.'

Pierre Clostermann.

We went off to bed and I closed the door softly, so as not to awaken the barman, who had dropped off to sleep on his stool, and also so as not to disturb 'the others'.

It was 9 May and the war already felt distant. Pilots were starting to make plans for their return home. One of the ADCs [aides-de-camp] working for Broady, as we called him, told me discreetly that we'd not be going home as soon as we might think and that we should continue training flights – things were beginning to turn sour with the Russians.

We were in the middle of lunch when we heard the familiar, characteristic throbbing of the aircraft engines. We rushed outside to see an immaculate formation of five Messerschmitt 262s preparing to land after a long pause. The RAF regiment AA [anti-aircraft] officer came running.

'What shall I do? Open fire?'

'Don't be a fool, old chap, the war is over. We aren't going to start it again just for your pleasure.'

The 262s landed faultlessly, except for the last of them, the leader, recognisable from the two black chevrons painted on his fuselage. He slewed round intentionally at the end of the runway, collapsing his undercarriage in order not to deliver his aircraft intact.

I rushed towards him in my jeep. The pilot was on his feet, checking his hair in the rear-vision mirror. His hair was too long, his helmet was broken and he was wearing a white silk scarf, a fine black leather flying suit at the neck of which was a Knight of the Iron Cross ribbon, with oak leaves. It was one of the *Wehrmacht*'s highest decorations and he was doubtless an ace, but I could not recognise his rank from his epaulettes. I jumped out of the jeep and headed towards him and we suddenly, almost unconsciously, found ourselves shaking hands. He had undone his holster revolver and handed me the weapon. It was a rare, genuine pre-war Luger with a squared wooden butt. He took me by surprise, speaking to me in impeccable French.

'I suppose I should give you this.'

I asked him why he addressed me in French.

'I saw the word France on your shoulder and your helmet is not English. You are a lieutenant so why do you have different stripes on your battle-dress? We always used to speak French at home. We come from Cologne and live on the edge of the Rhine. We used to spend our holidays in France before the war.'

At this point, two flight commanders arrived in their jeep. 'Go and collect the others,' I told them, 'I don't know what we are going to do with them, but while we work it out, take them to the mess and let them have a drink and something to eat – the Officers' Mess of course.'

My *Oberstleutnant* told me he would like to wash. I took him to my room, gave him my razor and shaving cream and he took a shower, emerging with my towel wrapped round him. He was well-built but had scars all over his body. He explained that he had been shot down five times, wounded on four occasions and forced to bail out on three.

An hour had passed since the 262s had landed and we suddenly heard the faint noise of a powerful engine. It was a small German four-seater liaison, a Messerschmitt 108, which landed without ceremony. It was the *Oberstleutnant's* orderly bringing his luggage. These Germans really were incredible. He had arrived from the besieged city of Prague, with two nurses whom he did not want to leave in the hand of the Russians. He carried the luggage into my room with a clicking of heels and a faultless salute – not a Nazi one since fighter pilots in the *Luftwaffe* didn't do that – but a classic salute, hand raised to peak.

My Teutonic companion was still in his underwear as he unpacked his case, taking out a pair of polished shoes and an extraordinarily elegant white uniform jacket. In Germany, fighter pilots were the aristocrats of the armed forces. He rummaged around in his things and handed me his log book, decorated with a large gilded symbol of a pilot, eagle and swastika. I glanced at the final pages. It showed over a hundred victories. As I took him to the mess for a drink, as requested, I showed him a Tempest at close range. I chose mine so that he could see the black crosses on the fuselage. However, they appeared to make little impression. The plane, on the other hand, did. He thought it magnificent.

I drank a beer in the mess with the German, who sat in a chair looking extremely relaxed. I hung on the telephone, trying to reach HQ of the 2nd Canadian Army in charge of the sector. I was just about at the end of my tether when finally somebody answered. It was probably an orderly and I could hear the armistice celebrations going on in the background, with people singing and shouting. The Lance-Corporal at the end of the line, no doubt with his feet on the desk and a bottle of whisky in his hand, did not give a damn about what I was telling him.

'I have five prisoners. What should I do with them?'

He laughed and told me that they had five million prisoners of their own and I could go to hell. Then he hung up.

Given the circumstances, we invited the Germans to dine with our pilots and the beer flowed freely. Despite our lack of a common language we managed to communicate with each other using the classic universal gestures of fighter pilots recounting tales of combat. A large map of Germany was spread on the table to help. We pin-pointed where we had encountered each other and where we had engaged in combat. It was the private world of the fighter pilot in all its glory!

This went on for eight days, but we could not keep the Germans secret any longer. All it needed was for some idiot from a ground crew who hadn't spent a single hour in the air in combat, but who now wanted to make up for it by at first protesting and then denouncing us. Two of the Germans asked for civilian clothes so that they could make their way home, and the others left for the prisoner of war camp, loaded down with oranges, chocolate and cigarettes. Why not? They had fought well and had always treated our downed pilots well. The war was over, and we had all survived with honour. In our swimming shorts in the underground swimming pool – we were in one of those wonderful peacetime *Luftwaffe* messes – you couldn't have told us apart.

MARGUERITE DIDDEN

HOME FRONT

Marguerite Didden (née Rodmell), aged 24 with an English father and French mother, lived in Brighton.

We half expected it. Any day now, our troops would enter Berlin, and the five long years of war would be over.

I was living back in Brighton on the South coast, one hour's train journey from London, a supposedly 'safe' town which, nevertheless, saw much atrocious bombing. It was on a direct route back to continental air bases and the town was used by German bombers to jettison left-over bombs creating untold damage and tragedy. I remember especially one sunny, quiet afternoon when a German plane, returning home, dropped its last bomb on a cinema in Kemp Town, where a children's matinée was in progress. The death and destruction in that innocent audience was horrific.

I had already seen such horrors living through the worst raids on London where, from the beginning of the war, I worked for a large firm employed in the making of component parts for radio and radar which eventually played a part in winning the battle of the air. I lived in Camden Town, and, after a particularly violent raid which destroyed many buildings in that area, I was allowed to go back to Brighton where my parents lived, and where I was thankfully spared the horrors of the doodlebugs which started to come over shortly afterwards.

And now, like everyone else, I was anticipating the final victory! That day (a sunny day, I remember) the bells of the Catholic church in our road started to peal, and others echoed them all over town; and factory hooters started to join in, blaring forth with abandon. Mummy and I were in the house when we heard them, and we laughed, and cried, and held hands, and kissed. For we knew what it meant!

Yes, the war was really over, definitively over in Europe. And Brighton seemed to be suddenly alive with a cacophony of sounds, and bells, and music of all kinds. We rushed outside. One or two of our neighbours ran over and kissed us. We had a celebratory drink with them. We couldn't contain our joy. My sister, who had recently had a baby and was staying with us while her husband was away, came down the stairs and joined us, tears streaming down her face. Daddy phoned to say he would be home for the rest of the day, so that we could be together to share this moment.

And for my mother, in particular, this day meant she would soon be able to go back to France to see her family. They had all survived. My aunt Suze had been cited for her work in the resistance, and my grandmother, at 94, had survived – alive and well. After D-Day we had managed to get regular news from them. But now – impossible to phone! Most lines were engaged so we had to wait till late afternoon before we could get in touch with them. Of course I didn't go to work that day, I think few people did.

In some ways it was pandemonium! Our time seemed to be spent in popping into friends' houses for a victory drink, or walking about, shaking hands, kissing, and hugging everyone we knew! A friend of mine, who had a flat in London, came round to invite me up to town for a celebration dinner and a night-club outing with other friends.

So I spent the rest of the day getting my clothes ready, and alternately laughing and crying with the neighbours, and enjoying with them this day of deliverance. Late in the afternoon, my friend Gordon came to pick me up to take me to London. In his reserve occupation he had a petrol allowance which he felt justified in using on this very special day. I'd managed to wash and set my hair, and to sort out an evening dress, which I had made myself out of an old curtain when clothing coupons were at a premium. And with my little vanity case, and a pair of dancing shoe, which had seen better days but still looked smart, I was ready for the party. We picked up two other friends on the way, and arrived at Gordon's flat on time to have a bath and doll ourselves up.

Dressed to the 'nines' and looking elegant in spite of the clothing restrictions of the past few years, we sailed into the Mirabelle, where Gordon was well known, and given a table not far from the dance-floor. The place was packed! Everyone was chatting and happy! It suddenly seemed impossible that we had all gone through five years of suffering, of privations, of fear, and worry, five years when families had lost dear ones, lost their homes, lived in shelters, or in the underground stations unable to wash or have a bath. It seemed scarcely possible that all those horrors which war brings about, and were our daily lot, should be over, and that we should once more be able to live normally, to reconstruct our lives!

That evening we were carefree! We dined, we danced, we sang. Everyone let their hair down! And, later, a little the worse for drink, we finally arrived back at Gordon's flat.

Jill and I happily fell asleep on the twin beds in the spare room and slept like logs!

When, at last, we had breakfasted and tidied up, we did what virtually all the people living in London did that day. We went outside Buckingham Palace and cheered the King and Queen, and the royal family every time they came out on the balcony. What better way to celebrate that special occasion than to share it with the whole world!

VIOLETTE WASSEM

HOME FRONT

Violette Wassem lived in Paris throughout the German occupation of the city between 1940 and 1944.

[The Germans] went East in haste, protected by the dangerously unpredictable SS Stormtroopers such as the two that were on the quay at Boulogne and made us remain bolt upright against the wall of the factory under threat of death. There were seven of us hostages, with our handkerchiefs as white flags; we all waited approximately three hours until the arrival of the Leclerc Division of the French Army released us. Then we regained our shelter (an 80-centimetre wide tunnel) to pass there the night. At midnight, a worker from my father's waterworks arrived, triumphant, to tell us that Paris and Boulogne were freed and illuminated, that the war was finished!!!

Alas, the following days were not so good, the battle was still intense around us. Germans still occupied many factories and buildings and these were summarily shot by the Leclerc tanks, the streets strewn with corpses. Eventually life resumed its course.

On the 26th [August 1944], the Germans had their revenge; they resumed bombings and these continued night and day until the end of the war on 8 May 1945, happy day for some, disastrous for so many when the wave of denunciations and revenge took place. I have seen women shorn bald because they were too friendly with German soldiers. Even our animals paid a price! Cats, dogs that it was necessary to have destroyed because they were driven crazy by their fear of bombs and sirens.

Finally, the 'Boches' left. Americans have taken their place in the general enthusiasm, distributing from their trucks, throwing at us food, kitchen furniture, spoons, forks, etc... carrying workers to work in their trucks to the great joy of all, and especially of the feminine population, where the beautiful black or white GIs made havoc.

The liberating forces in Paris were received with great enthusiasm and dreadful puns by the local population. French cartoon, VE Day 1945.

DAVID LANGDON OBE

FRONT LINE

David Langdon, an officer in the RAF and regular cartoonist for the magazine Punch, *was stationed in Paris.*

"Jeen Fizz, M'sieur?"

By lucky coincidence I was posted as an RAF officer to Paris the day the war ended.

I was allotted a room in a hotel only recently evacuated by *Wehrmacht* officers in their hurried retreat from France. At the bar on my first evening I was greeted by a smiling barman who, like all other hotel staff, had carried on with their work throughout the German occupation.

'Jeen fizz, M'sieur?' he enquired, 'Comme d'habitude?'

I soon learned that was the favoured drink of the previous hotel occupiers. It was a beverage unfamiliar to me in my years in the RAF.

But what struck me was the lack of any difference in the attitude of the hotel staff between the two occupying forces.

I tried the gin fizz, but it didn't appeal to my taste and I declined the offer of another helping...

RENÉE CHABANNE

HOME FRONT

Renée Chabanne was a 31-year-old housewife in Paris on VE Day.

There were a lot of people in the streets that day, but strangely enough not so many of the older generation. The main feeling was of relief that the Germans had gone. No more of that incessant marching over the cobbled streets and that dreadful German military music the army bands played... not to the French taste, I can tell you.

However, I have to say that the young German soldiers were extremely polite when you came across them and it was not diffucult to bump into them because they were everywhere, enjoying the cafés and going to Notre Dame and the Louvre. Of course it would be entirely different if you bumped into them after the curfew... they shot people. You see there was no aerial bombing and life on the street was as usual, people going about their lives under difficult circumstances, trying to get hold of food which was very scarce – if you had relatives in the country you might be lucky to get some from them. And we had to make clothes from almost anything. What I wanted more than anything was a huge bifstek with all the trimmings.

What everybody wanted was to get back to normal – or as near as possible – but everything had changed. But when you opened the windows optimism was in the air... people were returning to Paris. It was ours again.

GENERAL CHARLES DE GAULE, 8 MAY 1945
BROADCAST TO THE FRENCH PEOPLE

The war has been won. This is victory. It is the victory of the United Nations and of France. ... Honour, eternal honour, to our armies and their leaders. Honour to our nation, which never faltered, even under terrible trials, nor gave in to them. Honour to the United Nations, which mingled their blood, their sorrows and their hopes with ours and who today are triumphant with us. Long live France!

DUFF COOPER

HOME FRONT

Alfred Duff Cooper, 1st Viscount Norwich, was the British Government's liaison to the Free French Forces in 1943 and was made Ambassador to France in 1944.

4 May – During dinner we heard that all Germans in north-west Germany, Holland and Denmark had surrendered. There now remains Norway and Czechoslovakia. This piecemeal way of ending the war robs it of dramatic effect and must put something of a damper on popular rejoicing.

Arthur Forbes [British Air Ministry representative to SHAEF – Supreme Headquarters Allied Expeditionary Force] came to see me this morning. He told me that the

'The war is over': front
page of French daily Les
Nouvelles du Matin.

most rabidly anti-French influence in London is that of Professor Lindemann
[Lord Cherwell]. He is against the French Air Mission being shown anything
of importance and anticipates being at war with France shortly. The most pro-
French of Ministers is Stafford Cripps. Max is less enthusiastic about Russia than
he used to be.

5 MAY – The event this morning was the arrival of telegrams from the Prime
Minister and a personal message from him to de Gaulle, offering to withdraw all
British troops from the Levant as soon as the French have completed a treaty with
the States [of Syria and Lebanon]. I took this to the General this afternoon and
found him in a much better mood than on the last occasion. Palewski, whom I saw
first, told me he is now desperately anxious to conclude a treaty with England
which he believes is the only thing that can prevent another war. He is obsessed
by the Russian menace – and that is one of the many reasons why he is so anxious
to retain a base in the Levant. He [de Gaulle] told me that Beynet
[High Commissioner, Levant] was returning to Syria in a few days and that he
would hand over one brigade of the Special Troops to the States. I asked him to
make some announcement to this effect as soon as possible. He smiled and said
'Je ferai cela pour vous, Monsieur Ambassadeur.' It was a friendly interview.

7 MAY – General Redman [Head of SHAEF Mission to the French High
Command] came to see me this morning and told me that the unconditional
surrender of Germany had been signed in the early hours of this morning at
Reims. [He] also said that news was not to be divulged, which I said was
nonsense. Having mismanaged the war for five years the authorities are already
beginning to mismanage the peace. The declaration of war was bungled on
2 September 1939 and the announcement of unconditional surrender is being
bungled now. However it is great news. Diana broke down when I told her.

8 MAY: PEACE DAY – Wonderful weather – very hot. After lunch we listened to
Winston declaring the end of the war. It was disappointing. Then the sirens
sounded the all clear and the church bells rang. It was a very moving moment.
My eyes were full of tears. We dined at Maxim's. We went upstairs after dinner
and it was very amusing to watch the vast happy crowds. They danced downstairs.

LES NOUVELLES DU MATIN

Directeur: JEAN MARIN

La victoire en chantant...

MARDI 8 MAI 1945 Prix : 1 fr. 50

EN EUROPE, DEPUIS CETTE NUIT A 23 h. 1 m.

LA GUERRE EST FINIE

La capitulation sans conditions de l'Allemagne sera annoncée officiellement à 15 heures

MERCI
par JEAN MARIN

C'est à lui que je pense d'abord en cette nuit d'une immense douceur où, enfin, la guerre agonise à son tour.

A lui à ce jeune Français de vingt ans qui, en juillet 1940, me racontait son histoire, tournant entre ses doigts le béret alpin des premiers volontaires de la France libre.

Les rumeurs d'armistice l'avaient surpris, avant l'arrivée des Allemands, dans un fort de la côte bretonne. Il avait pris son fusil et cinquante cartouches, était allé embrasser une dernière fois sa mère et s'était embarqué dans un bateau de pêche à destination de l'Angleterre, dernier espoir de la paix en France de détresse.

A Londres, dans cette grande ville inconnue de lui et des siens, la première ville avait été pour lui, bureau de recrutement des Forces françaises libres. Posant sur la table du sous-officier ses cartouches et son fusil, il avait déclaré simplement : « On me dit la guerre finie. La guerre finie. La guerre n'est pas finie. Je viens m'engager. »

Peut-être ce Français est-il aujourd'hui quelque part en Allemagne, occupant le territoire ennemi. Peut-être est-il mort au service de la France. Mais, vivant ou mort, il est le symbole de ces Français obstinément français, grâce auxquels aujourd'hui notre pays doit se voir l'Allemagne capituler aux conditions entre les mains d'un haut commandement interallié où figurent des chefs français.

La fin de la guerre. La capitulation sans conditions du Troisième Reich ! On ose à peine y croire. On hésite presque à réaliser dans sa plénitude de ces mots bouleversants. Et, pourtant, de ces nuits, des millions d'être humains ont brevé pendant des mois et des années leur humiliation, leur douleur, leur immortelle espérance.

Certes, tant de morts, tant de souffrances, tant de tortures, tant de monstrueux charniers ne sont pas abolis par l'annonce de la victoire, par le retour de la paix en Europe.

Mais la victoire et le retour de la paix viennent justifier souverainement, consacrer comme par un sacrement ces morts et ces sacrifices.

Pauvres et chers yeux clairs des soldats tués, sanglants visages des victimes de la plus effroyable barbarie, reste sacrés de ceux qui ont voulu mourir pour que le puisse survécut, nous sommes devant vous, en ce seul inéluctable du docteur et de la fierté mêlées, soulevés par une admiration, une reconnaissance, un amour et nous mettons ains réserve la justice le meilleur de nous-mêmes. Parce que c'est à vous que l'heure, l'Allemagne dissout : la nation capitule et son gouvernement s'incline profondément devant les morts de cette guerre. Ils s'inclineront, en effet, aussi longuement qu'il sera nécessaire pour que leurs crimes historiques ne se répètent plus jamais.

(Suite en deuxième page)

LONDRES, 7 mai. — La B. B. C. annonce que le ministre allemand des Affaires étrangères, von Krosigk, a déclaré à la radio de Flensburg, aujourd'hui à 14 h. 30, que le haut commandement allemand avait accepté ce jour la reddition inconditionnelle.

La capitulation prend effet dans la nuit du 7 au 8 mai, à 23 heures 1 minute

A REIMS, DANS UNE PETITE ÉCOLE

REIMS, 7 mai. — On annonce officiellement que les Allemands se sont rendus sans conditions.

La reddition a été signée cette nuit, à 2 h. 41, dans une petite école en briques située dans le quartier général d'Eisenhower. Le colonel général Gustav Jodl, chef d'état-major général de l'Armée allemande, a signé la capitulation au nom de l'Allemagne.

Le général Bedell Smith, chef d'état-major du général Eisenhower, a reçu la reddition pour le commandement suprême allié, le général Ivan Susloparoff pour l'U.R.S.S., et le général de division François Sevez pour la France.

Le général Eisenhower n'a pas assisté à la cérémonie de la signature de la reddition inconditionnelle de l'Allemagne, mais il est arrivé peu après et s'est entretenu avec l'amiral allemand Von Freidenberg.

L'APPEL DE VON KROSIGK AUX ALLEMANDS

LONDRES, 7 Mai. — La radio allemande de Flensburg a déclaré :

« Ici, la radio allemande. Nous allons diffuser un appel du comte Schwerin von Krosigk au peuple allemand. Voici cet appel : »

« Allemands et Allemandes. « Le haut commandement des forces armées a proclamé aujourd'hui, sur l'ordre du grand amiral Doenitz, la reddition sans condition de toutes les forces combattantes allemandes. »

« C'est en tant que ministre du gouvernement du Reich désigné par l'amiral de la flotte pour traiter des problèmes de la guerre, en ce tragique moment de notre histoire, que je me tourne vers la nation allemande. Après une lutte héroïque qui a duré près de six ans, l'Allemagne a succombé devant la puissance écrasante de ses adversaires. »

« La poursuite de la guerre ne serait qu'un gaspillage inutile... »

« Le gouvernement, qui a le sens de ses responsabilités quant à l'avenir de la nation, a été forcé, à la suite de l'effondrement de toutes les forces physiques et matérielles de l'Allemagne, de demander à l'ennemi la cessation des hostilités. »

« La plus noble tâche de l'amiral de la flotte et de son gouvernement est d'épargner le plus grand nombre possible de vies allemandes dans cette dernière phase de la guerre. Que la cessation de la guerre n'ait pas été immédiate et simultanée à l'Ouest et à l'Est s'explique par cette unique raison.

« A cette heure grave, la nation allemande et son gouvernement s'inclinent profondément devant les morts de cette guerre. Leurs sacrifices nous imposent de très grandes obligations. Notre sympathie va, avant tout, aux blessés, aux orphelins et à tous ceux que cette guerre a meurtris.

« Nous devons accepter ce fardeau et remplir loyalement les obligations que nous ayons acceptées, mais nous ne devons pas être réduits au désespoir et tomber dans une prostration muette.

(Suite en deuxième page)

EN PAGE 2 :
● UN MESSAGE AUTOGRAPHE DU GÉNÉRAL KŒNIG
● L'ÉMOTION DANS PARIS
  par PIERRE SCIZE

Victory in Europe celebrations on the Champs Elysées, Paris.

ROLF WEINBERG

ARMED FORCES

Rolf Weinberg, a German Jew, escaped to Uruguay in 1938. He worked in British Intelligence in Uruguay and served with the Free French Forces.

We were NCOs lodging in the hotel La Opera. That day the order came that at three in the afternoon, de Gaulle would speak to us. To an enormous multitude of people he said, 'Friends, Hitler is dead, the war in Europe is won and is ended. France is free again!' It was such a moment, I fainted from emotion. They brought me up to my hotel room and a nurse from the Forces was holding my head. She said, 'I think you should enjoy yourself with the others, come down, let's have some champagne, don't lie here.' I said, 'You are right on one side but not for me, it's not the way to have a fiesta. Because I think of all my comrades and all of those who have been killed by this damned Nazi regime. The only thing I can tell you, I am so glad that I had the possibility to help to wipe the Nazi regime out.'

A few days later I went to Berlin. My contract with the Free French Forces was for the duration of the war plus another six months. After three months in Berlin I was called back to Paris. I was called to the President of France who was

Charles de Gaulle at that moment and he said, 'I've got here a telegram from the President of Uruguay, your mother wants you home. So I'll send you on Friday to Bologne and you will go on an official mission in uniform back to Uruguay. Because I want the French people to thank you by paying for the voyage back to your family.' That was very kind of him, and I went back to Uruguay where I was received in a way you can't imagine, all my friends and a big reception. I was received by the President. I was still in uniform. He congratulated me and I was demobilised in the French Embassy.

MARY PETTIT

FRONT LINE

Mary Pettit, a corporal in the Women's Auxiliary Air Force, was posted to Brussels — by then a leave centre for Allied troops from the front — as part of the Air Publications Distribution Unit.

We had settled in Brussels and May 1945 dawned. Something would soon happen — it would be VE Week! By 7 May there had been speculation for some days that the war would end soon. We all went across from the office to Curly's friends to listen to the wireless as it was rumoured that Churchill was going to speak. But no luck, only a programme about snails, so we went back to the barracks. About 7 pm, one of the girls dashed in saying there had been a news flash and that the war was over. Suddenly we all felt very homesick. When peace was signed, we had been told, we would get three days off. We got ourselves ready and went down to Wesley House for a couple of hours for a cup of tea and a natter. Most people were finding it hard to come to terms with their feelings. Predominant amongst them all was this intense homesickness; most of the British people felt that way. It was certainly the case with the girls. We went back to the barracks intending to get ready for bed. I couldn't settle and sat on the windowsill for a long time looking out over Brussels. What a sight! The whole city was lit up by searchlights, rockets, flares, Very lights everywhere. British, Belgian and American flags were flying; crowds were in the streets singing and laughing; car horns were sounding. As the evening sky darkened, the famous buildings were silhouetted against the glow from bonfires and fireworks. The old trams were clanking along as usual, but now with people standing or dancing on their roofs. The trams never seemed to run in a straight line as they swayed and rattled, reflecting the years of few repairs.

As they crossed the points at junctions they threw a weird green light across everything. It was a sight I will never ever forget. I did finally tear myself away and fell into bed, the noise below still ringing in my ears, and me quite unable to realise that in one part of the world the war was over.

Next morning, 8 May, I was up by 7.30 am, had breakfast and got ready for church. The service, a Thanksgiving for victory, started at 9.30 am with the British National Anthem, followed by the American and the Belgian – a very touching ceremony. The service was conducted by Padre Mainiel with the congregation of British, American, Belgian and many other nationalities. I sat next to a middle-aged Belgian lady. As we got up to leave, she asked me if I was doing anything, particularly during that day. I replied, 'No, I wasn't'. She asked me if I would care to come for lunch. I said that was very kind of her and I would be delighted to come. She stayed for a further service in French, and I met her outside the church at 11.20 am. She said that if we hurried we could catch her husband before he left and could then go by car, otherwise we would have to catch the tram. I have to say that my mind wandered a little, here we were in 1945, five years from the start of the war there and petrol was hardly an easily-acquired asset. As suggested, we hurried. To my amazement there appeared a very large car complete with chauffeur. We sat in the car for a minute or two before we were joined by her husband to whom I was formally introduced. This was Monsieur Tournier. They were exceptionally nice people and, on the way, they gave me a bit of a guided tour.

After about 15 minutes on the road, we turned sharp right, through a pair of large gates and up a long, winding drive, very well kept. There was not a weed in sight. The Tourniers' house was quite large and very tastefully and comfortably furnished. As you entered, the dining room was to the left; the drawing room to the right; while in the centre was a large room with French windows opening on to a terrace. The view from there was beautiful. Madame Tournier took me round the grounds and through the sunken garden with flowers of all sorts and colours. One particular thing that interested me was what looked like an old tombstone. Madame told me it was a 16th-century tombstone that had been brought from one of their farms. We had a look at the kitchen garden, too. There were beautiful lilies of the valley. The paths were so well tended it seemed a crime to walk on them. The remainder of the grounds were wooded with a little river running through. To wander through those grounds was indeed a haven of peace. They gave me the *Illustrated London News* and the *Picture Post* to read and, just sitting there on the terrace, one couldn't help feeling at peace with the world. It was a 'new' feeling after five years of being 'not at peace'.

WW2 People's War

IAN CARMICHAEL

Ian Carmichael, an officer in the 22nd Dragoons, had been seconded to HQ of 30th Armoured Brigade as a liaison and staff officer. He was stationed in a tented camp in a public park in a small town called Deventer in Holland with his friend John Moore.

It is difficult to describe to anyone who has not lived through six years of total war the immediate feelings of euphoria that burst when the news arrived that the final whistle had been blown; a tight cork exploding from a warm bottle of champagne would produce nothing in comparison with such effervescence. For six long years the people of Europe had never seen a light of any sort or description in the streets after dusk unless it had been either a blue one, the slim pencil-light of a masked down torch carried by a pedestrian, or the narrow – extremely narrow – letterbox slits to which the lights on all vehicles had been reduced. The fact that the maiming and killing had stopped; the fact that one had come through unscathed; the fact that that night every light in the town could be put on and the curtains left wide open, were all causes for unconfirmed ecstasy. Deventer now went mad. Lights were switched on everywhere and street after street was mobbed with Dutchmen of all ages carrying bright orange lanterns illuminated by candles. It was a warm May night and windows and doors were thrown wide open. Music blared from radios placed on window sills and dancing in the streets was wild and abandoned. On one normally busy crossroads the traffic had stopped completely. The area had been floodlit with unmasked headlights and dancing was in full swing to music pouring out of a large amplifier that had been rigged up on the side of one of the houses. Then the processions started and every house was 'open house'.

Sometime in the early hours of the morning, in a family home that John Moore and I visited quite often, the lady of the house tucked us both up on a camp-bed and a sofa (we were far gone) with tears pouring down her cheeks. Earlier that evening I had had no ears for a maudlin and, at the time I thought, cynical local journalist who told me to enjoy it all while I could because, mark his words, 'In fewer years that you can imagine, you will have to go through the whole thing again with Russia. They are the real menace, Ian, believe me.' But after the euphoria there was time for reflection. Despite the suicidal nature of their task, the casualties in my regiment over a year of hard fighting had been astonishingly light. Six officers and 26 other ranks killed, and 13 and 108, respectively, wounded.

But included in those figures were many of my friends.

Neither John nor I had had a single day off duty since we had each returned off leave in early March. Life had been hectic at HQ 30th Armoured Brigade during the intervening two months and we were all dog-tired. It was therefore with some relief, and even incredulity, that an apparently grateful brigade major came up to both of us later that day, Sunday, and said he thought we had earned a rest and that we were to take a staff car the following morning, go to Brussels, and that he didn't want to see either of us again until the staff conference on Friday morning.

The next morning neither of us moved out of his bed-roll until eleven o'clock. VE Day, we then discovered, had been officially announced for 8th May – the following day – and the thought of spending it in Brussels made us purr over an extremely leisurely late breakfast. Astonishingly, it is the mundane pleasures that linger. As on our brief trip to Rouen back in the previous September, the biggest and initial thrill was to be able to put on a clean service-dress once again and step out with creased trousers, brass buttons newly polished, a Sam Browne belt and, in my case, the 22nd Dragoons' gold piped, black and cream forage cap. The mildew had been duly shaken out of all of them by Musgrave, the Lothian and Border Yeomanry batman who had looked after me so solicitously throughout the whole campaign, and our battledresses were left, almost literally, standing up in a corner of our tent. Shortly after midday we stepped into a staff car (a great privilege for the likes of us) and set off for the, by now, bright lights of Belgium.

On our arrival in Brussels we checked into our hotel in the Boulevard Adolphe Max and went up to our room. As we entered it, the first comfortable room in a smart hotel that we had experienced for what seemed like eons, we both stood for a moment in silence. It was John who spoke first.

'This rings a bell,' he said.

For 'starters' we decided to soak for about an hour in a hot bath. In the early evening, refreshed and ready for the fray, we went out on the town and the whole thing started again. Two days previously we had witnessed and shared the elation of a small town with its street parties and orange lanterns; now we were in a big capital city with the lights of shop windows, neons, floodlit squares and even fireworks being sent heavenwards off the top of its trams. The streets were packed. Everybody loved everybody and rockets and thunderflashes were being ignited on every street corner.

After visits to innumerable bars, we wandered into Maxim's to watch the cabaret. There we joined the company of two half-cut but friendly GIs with their ATS escorts and after several bottles of champagne we emerged an hour or so later feeling in pretty much the same condition ourselves. Nevertheless, no time for bed yet we decided to sample a few more cafés, in one of which we got tangled up with two young Belgian married couples who shared a flat and who insisted that we went back to it for further celebratory glasses. Somewhere about 1 am, unable to keep up with John's fluent French, I passed out on the sofa. He, several cups of coffee and one bottle of cognac later, ultimately woke me at 7 am. We then embraced our hosts and, swearing eternal friendship and intentions of meeting for a yearly anniversary from then until the end of time (which, needless to say, we have never done), staggered back to our hotel where we fell asleep and slept until lunchtime.

STEPHEN DALE

PRISONER OF WAR

Stephen Dale, a German Jew, was imprisoned in the Sachsenhauer camp before fleeing to Britain in 1939. He served with the Pioneer Corps in Britain in 1942 and with SOE in Italy in 1944 before being taken prisoner and held in Coroneo, Stalag 17 and Oflag camps.

We were liberated by an American tank unit and allowed out of the camp immediately. I had no desire to go, though after a day or so I did go out. By that time we had much more to eat though we were immediately warned not to eat too much, because it would be bad for us. Diarrhoea was prevalent so the German guards were put to digging latrines for us as the normal lavatory facilities in the camp were not adequate. I don't think they minded for they were concerned with survival. They didn't know what they were facing. At the moment of liberation this millstone came off my neck. I knew that I was no longer in danger of being found out (as being a German Jew) and dealt with. That feeling lasted only for the moment I was liberated, for the next thing I was thinking was 'What happened to my family?' That suddenly and sharply came into focus. The war was still on when I was liberated but my personal and immediate war was over and consequently my thoughts turned to them.

...We were flown back to Kiddlington – and I remember when we arrived, I didn't kiss the ground like the Pope did, but I patted it with great affection. I'd come home – rather, England had become home after I got married. I always had a great affection for England. I contacted my sister when I got back and that was the moment she knew I was alive. My next question was what happened to the family. But by then we were both of the opinion that the chances of them being alive were slim. In due course we had confirmation from the Red Cross that none of them had survived.

The great day for me was the day I was liberated: VE day was not a jubilant date. My friend T. Turner had to go up to Glasgow and he suggested I go up there with him. We caught the train back by the skin of our teeth on the night of the 7th or 8th and somehow he managed to get us a sleeper going back to London. We arrived back in London and during the day it was announced that everything had been signed. There was not entirely spontaneous jubilation because people were prepared, but around Piccadilly and Leicester Square there were millions, it seemed, milling around and being exuberant and climbing on lamp posts and on bus shelters. People were very friendly, embracing each other and I was scolded on several occasions for walking around with a miserable long face. It was perfectly true. Naturally I was very happy that the war was over but it was also a moment of reflection. It was great that the killing in Europe had come to an end but for me it was really a depressing moment because I suddenly felt all the awful things that had happened to my family and to me come back to the surface. So, though they were perfectly justified, I couldn't join in these celebrations.

CLIFFORD BAILEY

PRISONER OF WAR

Clifford Bailey, an NCO with the Rifle Brigade, was captured by the Japanese in Singapore in 1942 and worked on the Thai–Burma Railway. He remained a prisoner in Japan until 1945.

The only definite news you'd get would be rather mixed up with a lot of rumours. All sorts of rumours used to come around. One rumour was that the *Queen Mary* had got sunk. Then that got rather garbled and became that Queen Mary had died, the old queen. And another rumour that went round, that the Eiffel Tower had been dismantled by the Germans and taken back to Germany for scrap and all sorts of things like that. But in between you'd get a snippet of something which could be the truth but disguised by all these other wild rumours.

The Japanese gave nothing away. But if things were going particularly bad for them you knew it by their attitude; they did take it out on us. One particular day in May we came back from the iron foundry and instead of being dismissed on the parade ground to go and get a wash and have our food we were kept on the parade and told that we must march round and round the yard and we must sing. We did that for about two hours. Didn't matter what you sang but you had to sing.

And if you didn't, if you faltered a bit or you weren't singing you had guards around with bamboo canes or pick handles and they would rap you across the legs. It wasn't 'till long after that we realised that that was the day Germany had surrendered and the Japs knew they were on their own.

HUGH JOHNSON

HOME FRONT

Hugh Johnson, later the famous wine writer, was a six-year-old child living in Amersham, Buckinghamshire, when VE Day was announced.

We were in the dining room at breakfast when my father came in and said, 'We've won. The war's over.' I'm sure we all hugged each other, my brother and sisters and I, the youngest, only six, but I just remember him, thin, grey and smiling, and the view through the French windows of the garden hemmed in with trees.

There were Americans everywhere in Amersham, I remember. We kids used to follow their marching columns shouting 'Got any gum, chum?' I don't suppose we even knew it was they who filled the sky with black bombers, almost touching wings as they roared overhead with a thunder I can still hear.

PHIL LOFFMAN

PRISONER OF WAR

Phil Loffman, an Australian NCO, served with the 2/28th Battalion Australian Imperial Forces in North Africa and was a prisoner of war in Italy and Germany 1942–45. In April he escaped and joined the Soviet forces before being flown to London.

The biggest surprise I got was when I got to England. I was expecting to see this bomb-damaged city, after the Battle of Britain and God knows what else and after we had just seen all this terrible stuff. But when I got to London you wouldn't have known there had been a war on. There were thousands of soldiers there.

London surprised me. When I'd left Australia girls weren't drinking in the public bar or anything like that. When I got to Eastbourne you had to push your way through, 'Excuse me girls, excuse me girls, I'm looking for a drink!' The place was full of women! We used the RAF's hospitality, and I was selling these Lugers I was getting – five pounds each for them, and that was a lot of money in those days – I had eight, and I sold them all.

I had a great old time in England. Wherever we went we dressed up. On one occasion it was a bloody stupid thing to do. I had this bush ranger corded hat on in one of the bars around Piccadilly and some sailor said 'Come on cowboy, reach for your gun.' I said 'Alright', and pulled this bloody Luger out in the pub. It wasn't loaded but I put it away and said 'Come on Stan, we're leaving.' He nearly fainted. The Yanks were overpowering. London was swamped with Americans.

Indeed, an amusing war
— FOR THE AMERICANS

Indeed, an amusing war
— FOR THE AMERICANS

German propaganda. The large presence of US servicemen in Great Britain is here exploited by the Germans in an attempt to damage the Allies' camaraderie.

I had been in Europe on VE Day, but it wasn't much of a celebration where I was. In the desperation and the gloom and the sadness of Europe, there was no VE Day. We were with the Russians and there was nothing celebrated. The war was over and there were still dead people and people being shot. I think Prague lasted another week or ten days before they shut down. We weren't far from there and the silly buggers were still fighting. When I was with the Russians, there were two big Tigers [tanks], apparently out of fuel. They put them back to back. There were two bloody Germans inside and someone said they had their families with them and they stood there and fired their last shot. They'd got all the Russian anti-tanking guns around them and blew themselves to pieces. If they were going to die, they were going to die in their tanks. Someone told me later that the Sergeant Major of the camp I left committed suicide. He shot himself with his own gun. VE Day wasn't a great thing in that part of the world, they'd lost and they knew. I wasn't there but they told me at the camp that the Sergeant Major got full of schnapps and shot himself at the front gate. Well, he may as well. The Russians took the camp over. Nobody wanted to fall under the Russians, nobody.

When I got home everybody was just glad it was all over. 'For Christ's sake, let's sort ourselves out and get back to work.'

JAMES EVANS

FRONT LINE

James Evans was a British officer who served with the 1/4th Battalion Gurkha Rifles in India and Burma, 1942–44. On VE Day he was in Kahat, India.

On VE Day, we were in a place called Kahat, back in India. We had had to forget all of our jungle training and devote ourselves to frontier work. When we moved furtively and close together the frontier people would tell us off, saying, 'God, these men, they're moving in groups, you can't do that on the frontier, you have to be well spaced out!' So we were learning all that on the edge of the NW Frontier Province when the news came through as we were having tea around the mess. We had a rather wild officer who ran off and got a revolver and fired shots into the air, which we thought was a bit un-British. He hadn't been to Burma.

Our men had lots of medals. Even Rifleman Mike Gurong, who we'd made a mess orderly, had a military medal. He heard us shouting and said, 'What's going on?' The mess food member said, 'Buddy, we've won the war. We've beaten the Germans.' He said, 'God, we were fighting them too?' He was a bit thick.

CECIL HOLNESS

ARMED FORCES

Cecil Holness was born in 1922 in Deeside, Jamaica. Like many other West Indian service-men, he was recruited into the Royal Air Force in 1944 and was in London on VE Day.

I was on leave then. I came out, to stay all night, watch the procession. We met a couple of girls – they were from Wales, you know – a chap and myself. And we entertained them, they stuck to us all through the time, because, like, to know you have a little companion until then – you know, they stuck to us. Oh that was great, man, oh we saw everything, saw everything.

We were so proud to have our flashes on. We were in the Second World War – that was great, man. But one thing – after all that now – one thing we didn't like was people asking us, 'When, now the war is over, when are you going back to your own country?' That's one thing I didn't like much. I said, God Almighty, England won the war and then goes to the people 'Alright! You came out to help us, you served your mother country well, when are you going back to your own country?' To me it didn't show much of an appreciation, none at all.

I remember we used to hitchhike into London. I was hitchhiking all the way from Tidnam – that's in Norfolk – and a bloke came along in a Bentley with his wife. He say 'Hey man, where you going?' I say, 'London, Sir'. He say, 'Jump in' and so I jump in and he congratulated me that we have risked our young lives to come and help England and we chatted all the way, man. So when, near the first underground station, I say 'Look, Sir, if you don't mind you could drop me to the nearest underground station in London.' So him say, 'Tell me directly where you are staying.' I say, 'Well, I'm staying at Arundel Street,' you know, 'cause they had a YMCA there. The man took me right to the door. I said, 'Thank you very, very much, sir.' Right to the door. He said, 'Good luck when you get back into civilian life.' Just like that. But most people after they talk – how we done very well – the question would follow, 'When are you going back to your own country?'

FATHER HILARY

HOME FRONT

Father Hilary of Mount St Bernard's Abbey, a Cistercian Monastery in Leicester, was a Bevin Boy during the war – one of many young men conscripted to support the war effort by working in Britain's coal mines.

I was a Bevin Boy aged 18 working down the mines for the war effort. I remember that on the day the war ended my parents and myself went to the pub and I stood on a bar stool and sang (I must have been drunk):

> *Mares eat oats*
> *And does eat oats*
> *And little lambs eat ivy*
> *Kids'll eat ivy too*
> *Wouldn't you?*

'Twas a big hit at the time, everybody sang it.
Next day it was back down the pit as usual.

JOHN DAVIES

John Davies was a child in Harrow and witnessed the local Victory celebrations.

I can remember the Italian POWs joining in the Victory celebrations and much calculation going on as local ladies by now had dark-haired, flashing-eyed two-year-olds – husbands that had been overseas for three years got over the shock or were hopefully less than knowledgeable.

My aunt Ethel (died three years ago) purportedly had some hideous experience in an air-raid shelter during a VE Day celebration in Plymouth. No one of my age group in our family ever found out what the experience was as it was only mentioned in hushed tones, but my father said whatever it was it should occur to her weekly as it was the only time he saw her happy.

Mr Gee next door to us in Harrow was on HMS *Swiftsure* in various oceans. At the end of hostilities us kids were hoping for tales of derring-do but apparently the *Swiftsure* just sailed through it all blithely, hardly noticing a war.

Charlie Gregory was another story, however. He was on HMS *Warspite* when she was hit by a glider bomb in the Med which struck her starboard AA sponsons and carried on into the armoured base of the bridge structure, tearing a hole almost to the water line. She was made watertight with concrete and sent to Bremerton Navy yard in the US for repairs. Mrs Gregory (cannot remember her name but she smoked a lot) accused Charlie (at the end of the war, as she did not think it patriotic to mention it sooner) of numerous amorous adventures in the US while she put up with bombs at home. Her spleen was vented on him at the VJ Day party by pouring something over him which may have been semolina pudding – but not sure.

On the first day of peace my father was instructed to kill one of the rabbits for a celebration dinner. Previously he had given them to Mr Jinks the butcher to do, but celebrations the previous night had rendered Mr Jinks perilous with a meat cleaver so father got the job. My mother, sister and I went to the park while the deed was done and returned to find him feeding it bread and milk so we had chips and, I think, scallops, which were then very cheap.

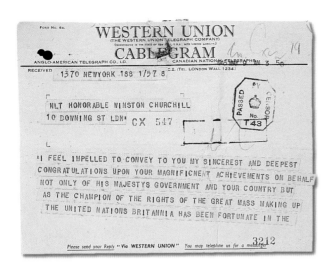

WESTERN UNION
CABLEGRAM
ANGLO-AMERICAN TELEGRAPH CO. L.D. CANADIAN NATIONAL TELEGRAPHS.
RECEIVED 1370 NEWYORK 188 1/57 8

NLT HONORABLE WINSTON CHURCHILL
10 DOWNING ST LDN= CX 547

=I FEEL IMPELLED TO CONVEY TO YOU MY SINCEREST AND DEEPEST
CONGRATULATIONS UPON YOUR MAGNIFICENT ACHIEVEMENTS ON BEHALF
NOT ONLY OF HIS MAJESTYS GOVERNMENT AND YOUR COUNTRY BUT
AS THE CHAMPION OF THE RIGHTS OF THE GREAT MASS MAKING UP
THE UNITED NATIONS BRITANNIA HAS BEEN FORTUNATE IN THE

3212

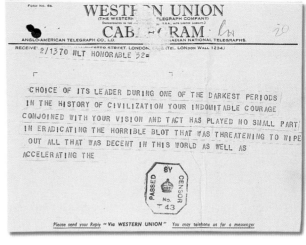

WESTERN UNION
CABLEGRAM
ANGLO-AMERICAN TELEGRAPH CO. L.D. CANADIAN NATIONAL TELEGRAPHS.
RECEIVED 2/1370 NLT HONORABLE 52=

CHOICE OF ITS LEADER DURING ONE OF THE DARKEST PERIODS
IN THE HISTORY OF CIVILIZATION YOUR INDOMITABLE COURAGE
CONJOINED WITH YOUR VISION AND TACT HAS PLAYED NO SMALL PART
IN ERADICATING THE HORRIBLE BLOT THAT WAS THREATENING TO WIPE
OUT ALL THAT WAS DECENT IN THIS WORLD AS WELL AS
ACCELERATING THE

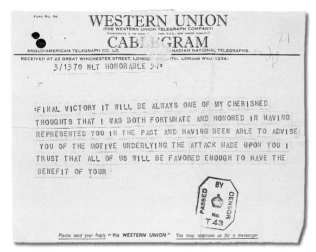

WESTERN UNION
CABLEGRAM
ANGLO-AMERICAN TELEGRAPH CO. L.D. CANADIAN NATIONAL TELEGRAPHS.
RECEIVED AT 22 GREAT WINCHESTER STREET, LONDON. (TEL. LONDON WALL 1234.)
3/1370 NLT HONORABLE 57=

=FINAL VICTORY IT WILL BE ALWAYS ONE OF MY CHERISHED
THOUGHTS THAT I WAS BOTH FORTUNATE AND HONORED IN HAVING
REPRESENTED YOU IN THE PAST AND HAVING BEEN ABLE TO ADVISE
YOU OF THE MOTIVE UNDERLYING THE ATTACK MADE UPON YOU I
TRUST THAT ALL OF US WILL BE FAVORED ENOUGH TO HAVE THE
BENEFIT OF YOUR

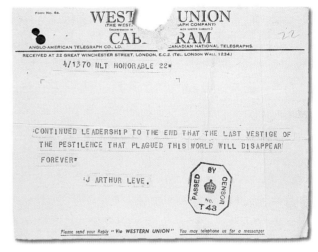

WESTERN UNION
CABLEGRAM
ANGLO-AMERICAN TELEGRAPH CO. L.D. CANADIAN NATIONAL TELEGRAPHS.
RECEIVED AT 22 GREAT WINCHESTER STREET, LONDON, E.C.2. (TEL. LONDON WALL 1234.)
4/1370 NLT HONORABLE 22=

=CONTINUED LEADERSHIP TO THE END THAT THE LAST VESTIGE OF
THE PESTILENCE THAT PLAGUED THIS WORLD WILL DISAPPEAR
FOREVER=

J ARTHUR LEVE.

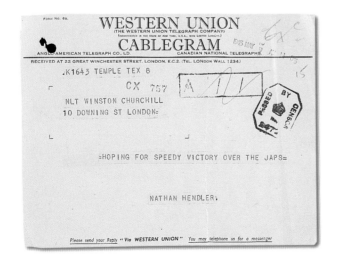

WESTERN UNION
CABLEGRAM
ANGLO-AMERICAN TELEGRAPH CO. L.D. CANADIAN NATIONAL TELEGRAPHS.
RECEIVED AT 22 GREAT WINCHESTER STREET, LONDON. E.C.2. (TEL. LONDON WALL 1234.)
K1643 TEMPLE TEX 8
CX 757

NLT WINSTON CHURCHILL
10 DOWNING ST LONDON=

=HOPING FOR SPEEDY VICTORY OVER THE JAPS=

NATHAN HENDLER.

CABLE & WIRELESS
LIMITED
"Via Imperial"

CW GBS460 ROME 33 USGOVT 5 1753 =

THE RIGHT HONORABLE WINSTON CHURCHILL PRIME
MINISTER LONDON =
I CANNOT REFRAIN FROM SENDING YOU MY
HEARTIEST FELICITATIONS ON YOUR VITAL
CONTRIBUTION TO THE GLORIOUS VICTORY OF THE
ALLIES STOP CORDIAL GREETINGS =
MYRON TAYLOR

*From the Great British
public: well-wishers' messages
to Churchill on VE Day.*

Congratulations

Sincere Congratulations
and
Best Wishes
on this
special occasion

Hon Winston Churchill
From Edith Clements

JEAN BARTLE

Jean Bartle was a schoolgirl in Brigg, north Lincolnshire, when the war ended.

We heard a lot of bombing around the area; there was a lot in Hull and in Grimsby. Mum wasn't so bad when the siren went off but as soon as the all clear went she used to faint. Our neighbour used to say, 'Oh for goodness sake, get the Johnny Jump Up out.' I used to wonder what the Johnny Jump Up was, but apparently it was some sort of wine that they used to get from gentlemen's clubs. It was supposed to be a tonic.

When it came to VE Day I was downstairs at the Manor House Convent in Brigg. The Sister came in and told us it had come over the radio that the war was over in Europe. We all laughed and cheered. They had big sash windows in the convent and they were swung up; it was a glorious day the sun was shining, beautiful. We were hanging out the windows and everybody was going down the streets on bicycles and the cars were sounding their horns. We were allowed to go home early because they thought, there's no good trying to keep them here because they're not going to do any work. After I'd had some tea I met up with all my pals and went on a tour of Brigg and then we went down in to the marketplace and all the lights came on. We thought that this was fantastic because we'd had no streetlights at all, no lights in the shops, nothing, everything had been blacked out. A lady I knew – Mrs Broom – her husband had got back that very day and he was a sailor. I can see them now dancing; she had his sailor's hat on. She had lovely ginger curls and his sailor hat stuck on the top.

ROGER FREEMAN

Roger Freeman, 16 years old, lived in Dedham, Essex.

While not going so far as to say they enjoyed the war, there are many septuagenarians who cherish nostalgia for that youthful period of their lives. Generally, children proved quite resilient to the fears and horrors of warfare. Terrified when the bombs dropped yet unaffectedly searching for bomb fragments while bodies were retrieved from destroyed buildings next morning. When an aircraft crashed, the predominant thought was what item could be liberated as a souvenir rather than the fate of the aircrew. It was as if children, at least those young teenagers, had come to accept the casualties of war far more readily than adults. My own collection of souvenirs included among prized items the wing tip of a doodlebug, the intact fins (complete with embossed Nazi symbol) of a bomb, and a cockpit instrument from an American fighter; the lot long since given away. Most were gathered within a mile or two from my home, during six years of war the village having been the recipient of some 30 high explosive bombs, many incendiaries, two aerial mines, one flying bomb and three aircraft crashes. All this resulted in two civilian and one airman deaths. There was nothing in the village that would qualify as a serious military objective and the *Luftwaffe*'s effort was somewhat wasted. Many other local villages have a similar story.

Roger Freeman aged 15, on the right, with friend: local boys up to mischief in wartime Essex.

Juvenile interest was not limited to harmless souvenirs. Indeed the acquisition of some piece of military ordnance had an unhealthy fascination for many. The 14-year-old who sat next to me in school somehow managed to appropriate a Mills hand grenade from the Home Guard. He would regularly brandish the lethal object around with threats to pull the safety pin unless he was given access to exam answers he did not know. The grenade could have killed several and maimed half the class. Like me the rest of his classmates were relieved to hear, true or not, that our tormentor had finally used the grenade to wreck a privy on a Clacton allotment. Getting hold of dangerous objects was not difficult, particularly as the military were often lax. The army carried out mortar bomb training in a nearby disused sandpit, the mortar bombs often failing to explode. Those that the soldiers couldn't find the village boys did. Fortunately, none of these retrieved missiles ever exploded when hurled at objects. Very fortunately!

Rounds of ammunition were quite easily obtained. A number of army .303 rifle rounds placed in the main school stove caused a series of violent detonations without, remarkably, the stove disintegrating. The wrath of the headmaster upon the perpetrator was terrible to see. An easy source of ammunition was the American occupied airfield in the next village. Jammed bullet traces often resulted in odd rounds being discarded by the side of an aircraft parking place for collection later. When the parking place was deserted non-authorised juniors often collected the rounds. Also, it was not unknown for portions of ammunition trace to fall from returning aircraft.

The standard US Browning machine gun fired .50-inch calibre rounds, the majority of which were classified as armour piercing incendiary. With the aid of a vice the bullet could be easily removed which allowed the explosive filling to be

Previous pages: At street
parties the length and
breadth of Britain, wives,
sons and daughters eagerly
anticipated the return of
husbands and fathers.

emptied from the round casing. Disappointingly, in its loose state the filling could not be made to explode, although it did have some interesting incendiary qualities when emptied onto a bonfire. It so happened that on the very day the Second World War officially ended I decided to avail myself of the contents of some 'point fifty' bullets in my possession. Whether or not this was to stoke some commemorative bonfire I do not remember, but after lunch that day I repaired to my father's workshop to make use of the vice. Having removed several bullets and emptied the rounds, I was then taken with the idea of detonating the percussion cap, the device in the end of the round that fired the round when struck. With the round case in the vice a large nail was held in my left hand and a hammer swung to strike the nail. The resultant bang was forceful enough to send me reeling. I found that two inches of my thumb had been split open and riddled with bits of brass from the cap. Unlike when in a gun breach there had been no retaining force on the cap to prevent blowback.

My mother was extremely cross, pointing out that but for my thumb catching the whole force of the exploding cap I might easily have got the fragments in my face and eyes. Although the thumb was a mess I was not despatched to the doctor for stitching and over the weeks that followed it healed quite nicely. The only problem was that periodically a small piece of brass would surface. The last emerging almost a year after the event. Today the scar, if very faint, is still visible as a personal reminder of the very last day of the Second World War – and my stupidity.

WYN EDWARDS

HOME FRONT

Wyn Edwards and her husband Bill lived in Coventry.

*Bill Edwards, guest of
honour, cuts the cake.*

VE day came and spontaneously a street party was quickly arranged. Everyone contributing something towards the 'feast'. For instance in order to make the butter ration go further it was beaten with evaporated milk to make it spread further. I made a sponge sandwich using liquid paraffin from my medicine cupboard, eggs from my own chickens in my back garden and I sacrificed some of my home-made jam. The sun shone, it was a glorious day and my husband Bill managed to get home as guest of honour to cut the cake.

WW2 People's War

MALCOLM GUTHRIE

ARMED FORCES

Malcolm Guthrie, of the RAF, was in Denmark.

There was a party on board a merchant ship in Oslo harbour for all the air crew. There was also a vast quantity of rum, and it was a hell of a party. I think it went on for a full two days. I don't recall any sleep anywhere in it, to the extent that the local military police came and collected us after about two days on rum and no sleep and not much food. They took us back to Gardermoen and we were supposed to be on our way. Unfortunately my skipper was in no condition whatsoever to fly out, so we loaded the aircraft up with troops and we were the last aircraft out, and there were no spare captains. So as second pilot I took the aircraft off, and Gardermoen was at a fairly high altitude, the air was a bit thin, and I can certainly recall being halfway down the runway and feeling that I was distinctly underpowered. I can recall a line of fir trees at the end of the runway, and then we went straight through the top of the fir trees and lowered them all by about six feet.

It was distinctly touch and go, but we came back across the North Sea and landed at Lossiemouth in Scotland, and disembarked the troops. And by that time the effects of the Merchant Navy rum had worn off and my skipper brought the aircraft back to Chelmsford.

We had done a lot of work with the Danish Resistance. In Denmark our reputation and standing was very, very high at the end of the war. I can see some of the German officers and NCOs now – they were lost, their leadership had suddenly gone and there was just an attitude that they just wished to please. The ground staff couldn't have been more helpful if they'd tried. In fact, even when we left, which would have been VE Day plus about 15, the Germans were still running the airfield, and I don't think it was until some time after that they were finally rounded up and taken to POW camps.

Perhaps two weeks after VE Day we went to Kastrup in Copenhagen, and the welcome we received was fantastic. I can remember taxiing round the perimeter track with literally hundreds and hundreds of people all waving to us from behind barriers. It was almost impossible to walk down the streets for more than about five minutes at a time without getting into conversation or having someone come up and wanting to shake your hand. After we'd left our aircraft, we went back to the airport lounge and we were given something we hadn't seen for years: vast bowls of strawberries were put on the table with bowls of cream. And I can still taste those strawberries and cream at Kastrup airport.

DAVID HUNTER

David Hunter, aged seven, lived on a farm at Aldbrough St John in North Yorkshire.

In 1944, a tractor arrived at the farm. Mr Fenwick told me it was American and had been sent over to help mechanise the farm so that it could produce more food. It was a Massey Harris, a great red beast with yellow flutes in the bonnet that reminded me of horse reins.

My dad was given the task of driving the thing. He did his best with it, but the transition from horses was really a bit difficult. There was no machinery that could be used with it; it all had to be modified by the local blacksmith and draw bars fitted instead of shafts that had been used for the horses. Dad was a good horse ploughman. He usually won the single furrow contest at the local ploughing matches but he couldn't keep a straight furrow with the tractor. It hurt his pride a bit I know.

A message from the monarch: the commemorative certificate presented by King George VI to schoolchildren, 8 June 1946.

8th June, 1946

To-day, as we celebrate victory, I send this personal message to you and all other boys and girls at school. For you have shared in the hardships and dangers of a total war and you have shared no less in the triumph of the Allied Nations.

I know you will always feel proud to belong to a country which was capable of such supreme effort; proud, too, of parents and elder brothers and sisters who by their courage, endurance and enterprise brought victory. May these qualities be yours as you grow up and join in the common effort to establish among the nations of the world unity and peace.

George R.I.

He did get a chance to show the Massey Harris off in 1945. VE day arrived and the population was very relieved, although the war in the Far East was still raging with great intensity.

It was decided that the village would hold a giant bonfire on the low green in celebration. Dad and the Massey were dispatched to the churchyard at Stanwick and a lot of yew trees were pruned; they are lethal to cattle and need to be trimmed when they overhang the churchyard wall. All the village youths went too, riding back with a full trailer-load of the branches for the fire. I rode with pride of place on the mudguard of the tractor, I felt very proud that my dad could handle so much power.

So the war came to a close. We had a celebration at the village school, Miss Pybus, one of the two teachers, gave all the 20 pupils a lovely red apple and a packet of dried egg powder, a gift from the people of Canada she said. I got my illuminated address from King George; 'Now that we celebrate victory' it read.

WW2 People's War

ELIZABETH CHAMPION

HOME FRONT

Elizabeth Champion lived in the East End of London with her husband Ted.

Ted was an Incident Officer with the ARP [Air Raid Precautions] and had to report on all the bombs. He didn't talk much about it, but I think he saw terrible things. Sometimes he used to come home covered in dust and very pale.

We were bombed out twice, and at the end of 1944 a church at the end of our road took a direct hit from a V2 rocket. It was Sunday lunchtime and I was making Christmas puddings. The blast threw me off my feet and under the table. I was three months pregnant and if the church walls had not been so thick I would have been killed. From then until the birth I was in a lot of pain and thought I would lose the baby.

The day the war ended I was in Poplar Hospital, having had my daughter 5 days earlier. In those days they kept you in bed for ten days after you had a baby! We were all in bed waiting for our elevenses when the Sister came running onto the ward shouting, 'The war has ended, the war has ended!' and we all started laughing and crying. Even the Sister was crying.

In the afternoon the priest came into the ward and held a service. He then came round to speak to each of us. He asked me why I was crying and I said I was crying because my young brother had died in this hospital, but that I was also happy that my brother Tommy would be coming home from India, and Billy would come home from Egypt and Albert from sea. I had six brothers, five serving, and it was the youngest who was killed, at home.

Two days later we were all taken onto the balcony of the hospital, which faced East India Docks, to see the King and Queen who were touring the East End in an open-topped car.

KEITH HINCHCLIFFE

Keith Hinchcliffe was a five-year-old child living in Darnton.

Through the eyes of a five-year-old the months leading up to VE day did not seem particularly dark, dangerous or depressing.

Rationing, although of course restricting clothing purchases and treats, didn't bother me unduly. In fact it provided areas of amusement and diversion. I'm sure that eating sticks of rhubarb dipped into half an ounce of sugar, spooned into the corner of a paper bag and running up and down the street sparking newly hobnailed boots was more enjoyable than the expensive pleasures that today's youngsters are persuaded to partake of.

The comparative lack of traffic on our streets and roads meant that we could enjoy a game of football, cricket, rounders, nipsy, kick can, etc., on the 'stadium' in the middle of our road, with little danger to life or limb.

The preparations for VE Day celebrations did, however, cause a fever of excitement that took our minds off our normal childish pleasures. Each household raided their carefully stored rations to provide sandwiches, cakes and buns. Ingenuity was taxed to the limit to provide street decorations. In our street several lines of clothing and bunting were strung across between each house to represent the Siegfried Line. Large Victory V signs were painted on the fronts of the houses. Flags of all descriptions were discovered in attics and festooned all the buildings.

The big day dawned and I think if there had been a camcorder working it would have looked like a Benny Hill show, with all the people scooting in and out of the houses.

Trestle tables had to be set up in the street with suitably patriotic red, white and blue coverings. Chairs, benches and stools were brought out and dusted down. There seemed to be enough food arranged on the tables to feed the whole village – not just our street. I remember going with my brother to fetch a wicker clothes-basket filled with individual trifles each covered with Hundreds and Thousands, and a few dozen marshmallow biscuits, that our local baker had kindly donated.

I think the actual bun fight was a bit of an anti-climax for me, in that, apart from enjoying a dozen or so potted-meat sandwiches, not much else suited my picky tastes.

When we'd finished with all the food and drink, the tables and chairs were removed and to my surprise a musical ensemble appeared in the front garden of one of the houses.

I remember that there was a chap playing a set of drums which I distinctly recall comprised of a big drum, side drums and top hat cymbals. There was also a trombonist, but I can't remember what other instrumentalists were part of the motley orchestra.

All the adults were behaving in a very strange manner, some were dancing up and down the street to the music, others were singing, laughing, cuddling and kissing. I thought the whole world must have gone mad.

To confirm my original impression that madness prevailed, two of the 'plumper' women decided to stage a mud wrestling match, clad in bloomers and vests. I'm not sure how a decision was made as to the winner in the contest because it was almost impossible to see which one was which.

I don't know how long the celebrations went on for, but I guess that I must have retired to bed at the very late hour of 9 pm, still unable to understand what all the fuss was about.

WW2 People's War

EDITH OLIVIER

HOME FRONT

Edith Olivier kept a diary for 60 years. In 1939 she became the first woman mayor of Wilton, Wiltshire, and for the next three years she led the town with a particular understanding of the needs of a rural community inundated with evacuee children, military personnel and refugees. She died in 1948.

Victory day called officially VE Day (Victory in Europe) and tomorrow is also to be a Public Holiday VE Day 2. These names show the lack of imagination engendered by nearly six war years. Official names are all initials and nothing else... Everyone feels rather stunned and unable to take in what Peace means... at 9 the King broadcast to the nation and Empire – a very good speech – and his delivery quite good. No real hesitation. It was heard in the Market Place thro' Mr Cook's loud speaker and his van played the crowd.

'It's a day for kicking your bloody hat about.' Mary Edwards is pictured with her three sisters, on the left, in the second row, in front of their mother who is wearing military uniform.

MARY EDWARDS

HOME FRONT

Mary Edwards (née Dimelow), aged seven, lived in Ashton-under-Lyne, near Manchester.

I was seven years old when the war started on 3 September 1939. A month before, an army vehicle with an officer in it had called to tell my dad to report to the armoury on Old Street in Ashton-under-Lyne within the hour and with his full kit. He was on reserve as he had served in the First World War and he was in the Territorials. He was sent to France and was in the Dunkirk evacuation.

One day a neighbour of ours, Mrs Winship (née Woolvin) knocked on the door and said, 'Your beloved husband is coming up the street,' and my mother replied, 'Not mine, Kit, he's in France.' I didn't wait to hear any more, I ran up the street to meet him. He was one of the lucky ones who got back safe to England.

You can imagine how thrilled we all were when the war ended. The kids collecting wood for a bonfire and mums getting food ready for a party in the backyard. I remember Albert Lowe, he kept the shop on the corner of Forester Street and Walmsley Street, walking up the ginnel dressed immaculately in a dark suit and green trilby which he took off, kicked it into the yard and said, 'It's a day for kicking your bloody hat about.' He went in their back door and came out with a white enamel bucket which he gave to someone along with some money to go to Fairclough's shed for a bucket of ice cream.

My grandfather, as the eldest person present, was asked to light the bonfire and the celebrations began.

NORA HORGAN

HOME FRONT

Nora Horgan was the wife of a cattle farmer in County Cork, Ireland.

I was out in the field counting cattle and Dan the postman came and shouted from the fence, 'Nora, the war is over.' And he cycled off and left the post on the kitchen table. Back at the house I thought about the war years and our country – neutral, but many of our citizens fighting for the Allies on land, sea and air. Well, I thought, this news calls for a celebration. So I took down the bottle of whiskey from the dresser and raised a glass or two to them all, friend and foe alike, wondering how much it all cost, and whether the beef trade would continue to flourish. We made a few bob out of it anyway.

KEES VANDERHEYDEN

HOME FRONT

Kees Vanderheyden was 11 years old when the war, and the German occupation of his home town of Oisterwijk in Holland, ended.

The war was very literally in my backyard with a German general's staff, his radio listening post, the Allied airmen hidden far away in the garden, and later the Canadian military field hospital in our living room with blood and wounded soldiers around us. It was a strange, terrible and sometimes even exciting period for the 11-year-old boy I was then.

In May of 1945, when the church bells in the village finally rung out to signal the end of the war, we got busy organising festivities to celebrate the Liberation. My mother used cloth, paper and cardboard to create twenty or more costumes for us and for our friends to wear in the parade. The gaily-coloured results of her work – bright costumes for princes, peasant girls, peasant boys and Indians – were draped all over our walls.

Cheered on by a joyous crowd and very proud of our motley finery, we paraded past shelled-out houses in the streets of Oisterwijk. After the parade, along with all the other children from our street, we went to the *Kapelleke*, the little chapel near our house dedicated to the Virgin Mary. There, we left an offering of thanks – a big thank-you card on which all our names were inscribed.

We were dismayed to learn that some people from our village had also organized a parade, ahead of ours: a very strange and very grim spectacle indeed. They loaded a group of women with shaven red-painted heads on horse-drawn carts: these were the girls who had gone out with German soldiers during the Occupation. The crowd booed them and spit on them. The children in our group all thought this was a very sad display.

With the arrival of real peace, after the Canadians liberated Holland, we lost our taste for war games. Nobody wanted to remember the old ghosts of fear and battle. The tank that my friend Leo and I made out of a little wagon and some boxes left by the Canadian army slept in dusty silence in its corner of the garage. We threw away our wooden guns and our tin-pot helmets.

JULIUSZ JASIEWICZ

ARMED FORCES

Juliusz Jasiewicz started military service in Poland in 1938, aged 18. After Artillery Officers' School, he was posted to the 19th Field Regiment of Artillery near Wilno (then Polish, now Vilnius and part of Lithuania) in 1939. When war broke out he found himself on active service. In 1944 he was posted to AOS (Air Observers School) Malton in Canada, to serve as a navigator.

In 1942 news began to spread that the Polish consulate in Stalinabad was arranging for Poles to be transported to the newly formed army. I had hardly recovered from typhus but I went to see the consul. Observing my sickly appearance he advised me to postpone my journey to join the army. But I was only too eager to join. Conditions in the army camp were not much better. Volunteers were pitched against the Russian winter with only a couple of blankets for shelter. Time dragged slowly from one meal to another. In the morning we had bread and boiled water and at midday a watery soup. There was something similar in the evening. As time crept wearily on, most of us who were former soldiers felt that we had been forgotten.

Like most of us I believed in a positive outcome to the war. For us this meant our return to a free and independent Poland – the only one we had known. When February 1945 came, I was well into my training at AOS Malton in Canada. News of the Yalta conference surrendering Poland to Russian domination was received by all of us with incredulity – we simply refused to believe it. How after all the sacrifices on many fronts of Polish soldiers we could be dispossessed of our homeland. There must be some misunderstanding due to our inadequate knowledge of English, I thought. All that was required was simply a clarification of ambiguous presentation in the newspapers was the general belief amongst us.

Juliusz Jasiewicz.

When it became absolutely clear that we were betrayed by our Allies in the most despicable manner, the reactions of my countrymen varied from suicide to a wait-and-see attitude. We in the AOS were made to believe by our officers that nothing was lost and that we would be used in the war against Russia. I accepted this assurance without reservation and continued my training with undiminished zeal, achieving top marks in all subjects. About a third of our Polish contingent refused to continue on the course, citing Yalta as the reason.

After the passing-out parade on 25 March 1945, I sailed to England to visit friends. While on board the ship in mid-Atlantic, I learned the war in Europe was over. I was given a week's leave to sort out my private matters. With the end of the war, British people were jubilant; their mood contrasted sharply with my feelings. For me and my countrymen the war was not over; we had lost it to Russia, with the approval and help of our Allies.

YELENA DAVYDOVA

HOME FRONT

Yelena Davydova, a student at the Odessa Polytechnic Institute, spent over two years in a Ukrainian village occupied by Nazi troops.

Odessa was liberated on 12 March 1944. The Germans started leaving long in advance. One day I saw Herr Kommandant Peters in a coughing German car on a bridge. He seemed quite happy to leave and was smiling broadly. Five or six German soldiers stayed on for some unknown purpose. A Soviet reconnaissance squad on motorcycles found them killing hens in a collective farm henhouse near the rail line. All those hen-hunters were expediently done away with. I'm at a loss for words to tell you how happy we were to see Soviet military uniforms again! There were fears for some time that the Germans might come back. They never did.

Late on 8 May 1945, all foreign ships in the port suddenly turned on their sirens. An air raid was ruled out, because a big map in Deribasovskaya Street showed the front line closing in on Berlin. I was at a loss. Late at night, somebody started pounding on our hostel door: 'Get up, the war is over!' The seaside boulevard where we ran was full of people, many of them crying, singing, dancing or playing accordions. More and more people came. The celebration continued all night. Foreign guests at the London Hotel opened their windows to look out. Shortly before dawn, my roommate and I sat down on a bench in Deribasovskaya Street to take some rest. In a hotel on the opposite side, a handsome officer appeared on a balcony and started firing in the air. That was his V-Day salute. The prospect of getting killed by a stray bullet on such a great day prompted us to stand up and take off.

JOSEF STALIN, 9 MAY 1945
VICTORY ADDRESS TO THE SOVIET UNION

Comrades! Compatriots, men and women! The Great Day of Victory over Germany has come. Fascist Germany, forced to her knees by the Red Army and the troops of our Allies, has acknowledged her defeat and declared unconditional surrender. The age-long struggle of the Slav peoples for their existence and their independence has ended in victory over the German invaders and the German tyranny. Henceforth, the great banner of freedom of nations and peace among nations will fly over Europe.

Comrades! The Great Patriotic War has ended in our complete victory. The period of the war in Europe is over. The period of peaceful development has begun. I congratulate you upon the victory, my dear compatriots, men and women! Glory to our heroic Red Army which upheld the independence of our Motherland and won victory over the enemy! Glory to our great people – the victor people! Eternal glory to the heroes who fell in the battles against the enemy and gave their lives for the freedom and happiness of our people.

GRIGORY SOROKIN

ARMED FORCES

Grigory Sorokin, fighter pilot in the Red Army, was selected for participation in the Victory Parade in Red Square in Moscow.

My last mission was on 10 May 1945. We were finishing off the remaining forces of Field Marshal Scherner holed up in the Czech mountains and liberated Prague. I then flew over Berlin providing air support for the 3rd and 4th tank armies commanded by P. Rybalko and D. Lelyushenko.

On 12 May 1945 our staff officers, telephone operators and radiomen asked me to show them around Berlin. We took a car and headed towards the Reichstag that was smoking in the distance. The air was filled with the pungent stench of decomposing bodies. The local metro was filled with water. There were about 50 of us there, together with people from the 1st, 2nd and 4th Ukrainian Fronts. Then someone invited us to cross the canal to the opposite side of the Reichstag where they were going to give an improvised concert. Catching sight of a brightly coloured shawl, someone cried: 'Ruslanova!' 'Valenki, Valenki!' cried out someone else. Ruslanova came out and bowing low, said: 'My dear victors! I love you all and I'm happy to sing for you this song called Valenki, the Soviet Valenki, which have walked all the way to Berlin.' When she was finished, I asked her to pose for a group photo with all of us.

After my last sortie, our Corps commander told that Josef Stalin had decided to hold a Victory parade in Moscow. 'You have flown more hours than anyone else of our staff did, that's why we're sending you there,' he told me. Only the most disciplined and decorated people, 165cm to 175cm-tall, were allowed to take part in the grand showcase. Of our three divisions they handpicked 20 men. Taking the list at the Corps headquarters, I headed to Dresden where we had a combined

Overleaf: The Soviet Union celebrates victory in the Great Patriotic War with fireworks over the Kremlin, 9 May 1945.

Soviet war heroes march in the Victory parade in Moscow.

regiment of the 1st Ukrainian Front – 1,015 men in all, a pilot battalion, a tank battalion, an artillery battalion and so on. Our uniforms were worn out so we were issued with brand new clothes complete with headsets. Then there came a new order saying that we would get new uniforms right in Moscow. All we got in Dresden was jodhpurs and blouses. General Baklanov was appointed to command the combined regiment. Arriving in Moscow we detrained and were ordered to march to Lefortovo. As the column of the 1st Ukrainian Front was moving through the city we saw a column of German POWs being convoyed back to their barracks. Youngsters lining up the streets were shouting and spitting at them and giving us a hero's welcome. We were overjoyed and filled with happy anticipation of the grand parade waiting for us ahead...

Serious as the preparations for the march-past were, there was no excessive drilling for us, all seasoned soldiers. The greenhorns, who had been sent to the battlefront without any prior training, were subjected to some pretty strenuous drilling though. After breakfast they were marched right to the drill square.

We were all issued dark green cloth uniforms, dry top boots and flyer's caps. The dress rehearsal was at the central airfield and another, night one, on Red Square. On June 24 we were ordered up at 3 am. After breakfast we marched to Red Square. There was a steady drizzle coming down. Soaking wet, we stood there waiting. Exactly at 10 am Marshal Georgy Zhukov rode out on his horse to hear a report from the parade's commander Marshal Konstantin Rokossovsky. Josef Stalin, who was also there, thanked the attending troops through the front commanders. Marching ahead of our combined regiment, with a banner in hand, was A. Pokryshkin, followed by our Front Commander I. Konev. Marching behind him was a line of army commanders, 12 in all, twice more than at any other front. We were all awarded Victory over Germany medals there. The parade over, we gave all our new and soaking uniforms back, except the caps and, putting on our old garb, returned to our stations.

YURI GRIBOV

FRONT LINE

The Red Army's Second Lieutenant Yuri Gribov, 19, led his machine-gun company into battle in the 1945 operations to cross the river Oder, capture Berlin and link up with the Americans on the Elbe.

In the dawn hour of 1 May, we took Brandenburg after reaching it in a 60-kilometre overnight march. We encountered white flags everywhere, and in one of the streets, piles of bodies of local civilians who had been shot by SS-men for hanging out such flags. One of my platoon commanders, Dmitri Frolov, was killed in action in Brandenburg. I replaced him with Sergeant Nefedov, the hero of the grove engagement outside Spandau. On the Elbe on 5 May, we collided head-on with a German division retreating from Berlin. Sixty percent of our regiment was wiped out in heavy fighting that day.

[House-to-house fighting] is so terrible that it defies description. This house is ours, that one is theirs. Near Spandau one day, we almost ran into a marching column of German soldiers after crossing a rubbled house wall. We hid behind trees and spent the following night in a cellar together with German civilians. Our Medical Corps man and I used civilian coats for cover. There were German soldiers upstairs, and sometimes they went down to the cellar to pick what looked like bottles. Our German neighbours knew who we were, but they did not betray us. In the morning, we slipped away through a hole in the wall.

My friend Second Lieutenant Dudnik, the same age as me, died in street fighting in Spandau. A Nazi sniper wounded him as we were crossing a tram line. Dudnik crawled for half a minute or so until the sniper finally did him in in our full view. We were powerless to help. By the time we pulled our friend away by his leather belts, he had been killed. One Soviet captain got a bullet in his leg as he and I were running across a street in Spandau. He cried of pain. Fortunately, we managed to carry him away.

On the 6th or 7th of May, sitting in a trench near the right bank, I spoke with Second Lieutenant Alexei Borisov: 'I suspect the war is over, Alexei.'

'Why do you think so ?'

'Because we have secure ground behind us, Soviet troops on the right, Soviet troops on the left and American forces in front of us.'

'Where is the official announcement then ?'

This came after some more rumours on 8 May. Colonel Buzykin assembled what remained of our division in a big meadow. He was limping along with a walking stick. Soldiers helped him onto a cart which he used as a podium to deliver the announcement and a victory speech. Hardly anybody listened to him. All started firing into the air instead. I took a bicycle and went for a ride. A German woman on the path got frightened seeing me but I told her in my fairly fluent German that she had nothing to fear and 'Hitler kaput'. That was the end of the war for me. Of the 32 boys who left the school in Krasnoarmeisk in December 1944, only 16 survived. Dying at 19 is a terrible thing.

ANNE SOMERHAUSEN

HOME FRONT

Anne Somerhausen was a resistance worker during the German occupation of Belgium. Her husband Mark had been a prisoner of war in Germany since 1940.

7 MAY – Am I a widow? Is my husband dead? Why has no word come through from him these long, long eight months? Must I fight on alone for ever? I am as tired as if I had lived for centuries – through centuries of war. How many, many days will this dreadful uncertainty last? Does life mean to crush me flat?

12 MAY – The miracle has happened. Five years ago to the day, almost to the hour, my husband kissed me goodbye and turned back to his anti-aircraft gun. Today he returned, an older, stronger man, tanned by the sun, hale in his battle dress – a very silent man, still somewhat a stranger in his own home. He walked into it, using his own latchkey, which he had carried like a talisman all these five years.

He walked straight into the garden, where Luke and Matthew were playing. He recognised Matthew and asked somewhat shyly: 'Is this Luke?' And Luke answered timidly: 'Are you my Dad?'

Johnny rushed down from upstairs to see who the soldier was. He recognised his father. But Mark was almost shocked, He had left a boy of 13; he found a young man, impossible to identify.

Johnny called up my office. I burst into tears. The office staff gathered around me. 'Put your hat on right.' 'You must powder your nose.' 'Put a bit of lipstick on.' I ran off in a daze.

There he stood in a doorway – my husband. We fell into each other's arms. No, this wasn't coming home after five years of war. This was Mark coming home from a somewhat leisurely trip abroad. Surely we had parted only three weeks or so ago? This was all quite natural and normal. Surely it was a little unbalanced to be crying?

...He is asleep now. He does not sense that I am watching him, or that from time to time I am holding his hand. There are many deep new lines in his face, and I am trying to read the story they tell. His hands are harder and broader – no longer the soft white hands of an intellectual. He sleeps profoundly – only, at times, there is a nervous twitching around his mouth.

He is asleep. He is here. I am holding my husband's hand at last. The children, too, are having their rest – each healthy boy sound asleep. No more war. My work is done. All, all is well.

PHILIP KELLY

HOME FRONT

Philip Kelly was a child in Essex at the end of the war.

Although very hard-of-hearing, when well enough I attended school and used to read books in the back row of class. Hours were passed in this fashion. Our lives began to change. No more air raids and more American planes than RAF. Then came the announcement that we could all have a day to celebrate the ending of hostilities in Europe.

On VE Day, we ran around with home-made flags and quickly built a big bonfire to joyfully burn an effigy of Hitler. Soon, the German POWs working in the fields were sent back to Europe. They were well fed here and at peace with only their German corporal to keep them working. We quite missed them when they had to go. But it gave us the chance to earn pocket-money picking peas and potatoes. Of course, many boys' fathers had gone off to the war. Some were still away in the Far East on VE Day and some never returned. One boy had a coconut posted home by his father who was later lost at sea.

WW2 People's War

CARMELLA DIGHT

Carmella Dight was five years old when Belgrade was liberated by the Red Army.

I was five when peace came to Yugoslavia in October 1944. The country was in ruins, particularly Belgrade, the city Hitler vowed to flatten in retaliation for disloyalty and the Partisan uprising against Germany. Yugoslavia before the war was not a rich country; after the war the country was destitute and in chaos. In 1941 the royal family fled to London, and in 1944 a Communist regime under the leadership of Marshal Tito came to power. Tito and the partisans liberated Belgrade on 20 October 1944. The Soviet army, partially instrumental in the liberation of Yugoslavia, arrived soon after.

I lived with my mother and aunt in the outskirts of the city at my aunt's house. Everyone listened to the news announcing liberation. When eventually it was confirmed, people hugged, kissed and downed the popular plum brandy. In Belgrade the partisans and the Red Army were received with open arms. However, there was a cloud hanging over the country. Tito and the new Communist government embarked on an internal battle squaring their differences with the Ustashi [Croatian nationalists who had supported Hitler's Germany] and the Chetniks [Serb royalists]. Within a few weeks most of the reckoning was done and the country cleansed of 'undesirable elements'. The anti-Communists surrendered to British or American forces rather than fall into Tito's hands.

We all waited impatiently for my father's return from the war. Each time the doorbell sounded, I rushed with my aunt to receive a returning family member or friend. If it was a male, I pulled my aunt's sleeve and asked, 'Is this my father?' the reply was always negative. She knew through Communist contacts that the Germans shot him in 1941, which was the fate of many Jewish males in Belgrade.

CELINA LIEBERMAN

REFUGEE

Celina Lieberman was a Jewish child living in the Ukraine when her family was sent to the Lvov Ghetto in Poland.

Lvov was a very crowded city, where we lived with my father's sister. They simply allocated some room to us. But now I wish we had gone to Siberia, because some people survived Siberia. I remember one morning in 1941 I got up and my mother was standing at the window. I joined her at the window and saw the first Germans going by on motorcycles, creeping by at dawn. My mother said, 'This is the end of us.'

The Lvov Ghetto started. It was miserable. At this point we were not in any danger, but I slept in a bed with my mother. Families were living on top of each other. There were nine people in a room. Conditions in the ghetto were beyond description. One of the

'They decided I was Aryan looking enough to pass in hiding.' Celina Lieberman, aged 5, her brother Artur, aged 11, and their Aunt Repa.

most annoying things was the lice in our hair. It was something to be ashamed of. You could not get a bar of soap and there was no hot water. You couldn't wash clothes. My mother made hamburgers out of chopped beet leaves and fried them in oil. I think the oil came from a car, because no one in the ghetto had cooking oil. The smell was horrible, and the taste was unforgettable.

At night I would hear horrible screams and I wondered if I would ever get these inhuman voices out of my head. I didn't know at the time that they were families being deported to the concentration camps. When our turn came to be deported, it was part of the routine that all Jews cleaned up their room. The Germans would come and check and see who was handicapped and who was capable. My father was deported and I never saw him again. He died in the Janowski concentration camp.

Finally, it was decided that I must be smuggled out to Zbarazh, where I was born, before the last board went up around the ghetto. We still had relatives there. My mother made arrangements with a non-Jewish person to smuggle me out. I asked my mother if I needed a coat and she said, 'No, the war will be over soon.' It was the spring of 1942. That was the last time I spoke to my mother. That was also the last time I saw my brother Artur. I had hoped that because of his blonde,

Aryan looks, he would survive. But he died in Zytomir forced labour camp.

It must have taken me three or four days to get to Zbarazh. I remember riding, walking and then sitting in a forest. I stayed with my Uncle Adolph and Aunt Rozia for a while before they decided that I was Aryan looking enough to pass in hiding.

Above: Celina Lieberman, aged 14. Below: Celina's ID card from the Displaced Persons camp she was sent to after the war.

They gathered up whatever they had — silverware, candlesticks and money — and gave it to a Ukrainian woman in the village of Berezowice, to hide me until my parents could come and reclaim me. I was hidden in an attic on her farm. She was kind to me and fed me three times a day. Then people in the village began to suspect that she might be harbouring a Jew and she got frightened and threw me out.

I walked back to Zbarazh. I was eleven years old at the time. Helena Zaleska, a Polish Catholic farmwoman found me and asked if I wanted to be her child. She was childless and wanted me for her own. She hid me, gave me the name Marishka and taught me how to behave in church. She and her brother had good hearts. They were very religious and for the record, I say that they were righteous Gentiles. They were good to me. They gave me love. I worked awfully hard, but so did they. I had fresh air and whatever food they had.

I learned to be a very good Catholic and go to Church. I'd wear Helena's only pair of boots to church and when I came home she would wear them to church. It was a relay. What bothered me was the absence of any reading material. There was only one book and that was on the lives of saints. I know every saint by heart. I developed a prayer that went something like, 'Dear God, I'm not doing this to offend you, but to survive. I don't want to go to Church,' and I did it in rhyme. This was my way of apologising to other Jews.

At the end of the war the Russians started to advance. A detachment came to the farm. I didn't know until a week later that this was liberation. The shooting was very frightening, but the war was over.

I was 14 at the end of the war and believed that I was the only surviving Jew left on earth.

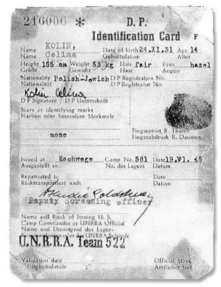

MASS-OBSERVATION ARCHIVE, 7 MAY 1945
OVERHEARD AT RIBBON COUNTER, WOOLWORTHS, OXFORD CIRCUS

'I'm sure I wouldn't buy any bloody victory ribbon. My boy's just been killed outright in Holland, and they say the fighting in Holland's over. Well don't you believe what they say. My boy wasn't even wounded, he didn't stand a chance, it's going to be no bloody victory for me.' [People at ribbon counter look up, and nod sympathetically.]

TERRY SHAW

FRONT LINE

Terry Shaw, 18, of the Royal Navy, was at sea when he heard the news that the war in Europe had ended.

Where was I on VE Day? Somewhere in the North Atlantic, on a troopship in convoy, four days out from Greenock, bound for Gibraltar. I remember the scene vividly – the brilliant foam-flecked ultramarine blue of the rolling, sunlit Atlantic, the lines of merchant ships behind and about us; the protecting, bucking corvettes, away on the horizon, sometimes all but disappearing as they ploughed through the heavy swell. The announcement came through on our ship's intercom, grave, measured – Germany had surrendered, the war in Europe was over. But it added a warning, our vigilance must remain total, a caution reinforced by the occasional thump of a distant depth charge.

How did I feel, as a young sailor (not quite 19), en route on his posting to his first ship? Relief that the killing was all but over, and that – save possible involvement in the war against Japan – I had been spared. Certainly there was no gung-ho youthful regret at missing the fighting. After nearly six years of war, I was becoming aware of its horror and tragedy, and of the sacrifice and suffering of millions.

I am reminded of a parents' epitaph on the headstone of their 18-year-old boy in a Normandy war cemetery, which spells out that suffering so poignantly and which, many years later, brought tears to my eyes:

'Only one to all the world

But all the world to us.'

WW2 People's War

**GENERAL BERNARD MONTGOMERY, 8 MAY 1945
VICTORY DAY SPEECH**

What I have to say is very simple and quite short. I would ask you all to remember those of our comrades who fell in the struggle. They gave their lives so that others might have freedom and no man can do more than that. I believe that He would say to each one of them, 'Well done, thou good and faithful servant.' And we who remain have seen the thing through to the end. We all have a feeling of great joy and thankfulness that we have been preserved to see this day. We must remember to give the praise and thankfulness where it is due. This is the Lord's doing and it is marvellous in our eyes.

LEN SCOTT

ARMED FORCES

Sergeant Len Scott of the Royal Army Pay Corps had been stationed in Rome since November 1944. Having been a journalist, he had volunteered for service in 1939.

On 10 May 1945 I wrote this letter to my Danish wife, Minna, from No. 8 Command Pay Office in Rome:

'I suppose I should have started this letter with a howl of joy about the armistice, but I feel more like weeping than rejoicing – weeping from sheer relief and thankfulness that this long drawn-out slaughter has ceased at last. Two days, Tuesday and Wednesday, were set aside here for celebration, but everything was very quiet. Even in Rome where a certain amount of high spirits might have been anticipated, the atmosphere was sober and calm, even among the civilians. When the sirens sounded a long All Clear there was a certain amount of hand-shaking between strangers and some feeble cheering but the evening passed away as uneventfully as a Church Parade. The troops seemed actually subdued.

'I was in the company of two infantry sergeants and a paratrooper. On asking the last-named how he felt about the news, he said: "Well, it seems to me that the main thing is that I'm not going to get killed – and that my friends are not going to get killed either." This seemed to be the general attitude. Me? The war was over and I had never seen a German soldier dead or alive, had never aimed my rifle at a living target. On V Day itself I spent the afternoon in town where I saw *Mutiny on the Bounty* and then sat at my ease under a tree in the Borghese Gardens.'

Writing these lines I wondered why I felt no guilt at my passive and comfortable war. No. No guilt. On 6 March 1940 I had placed myself at the disposal of the military authorities. For the following five years I had been moved on their chessboard - the paltriest of pawns. I could have been at El Alamein, Anzio, Cassino or Normandy. I was sorry for those whose fate it had been to enter those slaughter-houses. I had merely drawn a lucky card, aided by one dud eye. But I was glad I had not had to kill anyone, delighted that I was still alive.

I continued: 'Yesterday I took a tramcar out to the hills – to Castel Gandolfo – and spent my afternoon beside the huge blue lake, letting the water ripple over my bare feet. It was very quiet up there and very lonely. I was able to think in peace. Yes, it was strange to realise that for the first time in many years there was peace in Europe and that I might even think about such unlikely contingencies as going home. For "going home" was something that might happen when that huge and unlikely miracle happened – the end of the war in Europe.

Minna Scott.

'Now the sun is blazing down though it is six o'clock in the evening. In the distance the blue ridge of the mountains stands out against the lighter blue of the sky; next door, in the girls' orphanage, a choir of tots is singing Italian songs to the accompaniment of a piano-accordion. A most un-English scene is it not? But by virtue of that very possibility of my return to you the mountains seem less clear than usual, the voices less audible. Instead I seem to see the wooded hills of Marden Park, the chuffing of the train far down the valley, your steady grey eyes.'

Our cinema now screened newsreels of the VE Day celebrations in London – the hysterical crowds, Churchill and the royal family on the Buckingham Palace balcony; the kissing and dancing. Many of us – including myself – watched with fishy eyes. Some of the men had been overseas since 1939 and for them London had become just another foreign city. Many had long since lost touch with girls and wives. I counted myself lucky.

The eventual departure of the *Alleati* aroused apprehension in some sections of the Italian people. My friend, Staff-Sergeant Gordon Milne was billeted with a hard-up Contessa who was sure that the Communists would take over the State. There was a possibility of a right-wing backlash. Civil war. Tito's doings in nearby Yugoslavia ...

Warlingham, Surrey. Minna wrote on 8 May: 'So the danger is past. This is as far as I am able to get today. The thought of your return is too tender to be handled. I have made a Danish flag and it flaps merrily on our hilltop at the back of the house to avoid competing with our landlord's Union Jack flapping from the verandah. It seems that everyone has gone mad and the crowds in London are enormous. Do you remember our flight from the Coronation? Well, I just could not face this show either and I have been pondering the fact all afternoon. Am I completely unable to celebrate? Have I lost the power to be happy? Oh Len! All I can think about is your return. Even my hope of an early communication with Denmark is vague and unreal. It is as if all life has been crushed out of me and I cannot grasp reality. And then your letter came. Len, you do make me so happy. I have nearly forgotten how it feels to be kissed. Yes, we will go stark, staring mad together – unless we are so overcome by happiness that we fail to speak and merely stare at each other in open-eyed wonder.

'The best description of me at the moment is that of a dry sponge, thirsty for knowledge, love, you, adventure, peace, travel, excitement, family life, animals, the back-of-beyond and Denmark all in one and the same breath. How are you going to cope with this mouthful? You will probably want to spank me before you have been with me for more than five minutes. But, seriously, I do not think I can be quite serious tonight. It is a strange, thundery, evening and anything might happen.'

12 May: 'Everything would seem more real if I could hear from home. The news that the Germans will be going in a matter of weeks is wonderful – but how are they all? As you see – celebrations with lots of reservations. I do know I have much to be thankful for and will have to train myself to be happy. I have been making discreet enquiries from other people and am relieved to find that I am not the only one to be feeling 'queer'. It is going to take more than victory to live down years of anxiety and loneliness. Gudrun, my Danish friend, wants me to go to London tomorrow to see the royal family or something... and in the heat of the moment (it is very hot) I said "Not b****y likely!" I should have pleaded my sore throat and sore eyes, but I think I upset her. Imagine if I behaved so ruthlessly when you come home.

'I must be a drivelling, sentimental idiot for I writhe to imagine the homecoming of some of the enthusiastic lads who set out on Hitler's world-conquering quest. They cannot all be bad, any more than all the Allies can be good, and they have some dire sights in store for them. Is it being 'soft' to be uncomfortably aware of mankind in distress? I know they brought it upon themselves, only they cannot all be bad and there is bound to be unspeakable suffering in defeated Germany. Or am I still wearing blinkers? If it is possible to trace the blame to individuals, by all means do so. But I am convinced that the old saying I remember from Denmark will still hold good in a new version, "The small thief we hang; to the big thief we bow." I cannot voice my opinions here, least of all to Gudrun.

'Mercy has become an obsolete word at present. I am told that I would not recommend it if I could see some of the gruesome tortures indulged in by the aggressors applied to a member of my own family. I just do not understand anything any more. My mind is a vacuum or worse – sometimes a boiling cauldron of conflicting emotions. I need someone like you to tidy up my mind for me.'

But later: 'Such a relief to hear how you feel about it all. I felt I was an odd-number, unable to feel exhilaration at the reprieve or the liberation of Denmark. Gudrun makes me feel that way. She has been frantic most of the time and taking it out on me. She had no idea about my attitude until last night. Then your letter came, describing VE Day in Rome and I knew that everything was all right, that to you too it all meant the end of the worst madness. How could I go celebrating in London or anywhere else without you? I am not ungrateful – far from it. I am profoundly thankful that the murder is over, the imprisoned peoples liberated, given aid and food, that Denmark was not made into another battlefield. It will be time enough to celebrate when I know that they are all unhurt and well. Meanwhile I must work, work – and not get feverishly impatient for your return. To be able to write about that as a certainty fills me with awe.

'Gudrun has made it clear to me that I shall never return to Denmark for good if it means behaving as she wishes Danes to behave. She and her friends still believe in shouting for joy, embracing and kissing each other and dancing round the room waving Danish flags. I suspect that I am the happier in my quiet way which appears to correspond to your reactions, for which Heaven be praised.'

WW2 People's War

MARIETTE ROZEN

REFUGEE

Mariette Rozen, a Belgian Jew, was ten years old when the war ended.

Mariette Rozen's parents, Chanah-Malka and Aaron Rozen.

One day, my mother came home and sewed a yellow star on my jacket. I remember my brother Jean saying to me, 'Mariette, take the star off.' I used to always take it off and my mother used to sew it back on again. Then the Germans told everyone to register the names of all family members at the police station or be deported. My mother did what she was told and registered all our names, even those of our aunts, uncles and cousins. My oldest brother Jean yelled at my mother for this. I remember this clearly because at that time

Above: Of eleven brothers and sisters, eight survived. Mariette (right) with her sister Esther and nephew Gigi.
Right: Mariette in an orphanage after the war, in the centre with her hands together. Nuns had taught her to always look like she was in prayer in order to pass as a Christian.

no one dared to raised their voice to their parents. I was frightened.

I remember Esther, Henri, Jacques, Maman and I trying to walk to Paris, where Sarah was living. There were lots of people walking on the road. A plane dive-bombed everyone and Henri saved us all by pushing us into the ditch.

Eventually, Jean separated us all and placed us in different hiding places. I remember him telling me to kiss Maman goodbye. My next memory is of being with a strange family. I think that my mind went into shock. I never cried. I became a child of silence. I was so hurt. While the children in the house went to school, I used to sit under the kitchen table. I wasn't allowed to go outside.

Afterwards, Jean moved me around to many different hiding places and I lived with so many different people. Jean told me to always remember who I was and that I was Jewish, but never to tell anyone my last name, for fear that it would reveal that I was Jewish. I don't think I really understood but I knew not to ask questions. Henri was the one who kept track of where we all were during the war and would always keep in touch with me.

On my seventh birthday, I was taken by a woman I didn't know to meet my mother. As we neared the house, we saw the Germans putting my mother and brother Albert on a truck. My mother was all dressed up for my birthday. The woman grabbed me and told me to stop screaming. That was the last time I saw my mother.

Eventually I was hidden in a convent. I remember the Mother Superior waking me up in the middle of the night and telling me to hide in the sewers of the convent. One of the nuns had found out that I was Jewish and had reported me to the Gestapo for the reward money.

Afterwards, I was moved to a Catholic orphanage. I stayed in a few different orphanages in Belgium, Luxembourg and Paris. I was never in one place long enough to remember their names. I learned to speak many languages, Yiddish, Polish, Flemish, French, Dutch and Swedish. I was very lonely. I became a void, without any feeling at all.

I was ten years old and still in an orphanage when the war ended. One of the other little girls in the orphanage had a sister who happened to know where my sister Esther was living. That is how Esther found me. She took me to live with my brother Charles in Brussels. Of the eleven brothers and sisters, eight of us survived. Jean, who had been a member of the Resistance, was killed by the Germans during the war. Simon died three weeks after liberation in Auschwitz.

JAMES ROFFEY

HOME FRONT

James Roffey, aged 14 at the end of the war, was one of the many children evacuated from London. He was sent to Pulborough, West Sussex, with his younger brother and elder sister.

After years of waiting and longing to go home I quite unexpectedly received a letter from my mother telling me that John and I could return home and enclosing the money for our train tickets. I was wildly excited and went round the village saying my goodbyes and paying one last visit to all my favourite places, little realising the disillusionment that awaited me when I finally arrived back in London.

Our mother met us at Victoria station and we caught a tram to Camberwell. The tram was dirty; its windows were boarded up, so I couldn't see much outside. Even then I found that our mother would not talk about the evacuation. Our old home was in a very battered state from the bombing and everywhere looked dilapidated. I think I was expecting some sort of welcome home, but nothing happened and no one was at all interested in what I had to say; perhaps that was because I then spoke in a strong Sussex accent and therefore seemed alien to them.

On one occasion I was out with my mother when she met a neighbour who looked at me and said 'And who is this boy then?' To which my mother replied, 'Oh he is my youngest son, he has just come home from being evacuated.' Then the woman looked at me and said 'Oh you were one of the lucky ones having a nice time in the country. I don't suppose you really knew that there was a war on!' That really annoyed me. So after being machine-gunned, suffering years of

homesickness, having had to be grown-up and self-reliant for four years all that could be simply brushed aside and told I was one of the lucky ones. I complained to my mother about it but she told me not to be so silly.

Within a few weeks of returning home all the feelings of not really belonging that I had experienced as an evacuee returned. I felt no affinity with London or my own home. I wanted to be back in the country, but had to wait a few years before I could achieve that aim.

It was inevitable that my education would suffer due to the war and evacuation. In 1939 I was about to move up from the infants to the junior school, (the big boys), but the evacuation intervened. At Pulborough I was put in the junior class with the village boys and a few other evacuees. After a few years they moved me to the village hall where the Peckham Central Girls School had their lessons. There were about six classes held in the main hall and we all sat round trestle tables trying to listen to our teacher and not one of the others. They did their best but under such conditions I don't think we learnt much.

Things were not much better when we returned to London. In an attempt to sort us out we had to sit examinations for which no preparatory teaching was given. If you passed you could go to a Central school, which you would leave at the age of 15, but if you failed, which I and most other former evacuees did, you moved on to an elementary school, the leaving age of which was 14.

My school was to be in Grove Lane, Camberwell. It had been badly bombed and closed as a school for many years. The ground floor classrooms were still in use by the ARP and one had its windows and doors painted black and continued to be used as a mortuary to which bomb victims were brought.

The school was to reopen using only the remaining upper classrooms, but first the teachers and local boys had to shovel out the heaps of broken glass and fallen plaster from the bombing. Eventually it was made ready and we were told to report there.

On average there were 50 boys in each classroom and the teachers were elderly men who had been recalled from retirement. There was virtually no equipment, few books and even less interest. As leaving age drew nearer a few of us became worried about how backward our education was. We asked our teacher to give us homework that might help us to catch up, but his reply was 'If you think I am taking on all that extra work you are wrong. Besides, what is the point, within a year you will all be sweeping up factory floors.'

Many years later I met a man who had been a teacher in a London school like mine, and he told me what it was like for them. 'I had taught hundreds of boys over the years and thought I knew how to handle them, but found I was totally unprepared for what I was asked to do towards the end of the war. There were boys in my class who had lived through all the bombing, some had been buried alive, and others had helped to dig out people from bombed houses. But the hardest to understand were the boys who had been long-term evacuees. Generally they were quiet and well behaved, but would flare up and lash out if they thought they were being belittled in any way. Also they could all put on a "dead-pan" face, making it impossible to know what they were thinking.' He told me that in his opinion the education system failed the boys who had lived through the war. 'We tried to stick to the pre-war methods that had become totally unsuitable. No wonder some of the boys rebelled and others simply "opted out".'

I left school just after VE Day. I shall never forget the elation we all felt when the news finally broke that Germany had surrendered. Out of the upstairs windows of every house appeared the flags that had survived the bombing, people just stood around grinning. My mother said 'Come on. We are going up to the West End!' Soon we were on a bus that was inching its way through the crowds, eventually we were outside Buckingham Palace and shouting, 'We want the King' along with thousands of others. Then mounted police gently made a way through the crowds for on open-topped car, in which stood Winston Churchill waving a huge cigar. Soon afterwards he appeared on the balcony with the royal family and everyone cheered even louder.

Eventually we made our way home, where we found a huge bonfire already blazing at the top of our road. Men and boys were ripping the doors and floorboards out of bombed houses to burn, and then they went into the street shelters and dragged out the bunks, saying 'We won't need these any more!'

From our road you could see all over London and that night the sky glowed redder from the bonfires than it had done at the height of Blitz, but the best sight of all was that of the dome of St Paul's Cathedral, behind which were two searchlights making a huge V sign.

However our eldest brother, Edward, was still in the Army, somewhere in Italy. He had been missing for many weeks until found in a military hospital suffering from jaundice. But even when he finally made it home our family could not be fully reunited because our dear sister Jean had died in 1943 at the age of 18 of meningitis. We had all changed; the war had taken its toll and things could never be the same again.

WW2 People's War

ED EVANS

ARMED FORCES

Ed Evans, a Nav/B (Navigator/Bomb Aimer) in the RAF, was on leave at home in Dagenham, Essex when victory was declared.

The recent anniversary of the bombing of Dresden prompted memories of the celebrations which erupted when VE Day was declared. I was home on leave. I joined in with the hysterical rejoicing which took place at the top of the road where my family lived in Dagenham. Someone had loaned an old piano which was taken on a wheel barrow from the front gardens of one house to another. 'Roll Out The Barrel'; 'We're Gonna Hang Out Our Washing On The Siegfreid Line'; '(There'll Be Bluebirds Over) The White Cliffs Of Dover'; all were thumped out and lustily sung again and again. The war was over. Now, some 60 years later as I watched on TV the scenes of destruction and devastation in Dresden for which I was partially responsible – I had dropped our bomb load – I experienced the remorse, and the heartfelt wish that governments will one day refuse to resolve their differences or achieve their goals by warfare.

Ed Evans (back row, right) with his crew.

**GENERAL ALFREID JODL, 7 MAY 1945
ON THE SIGNING OF THE SURRENDER AT REIMS**

With this signature the German people and the German Wehrmacht are, for better or for worse, delivered into the victor's hands.

HEIDI KIRSCH

HOME FRONT

Heidi Kirsch was an eleven-year-old child in Leipzig, Germany.

The spring days in April 1945 were beautiful. The linden trees lining our cobble-stone street in Wiederitsch, a suburb of Leipzig, had young light green leaves, and the flowers of the white lilac in our front yard filled the air with their fragrance.

Yet we were sitting in the dark damp cellar underneath our house – cold and afraid. My mother watched us five children closely, insisting that it was too dangerous to go upstairs or outside. We listened to the high-pitched sound as heavy artillery shells whistled across our house and then heard the crash of their detonation in the centre of Leipzig. My mother read us the proclamation of Leipzig's mayor to all his citizens:

> Do not resist the enemy! Surrender quietly without any struggle! Display a white flag! May God protect our city.

Hours later the guns were quiet and we left the cellar. We did not have a white flag, but we hung white towels and tea towels out of all the windows facing our street. The next day was 20 April 1945, Hitler's birthday. We heard no sounds of danger, so we had breakfast upstairs and looked out of the window at our beautiful trees and shrubs in their spring garb. The sun was shining brightly and my mother was combing and plaiting my sister's hair, when we saw the USA soldiers coming. They all were carrying guns, pointing them in front of them, ready to shoot. It all seemed unreal, like a movie. For the first time in my life I saw someone with a dark skin. There were no loud noises; no one was in the street. People just watched from their windows.

We hoped that nobody would be so mad as to shoot or throw a stone. The government in Berlin had ordered all Germans to resist to the last drop of their blood, but we all surrendered without a shot. (In his last address to the nation Joseph Goebbels said, 'One would have to spit on Leipzig – *Auf Leipzig müßte man spucken*.') Following the walking soldiers, the tanks rumbled along our narrow street, crushing the cobblestones and having great difficulty negotiating the corner at the end of the street. The occupation forces settled in.

The next day a USA soldier came to our house. He was wearing a big wristwatch and pointing to it, he ordered us to leave our house within two hours. The US Army needed it to house their soldiers. So we took some of our belongings to our neighbour's house and waited. I had taken my feather bed and a book, and blissfully read a teenage novel titled *Bighead* (*Trotzkopf*) in the front parlour at our neighbour's. My mother went to the commanding officer and pleaded her case in her rusty high-school English. Would it be possible to let her and her five young children stay in the house and make some other arrangements for the army soldiers? She succeeded and we were allowed to go back to our house. I was quite disappointed, because I couldn't finish reading my novel, but had to help in the house instead.

On each second step of the wooden staircase in our two-storey house stood a large paper bag of sand and buckets of water had been placed where there was room, in readiness, should the house be bombed. Now my older sister and brother and I carried the sand bags out to the garden and emptied them in the sand pit. We were so happy. No more air raids! No more sitting in the cellar at night shivering, waiting for the bombs to fall! The war was over.

My father had returned home from the Front shortly after 20 July 1944, the day of the failed assassination attempt on Hitler. A doctor friend had declared him medically unfit to fight. He now was teaching the young high-school students, who had been conscripted to assist the anti-aircraft units around Leipzig. As a high-school teacher he was teaching school subjects to prepare them for life after the war. Unfortunately he was still an officer in the Air Force and had no discharge papers. He still had his weapons. Encouraged by a friend, who had his discharge papers, he went to the commanding officer of the US Army in our suburb to hand in his weapons. There he was taken a prisoner of war. He only came back home in October 1948. At first he was in US prison camps and then the Soviets took him to the Soviet Union in February 1946. He had not been a Nazi and never talked to us children about his wartime experiences or his years as a prisoner of war.

When Germany surrendered unconditionally on 8 May 1945 we were so glad that the war was over. We were grateful that our house was still standing and we were alive. But our future was uncertain. My father had been taken away and we had no income. The social welfare benefit was not even enough to pay the rates. How would we survive?

The Kirsch house in Leipzig.

JOHN HALL-WILLIAMS

HUMANITARIAN RELIEF

John Hall-Williams was a British conscientious objector to the war, volunteering in the liberation of Bergen-Belsen concentration camp as part of the Friends Relief Service.

I think the recollection I have [of first entering Bergen-Belsen] is of chaos and difficulty in finding the way. What you didn't want to do was lose yourself because there were various routes to go. What route to take to the children's camp, we had to enquire – there were various huts and they were all occupied with 600 or more live or dead persons. There was an indescribable smell but I don't even recall that. I have a vision of a smoke haze and these piles of bodies were everywhere and people were huddled over wood fires and helplessly staring out and picking over the bodies to see what they could find which could be useful clothing to be rescued, so there's a scene of almost medieval horror – and you can't easily describe or imagine what it was like. But it had a profound effect on some people and I've been asked many times what effect it had on me. The answer is there was no time to have any thoughts about it – we just had a task to do and got on with it. We thought about it only in retrospect, afterwards. Indeed I gather that is quite general among the people who served in the forces. There are some who have had nervous collapses, nervous troubles ever since, some who have only now come to terms with it after 50 years because it was so awful. Even anger was postponed at the time.

There were something like 60,000 people living in Camp One, and 20,000 lived to be evacuated on their feet, 20,000 were buried and 20,000 were placed in hospital. And we don't know how many of those survived although the death rate declined rapidly but it was very high at first in the hospital blocks.

[On VE Day] I was en route to Osnabruck to the NAAFI depot there where we had to draw rations of cigarettes and liquor for the whole of the army units we were attached to, including ourselves ... and on the way there nothing untoward happened. On the way back we were conscious of some celebration going on, the firing of Very lights and maybe the signal lights were in the sky, and a Russian soldier stepped out into the road and I stopped and he handed me his pistol and said, 'The war's over.' So I accepted graciously and being a pacifist, not knowing what to do, I drove to Belsen and when I got there I presented the gun to the padre because it was no use to me. And we were conscious that we'd missed Churchill's speech and the King's speech and all that which was to do with the end of the war. So that was the VE Day ceremony.

A ceremonial burning [of the huts at Belsen] took place organised by all the units to attend on 21 May at 6.00 in the evening. And we went down there. I went with a British Red Cross person, Ted Batty, and we attended and the army flamethrowers were lined up to ceremonially focus on two huts with Hitler's picture on one place and the German flag on the other place and they had a signal to point the fire towards them. Before that we had speeches from two or three guards and we were all in a very happy mood because the task of clearing the camp had been accomplished. That's all I remember.

At the time it was a camp clear of inmates so apart from any employees of ours there wouldn't be any there. The inmates, however, joined in the celebrations which we had in part 2 of the camp round about that time and the girls I noticed were dating the soldiers. The girls among the inmates having found powder and rouge for their cheeks and lipstick were happily doing what girls and boys always do together and dancing, and the dancing went on to the small hours.

VICTOR BREITBURG

CONCENTRATION CAMP

Victor Breitburg, aged 17, lived in the Lodz Ghetto in Poland.

The Germans told us they were going to send the children to farms and we would see them after the war. We hid our sister. My aunt believed them and gave them her daughter. Those children never saw daylight again. I learned later they were gassed and burned.

In July, 1944, the Germans came to take us to the country to work. My family hid in the basement for days. By day six, we were out of food, the children were getting sick and my sister was turning yellow. So we took our knapsack with our pots and pans and clothes and we boarded the train. Day one we were given a loaf of bread and something to drink. Day two, we saw guys in stripes working in the fields. The train stopped near the fields and there was a lot of noise, and a lot of dogs barking. Women were told to go on one side and men on the other side. I was 17. I didn't want to leave my mother.

She said, 'You go.' When I turned around, they were so far I didn't see them. On the third day I noticed somebody from Lodz and I asked him where the women and children were. He took me to the end of a wire and he said behind those buildings there was a crematorium. He said they were all gassed and cremated.

I could not understand cremation. I couldn't understand gas. I stood there for about an hour. I looked at the smoke. I still couldn't believe it. I didn't care if I lived or died. But after some time passed, I had the will of survival. The hate was so strong that I had to live.

I never forgot looking at skeletons and dead people. We were skeletons, and as we rode by on trains, the people outside would spit on us. I continued to work. I would dig up bombs that did not explode. I figured if I don't do it I won't get food and I'll die anyway.

On 8 May 1945, I was coming out of the bathroom and I saw people running. I said, what's happening. I didn't move. The war was over. Somehow I survived. I was the only survivor out of 54 people in my family. I went back to Lodz to see if I could find some of my family members, but there was no one.

WILLIE GLASER

FRONT LINE

Lance-Corporal Willie Glaser, 23, a German-born Polish Jew in the 1st Polish Armoured Division, was fighting the German Army in Belgium in April 1945. He was decorated with the Krzych Walecznych, the Polish 'Cross of Valour'.

In April 1945 we crossed into Germany. Again fighting was very heavy, the Germans were defending their own soil. On 4 May, the 10th Mounted Rifles Reconnaissance Regiment, preceding as usual the 1st Polish Armoured Division, faced fierce resistance near the town of Astederfeld. This was my last combat. On 8 May 1945 Germany surrendered unconditionally.

Here I was, Willie Glaser from Fuerth in Bavaria, back on German soil. Deep down in my heart I knew that I would never see my family again. I was in contact with my uncle Benjamin, my father's brother, who in 1935 had emigrated to Palestine. Later he told me that even in 1944 he was already sure that my family had perished. Nevertheless, in his letters he was trying to give me hope about the fate of my family.

I just did not understand how my Christian playmates from Blumenstrasse, when we were five and six years old, could be guilty of such crimes. After all

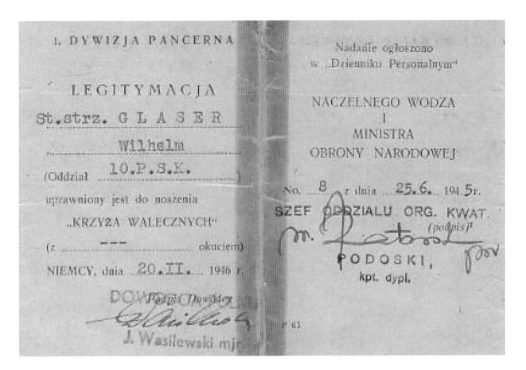

Left: Lance-Corporal Willie Glaser's certificate for the Polish Cross of Valour.
Right: Willie Glaser in Meppen, Germany in 1945.

I came to their houses after playing 'Cowboys and Indians' where their mothers fed me a *Butterbrot* (bread and butter) with marmalade. Franzl and Fritzl also came to my house to get a slice of my mother's *Apfelkuchen* (apple cake).

Everybody knew we were Jewish and there never was a problem. When I visited my grandmother in Koenigstrasse, I loved to stroll to the fire station, which was situated right behind my grandmother's house. It was a big thrill to help the firemen cleaning their fire engines. They knew I was Jewish. They helped me climb into the driver's seat. I was so proud and wanted to become a fireman when I grew up. Were these firemen also guilty of the atrocities inflicted on their Jewish neighbours?

In Fuerth everybody knew everybody. My grandmother was well known as Ester Glaser, the shoemaker's widow. When I accompanied her to the market, many men took off their hats or caps in a friendly greeting, ladies said, '*Gruess Gott, Frau Glaser?*' ('How do you do, Mrs. Glaser?'). Were all these people directly responsible for the murder of my family?

DAVID BRADFORD

David Bradford, a British medical student, was engaged in relief work at Bergen-Belsen concentration camp with the Red Cross.

The inmates were pretty apathetic when we arrived. They didn't really know who we were at first. They were very grateful for any food. If you actually took the trouble to lift up their heads and try to get fluid into them or food, because a lot of them had to be hand-fed, they would be very grateful. Occasionally you had chocolate or something like that which became available. They thought that was marvellous. And we used to dole out cigarettes.

The terrible thing was, the fitter ones were so greedy and didn't take any notice of the ill ones. The Czech doctors and people, they were pretty ruthless, they looked after number one. We had to be a little bit strict with them to try and get them to do something for the patients. But in those circumstances there was not an awful lot you could do except see that they had their fair share of food.

I remember one family, two brothers and a sister, all under twenty. The girl was able to look after the men – her brothers. One of them died and it was a terribly tragic situation. His sister clung on to him and we had to forcibly separate her to get him taken outside. This was the sort of thing that you read about, and we'd never encountered this situation before. She wasn't apathetic obviously because she was relatively well. But the ones that were just lying, they really were just vegetables.

They probably couldn't see any future – what was VE Day to them? Even if they managed to live, they were left only with the prospect of going back to ruined cities in Poland and Czechoslovakia.

KENNETH BUNGARD

Kenneth Bungard was serving aboard the HMS Zenith in the Arctic and Germany 1944–45.

Almost immediately when the war was finished we sailed through the Kiel Canal to a place called Travemunde, near Lübeck. Crowds of German people used to stand up against the quay and look at us. The fellas on the lower deck got together and they asked permission to have some of the very young children aboard. We knew that they couldn't be responsible for the war and they hadn't seen any decent food. So we gave them a tea party and we gave them sweets out of our ration, things they'd never seen before and we got them swinging on the hammocks and riding on the guns and so forth. We did that for several days and the children got to know us quite well. We managed to get hold of a lot of Polish children as well as German children. We didn't mix them though, they don't mix. It all went very well, they were very well behaved. The strange thing was that when we suddenly got sailing orders and we had to leave, the children knew it before we did. As the ship left in the morning, the children were all there, on the quay throwing flowers onto the ship. The German children, strangely, we got on better with than the Polish. The war was now over, they weren't to blame and we thought it might do a bit of good.

EDUARD WINKLER

PRISONER OF WAR

Eduard Winkler served with the German Air Force and was captured by the British in March 1945. He was held at camps in France, Belgium and England until 1948.

We were treated perfectly well until we lost the war completely – until the surrender. When the surrender came we didn't get any more razor blades, cigarettes or soap. That was one of the things that rather surprised us. The change in treatment was quite sudden. Before, we used to get tins of 50 cigarettes, razor blades, soap, which was very good for bargaining with the French people – Lux soap – and exchanged it for bread or whatever. I started a bit of a business at the camp at Ranville in France. I sold soap and asked the chappie there to get me some flints for lighters in exchange. I made lighters and sold them to the German POWs who were drivers and had the opportunity to sell petrol to the French farmers. From there they sent us to a camp, non-working, in Belgium. We couldn't get out. This was the worst experience of my life. We got very little food, hardly anything to drink and we lost a lot of weight. I came in to that camp as a fairly fit German paratrooper. When I came to England, I'd lost several stone and I used to lay down to comb my hair. The commandant of the camp was a

The Allied Safe Conduct Pass, or Passierschein, *one of the most effective leaflets of the war, was dropped from 1944 onwards in German-occupied zones. This surrender pass, deliberately designed as an official document to appeal to German soldiers, was developed by the Psychological Warfare Division of SHAEF.*

German Jew, who had joined the British Army. He was saying he was going to give us the rations which the German Jews had had in the last few days at Bergen-Belsen, or wherever. We used to get a small pound loaf of bread and we had to divide it by 16 men in the morning. We had one flat teaspoonful of jam to divide, by 16 people. For dinner we used to get dishes of potatoes which were not permitted to be washed, peeled or anything. No salt, just potatoes boiled and we had beetroot or leek flavouring. For every hundred men there was one tin of corned beef added to the stew. We got tea but it was not enough to satisfy most of our thirsts. We were always happy for the rains because we could soak up some water. There were people even going to the latrine and sucking the moisture out of there. It was winter time and in this place I actually had a taste of a bit of rat and pigeon. Somebody had caught a rat. We were stuck in the barracks and we couldn't move, we weren't very keen to move, most of the time we were laying down.

KENNETH AMBROSE

FRONT LINE

Kenneth Ambrose was a German Jewish schoolchild living in Stettin, Germany. After escaping Germany he went on to serve with the RAF and the British Bombing Survey in Great Britain and north-west Europe. He returned to Germany after the Allied victory.

I was very conscious of the way that I was in charge now, and that they [the Germans] were now bowing and scraping. Before the war I had to keep out of their way, now I could walk on the pavement and it was they who would have to step into the road if there wasn't enough room. If a train was full, it was now all the Germans who were made to crowd together in one part of the train. We, as the foreign occupying army, had lots of room and travelled in comfort in another part of the train. I felt there was some poetic justice in that and I did say so at the time. They are not very nice feelings, but nevertheless that's what they were. Although I was invariably polite to the Germans, I nevertheless made it clear who was in control now.

The greatest puzzle was that all the Nazis had suddenly disappeared – 'nobody's ever been a Nazi, we had to join the party but I'm not a Nazi, never have been, we love the Jews, some of my best friends were Jews before the war' – I was considered half ambassador, half servant, half social worker for the Jews.

We were closer to my mother's family and we found out from one of the ten survivors who wrote up about as much as he knew of what had happened to the group when they were deported. We found that in 1942 they'd disappeared in *'Achtung'* as the Germans called it, a mass shooting. Of course, a few of them, including the person who had written the report, had hidden away. They heard the shooting, so I did know what was happening by then.

HANNA ZBIROHOWSKA-KOSCIA

PRISONER OF WAR

Hanna Zbirohowska-Koscia was liberated from Oberlangen prison camp in 1945, aged 17, and rescued by her mother, a member of the Polish Underground Movement.

Of course I was very happy that the war ended. But for me, who was only 17 at the time, it was a time of great contradiction. I could say I would like to go home, but my home didn't exist any more. My family comes from eastern Poland, which was occupied by Russians.

The liberation of Oberlangen in April – but outside its confines the war continued. On one of the 'joyrides', pictured, the liberators got carried away and took the girls beyond the camp, where two were sadly murdered by German soldiers.

Previous pages: Thousands
of German prisoners of
war are marched through
the Fatherland.

I heard the news on the radio, through the megaphones at the POW camp at Oberlangen. Every morning we had our roll call, we had to stand in front of our barracks, and the commandant read the orders and we would say our prayers or sing. It was announced on such an occasion that the war had ended, and of course it was hip-hooray and a happy occasion. But the war had not yet ended for me, and I was not the only one.

In 1941 I had joined the Polish Guides at the age of 13. But the atmosphere was such that everybody wanted to do something and get involved. We were trained in first aid and as couriers. We had to get to know all the secret passages and eventually prepare for the rising in 1944. That was what we were really looking forward to. I survived somehow, but it was not easy. My superior had to choose where to send us to survive and I was chosen to go to prison camp. I didn't want to leave Poland, I was happy to be there – well, maybe happy isn't the right word, but it was important to me. They took us to Oberlangen, near Meppen. It was not really a concentration camp, but a camp where people were punished for something.

It was very lucky that the Polish 1st Division Army liberated our camp. The Front was coming forward, but because we were so near the Netherlands frontier we could hear the Germans blowing up bridges on the canals. We heard the artillery, we heard everything. We waited and finally they came. It was marvellous, the sun was setting and a Polish tank approached and burst through the four layers of barbed wire. It was an extremely happy occasion. But as far as I knew, my mother was in Auschwitz. In fact, she had been evacuated to Bergen-Belsen, which I think was the worst concentration camp you could be in, you were starved to death. All I knew was that she was somewhere in Germany and I had to find her. It was so difficult to imagine how to move. Germany had been so badly destroyed.

My mother was at Bergen-Belsen when the war ended. She could hardly stand on her feet, but immediately she tried to collect and verify the ladies who had survived and who had been in the Polish Underground Movement. She asked the liaison officer who was heading towards Oberlangen to take her with him. So she came and she, of course, went to the lady in charge and asked about all the women who used to be in the Underground Army and so on here. I was walking on those marshes where I would spend hours. I had such a longing to be free. And my friends called to me, 'Come, your mother is here.' I thought, what a joke, how could it be? I couldn't recognise her, she was so changed. When people are starved they have liquid in their faces which causes blisters, her hair was cut short and she was of course very thin. She never was very big, but this was different. And she used to sing beautifully, but her voice changed because she had such a throat illness. We were very happy to meet and thankful to have both survived.

We soon began to discuss what to do next. She said there are so many camps in Germany with Polish prisoners, not only from the Warsaw uprising, but political or otherwise, sent to labour camps. So she intended, fragile as she was that she wanted to travel around Germany and pick up those people. It was really amazing – her attitude, her sense of duty and her realisation that these people needed help, because in those civilian camps they didn't have any hope. They were fed somehow, they had a roof over their heads but it was a kind of stagnation. She explained to the Polish authorities what she wanted to do, but I wouldn't let her go on her own. We didn't have any transport so we had to hitch-hike with lorries or military vehicles. We travelled around Germany with a list of people and contacts – there was a big POW camp in Lübeck, we went to the place where the survivors of Belsen and lots of friends were staying, near Lüneberg. We went back to Oberlangen from where we were moved nearby to Nierderlangen. There we found my two friends from eastern Poland, who crossed the border as we did and went to the same underground school in Warsaw. We heard news that my father had not got out of Russia. It was such a blow to my mother; she had trusted that he would be strong and that he would survive. This trust had helped her to survive as well. I felt I mustn't leave her, especially after the news of my father. We discussed the idea of going back to Poland but she said she was still on duty, that the war may have officially ended, but not for us.

BILL GLÜCK

CONCENTRATION CAMP

Bill (originally Bela) Glück, a Hungarian-speaking Jew from Romania, was imprisoned in Auschwitz-Birkenau and then Muhldorf concentration camps in 1944, aged 13.

At the last stop we were relieved when the doors were finally opened amid much noise and mayhem. Prisoners in striped uniforms screamed at us and forcefully dragged the weak and old out of the wagons. I saw smartly dressed SS guards whacking at people with heavy walking sticks in order to make us move faster — 'Schnell! Schnell!' ('Faster! Faster!'). We were herded into two lines — one for men, the other for women. We did not know what was at the head of the line.

My father kept me in front of him and told me to make

myself appear taller. When it was my turn to be in front of the officer, I told him I was 17 years old, a tinsmith by trade and a good worker. It was a lie on all three counts. My father theorised that as long as we were of some use to them, they might keep us alive a bit longer. It worked. The officer looked down at me, smiled, shook his head, and sent me to the right. As I was running I looked back and saw my father behind me. That gave me some comfort, but soon I was separated from him and put into a group with other boys about my age.

The Glück family before the war. Bill (left) and his brother Ernest are in the front, behind them their great-grandfather, then over 100 years old.

I was 13 years old, the youngest of the three children in my family. It was the first time I had been separated from my mother. Suddenly I found myself alone, lost in that inexplicable hell and completely bewildered. I began to cry as soon as I had a moment to myself. In spite of the masses of people around me, I was all alone. I must have fallen asleep, because suddenly I was dragged out of my bunk by two large prisoners. They held me by the shoulders, ran me out of the barracks screaming very loudly and shaking me like a rag.

Outside they put me in a line of people waiting their turn to get some food. They gave me a metal dish, ordered me to get in line every time I saw food being given out and to eat it all no matter how vile it might be. They also told me to never cry again. I was petrified of them. When they were satisfied that I was really paying attention, they softly told me that I looked like a strong and resilient boy and therefore I must do everything in my power to survive and tell the world what happened to our people in Auschwitz-Birkenau. I never saw them again. I have no idea who they were. All I know is that they spoke Yiddish.

That was my introduction to the infamous Auschwitz-Birkenau concentration camp, where I remained for a few weeks. I quickly learned which buildings were the gas chambers and the crematoria. The very tall chimneys were spewing foul smelling smoke, day and night, night and day, without end. When I first inquired about those chimneys, I was told that they were part of the crematorium.

'What's a crematorium?' I asked.

'That's where your parents were gassed and burned,' came the answer. I was stunned.

I was soon given a prisoner number, 'processed', and sent with a large group to Mühldorf concentration camp, a work camp. Our task was to build an underground cement aircraft maintenance bunker. That camp did not need gas chambers — people were dying quicker than flies. We were fed below the minimum calories required for normal existence, and were forced to work very hard. Beatings, injuries and diseases made people succumb at a rapid rate.

Being smaller than the average prisoner had its advantages; I could exist better on the meagre amount of food received. The disadvantage was that I could not hold my own when it came to physical altercations. I quickly became 'camp smart' and learned the rules of survival. All my attention was focused on survival — every day, every hour, and every minute. After a while, I knew that I could survive for a long time.

Josef Glück, Bill's father, in 1945, age 49.

At times, however, I wasn't sure if I wanted to survive. I wasn't sure if I wanted to return to a hostile world. I didn't have much reason to hope that anyone else from my family would survive. In spite of all this, I had a great urge to push on and to survive. I was very careful not to exert more energy than I absolutely had to and I certainly didn't want to help the German war effort. Sometimes, I was able to barter things to get more food. I was able to secure additional warm clothing and some Polish army boots.

On 25 April 1945 they loaded many of us into cattle cars again, and transported us towards an unknown destination for mass execution. We sent some prisoners to make a deal with the officer in charge. We asked him to take us towards the oncoming American forces, instead of the execution site. In turn we guaranteed him safe passage as soon as we reached the American forces. If he had not agreed, he would most likely have been executed as a war criminal. We were very lucky that he agreed.

Our train stopped near a small station and waited. In the morning we found our guards had all disappeared. People drained of all strength lay in the wagons. I searched for some food nearby, but there was nothing. I had a quiet conversation with a young man sitting next to me. I looked into his eyes and I knew he would die soon. We spoke of unimportant, trivial things — as if we didn't have a care in the world. He had the appearance of a man who had made peace with the idea of dying. He looked at death as an escape from the kind of life he had known. At dusk, he got up and slowly walked into the nearby woods. I did not follow, but found him in the morning, sitting, slightly covered with snow, his head resting on his arm over a fallen tree. He looked as if he had just sat down for a nap.

At dawn, on 1 May 1945, we saw a column of tanks approaching in the valley below us. Someone recognised the white, five-star markings on them and let out a very loud scream: 'Americans!' Those who could ran down the embankment. Others rolled down toward the tanks, which had stopped moving and turned their gun turrets in our direction. We kept running in spite of the guns aimed at us.

They gave us rations and emptied their pockets and gave us chocolate. They told us in Yiddish or in German that they had to move on, but that another column would look after us. Some of our group died from over-stuffing their stomachs. The doctor who came in the next column had his soldiers collect our food and fed us with controlled amounts of soup until he thought we could be transported to a nearby military hospital.

We arrived at the hospital on 4 May. German military doctors and nurses were there to receive us. They took our lice-ridden clothes, disinfected us, and bathed those who could not bathe themselves. They put ointment on our rotting bodies and gave us light brown pyjamas to wear, all under the watchful eyes of American military personnel. On 7 May we received a 5-kilogram box of food from the Americans. There is no way to explain how grateful I was then, and still am, to the kind Americans who saved us from certain starvation.

Official documentation permitting father and son to return to their home in Satu Mare, originally part of Romania but transferred to Hungary in 1940 on the orders of Hitler.

As soon as we were able to be on our feet we were moved to Feldafing Displaced Persons camp. Our group was easily recognised because we all wore the same brown pyjamas until we received regular clothes later. People recovered their health slowly. Some never recovered mentally, others did not want to. I and other young people fared better. We stayed in large spacious barracks and had ample food. After the concentration camp all food tasted great. We could never get enough of it. At the beginning, we constantly searched for more food. We needed it mentally and felt we could never have enough. Slowly, I came to be less anxious about having enough food for tomorrow.

I discovered a small group of boys my own age. We were drawn together like magnets. We only trusted one another and came to rely on each other for support. We were ready to defend each other at any cost. The only people we respected were the Americans. The only orders we were ready to obey were the American Military Police. We moved around freely in the DP camp and even in the German cities. We were rough and troubled. We were not afraid of anyone or anything.

The Munich railway station was always teeming with different people, remnants from the war. We often got into vicious fights there. We were an embarrassment to many adults in the DP camp, who were keen to return to a 'normal' life and to start over again. We were loose cannons with no family or reputations to worry about. Luckily, one of the survivors, a Hungarian ex-boxing champion, got a hold of us. He trained us and made us fight in the ring. Soon there were boxing matches between the DP camps. Now all our attention was focused on winning and on pleasing our coach. He was great, tireless and we respected him.

One day one of the boys came to tell me that he had noticed a survivor named Josef Glück posted on one of the lists. 'Could he be your father?' he asked. It was the dream and fervent hope of everyone who made it through the concentration camps that by some miracle they would find at least one member of their family alive.

Word spread quickly in the camp. Everyone was excited to learn of the outcome — everyone except me. I could not understand what the fuss was about. I knew my father was a decent man and that he deserved to live, but I was unable to care about anybody at that time. When we finally met I could hardly recognise him. The old dirty jacket he was wearing hung half empty on him. His bony shoulders were bent over from the strain of starvation and suffering. I could see that he had difficulty standing. I recognised his sparkling eyes that radiated with happiness when he saw me. He hugged me and began to cry. I could not understand why he was crying. Many in the crowd were crying as well — but not me. I was standing like a log when my father hugged me. I was completely devoid of any emotion or feelings. My father was still holding me when I realised something was wrong with me.

After a while, I began to spend more time with my gentle father and less with the boys. I lived with the group a bit longer and then decided to stay with my father. He was wise and had all the patience I needed as I tried to pull myself together. We began to make plans for our return to our home in Hungary.

UNKNOWN

HOME FRONT

This testimony is from a German-speaking civilian from Sudetenland, Czechoslovakia, suffering the reprisals from Czech forces upon Germany's surrender.

The robbings and beatings began at dawn on the 9th [of May]. The Czechs, punctilious as always to the letter of the law, did not attack us during the night of the 8th/9th even though the war had ended and we were their captives.

The *Reichsdeutsche* and *Volksdeutsche* were marched away and we Sudeten Germans, about five hundred in number, were soon alone. The men were separated from the women and children. We all had to stand in ranks and we had been standing there for some time when groups of partisans walked through our ranks and selected men at random and led them away behind some carts. There were shots heard and the Czechs came back and laughed at our fear. Then they picked out fresh victims. There were about twenty in number. This group was ordered to kneel down in front of the rest of us – about 50 yards in front of us. There was a clicking of bolts then one of the partisans swung the barrel of his rifle along the line of kneeling men. He fired. One of the men fell forward. Another partisan stepped up and traversed his rifle along the line of men now shaking with fear. There was another shot but this time nobody fell. The partisan had deliberately aimed wide of his target. A third Czech pointed his rifle and pulled the trigger. There was no explosion. He roared with laughter. He had not loaded the gun. It was a huge joke. Then a fourth partisan fired and killed a man from my own village. So it went on. How long we stood there while they slowly selected their victims in that line and tormented them before murdering them, I do not know. Eventually, all the twenty or so were dead.

DANUTA KUJAWINSKA

REFUGEE

Danuta, bottom left, with her mother, top left, aunt and cousin.

Danuta Kujawinska (née Wojtowicz), of Stolin in eastern Poland, was eight years old at the outbreak of war.

I was born and brought up in Stolin in the east of Poland (as it was before the Second World War). There, we were subjected to the Soviet invasion in September 1939. One night, soon after war broke out, my father was arrested by Russian soldiers and imprisoned. He was interrogated and beaten up (he had his teeth knocked out when he refused to confess to false conspiracy charges), before disappearing from the prison in Stolin around six months later. My mother was left with my two sisters, Irena and Ela, and me. I was eight years old at the time, Irena was six and Ela was a few months old having been born in April 1939. We lived under Russian occupation for two years until Hitler broke the Nazi–Soviet pact in 1941. After this, the Russians retreated and the Nazis took over our town. We lived under Nazi occupation until early 1944.

At the beginning of 1944 we were rounded up by German soldiers and taken in horse-drawn trailers from our home to the train station, where, along with many other people, including my mother's sister and her two girls, we were loaded into cattle trucks that would take us to Germany. It took about a week to get to Berlin, where we spent some weeks in a transitional camp, until we were transported once again.

And so, at the end of the war my mother, aunt, two sisters, two cousins and I found ourselves in a little German village called Heinrichsberg, about 15 miles from Magdeburg. We had been sent there to work the land of the local estate, along with other Poles and a handful of Russians; there were a hundred or so of us in total. We lived in very basic huts in the village and our work was seasonal farm labour: sowing, thinning, harvesting. We were always overseen by one or other of the German supervisors, some of whom were kind to us, offering the children sweets and chocolates and letting us take it easy if the master of the estate was not around; whilst some could be quite brutal, administering a sharp slap or a whack on the back with a wooden stick if our work was not satisfactory. We cleaned out storehouses and stables in the winter when there was nothing to do outside. I worked with my mother, my aunt and elder cousin, Halina, while my younger sister, Irena, stayed in the hut to look after the young children, Ela and Krystyna.

Just before the war ended, a kind German lady who lived nearby and whose husband was an SS officer working away fighting the Allies, came in secret to our hut to tell us that next time the sirens go off for a long time (at least five minutes), it will be a sign that the war is over. My aunt spoke a little German and was able to understand.

One day, in April 1945, we were in one of the fields of the estate thinning sugar beet seedlings with hoes with handles that were only six inches long – it was backbreaking work – when all of a sudden the sirens went off. Normally we would have assumed that they signalled an air raid and would have dashed for cover, but in this case the sirens went on and on and on. We knew then that we had been liberated.

The workers cried out and jumped for joy. The German supervisor just looked at us. We dropped our tools and went into the village. The village was deathly silent and we did not see a soul. No one really knew what was going on, least of all me.

A group photo of workers on the estate in Heinrichsberg. Thirteen-year-old Danuta sits immediately to the left of the estate supervisor, centre. Above is the Arbeitsbuch, or workbook, used to keep track of foreign labourers in Germany.

Soon we noticed a man at the top of the hill just outside the village. He was waving a huge white sheet. My mother and my aunt burst into tears. I asked them why they were crying. They answered because we were free.

We went back to our huts and waited. A day or two later, American tanks rolled into the village. We showered them with flowers we had picked from nearby gardens. We were free to do this because there was not a single German around. They must have fled. The Americans installed themselves in the village. They were very friendly and most kind. They took whoever wanted to go to the manor house of the estate, to the cellars where there were stores and stores of food: of jams and preserves and all sorts of sausages. They told us to just help ourselves and take and eat as much as we wanted. This was most welcome after our diet of primarily peas and potatoes. Although we occasionally managed to supplement this by stealing a little flour from the store and once, my sister Irena, who was a real little tomboy, actually stole a tiny piglet from the swineherd's flock in the field adjacent to the estate, and she killed it for us to eat. We roasted it on the open hearth in our hut.

I remember one American soldier in particular who came to our hut to check on us. He played with the toddlers and picked them up. He took out a picture of a little girl and showed it to us. I think he was showing us his daughter. I recall he spoke a few words of Polish (his father may have been Polish). I admired his fine-looking wristwatch, which he took off and very generously presented to my youngest sister Ela. I have always retained a great fondness for Americans for their hand in our liberation.

We did not stay in Heinrichsberg for long after that. We were taken back to the station at Magdeburg, which I had thought so beautiful on our way to Heinrichsberg, but which now lay in ruins. Our next destination was to be a Displaced Persons camp near Hildesheim. There, we were fed and clothed by UNRA (United Nations Relief and Rehabilitation Administration), which had been formed by the United States in 1943.

While the war may have ended, there was no way that we could go back to the life we had before the war. My father had disappeared; every time my mother had made enquiries with the Red Cross as to his whereabouts she had received the same answer, that he was missing, presumed dead. And we had nowhere to go. So we stayed in the camp, which was called Trillke-Werke. The camp was like a little village. It became a real hive of industry while it was being decided what was to be done with everybody. Those who had relatives abroad in England, France or America, for example, were able to go there to join them, while those without waited for transport back to Poland. My family fell into the latter grouping, though, at that age, I was not aware of the political situation in Poland and the fact that the town we came from would no longer be in Poland. In the meantime, the educated, professional Poles in the camp set up courses to give us youngsters some schooling. I had had one year of school in Poland before the war, a couple of years in school under the Soviets (in Russian) and then the Nazis closed down the schools. So I was 15 years old and barely literate. In Trillke-Werke I completed a three-month crash course to obtain a certificate confirming I had a junior school education and another to confirm I had the first year of high school. It was good to have these certificates, even though I had nothing in my head! A choir was set up, as was a drama society and I took part in both. We put on a play about the uprising in Warsaw in 1944. The director was a real theatre director from Warsaw, whose wife was a ballerina. I played the leading female role: an AK (*Armia Krajowa*/Polish Home Army) operative whose code-name was Wanda. (The director said he thought I had talent.) During the course of the play I was shot by a German soldier and fell 'dead' on the stage, at which point my youngest sister Ela, who was in the audience (and seven years old by that time), stood up and started crying and yelling that someone had killed Danusia, her sister!

We stayed in the DP camp for about a year and a half. I had a most memorable Christmas at the end of 1946 because of what was about to unfold. One day in December that year, a woman from the choir called to say she had a nice Christmas present for me. I asked why she had not brought it to me. She said it was too heavy to carry, but she would take me to collect it. She introduced me to a man dressed in a Polish soldier's uniform. I did not recognise him, but it was my father, whom I had not seen for seven years. From a child of eight I had become a young lady, I was 15 years old, so he had some difficulty recognising me too. It was a very emotional moment.

While happy endings are always good, life is often too complicated to allow too many. The reason my father asked to see me, not my mother, was because when he arrived at the camp that he had traced us to, someone had already told him that my mother had re-married and was having a baby. After he had seen me, he asked to see my mother. They talked and talked for hours and hours and my mother cried and cried. My father had proposed that he take us all to start a new life in England, on condition that she abort the child she was carrying and leave everything else behind. She could not agree to abort the baby, so she was to return to Poland after all, with her new family. Ela, she argued, was too young to leave her mother and would go too. Irena and I were deemed old enough to make up our own minds: we could go back to Poland with our mother, or follow our father to a new life in England. Which is what we did.

JULIA FLEISCHER

CONCENTRATION CAMP

In May and June 1945 the tables were turned on the German-speaking population of Czechoslovakia, who formed a significant minority of the overall population. From being masters they became the hunted and were threatened by the understandably vengeful Czech majority with confiscation, internment and expulsion.

This affected Maria Bondi, a 74-year-old widow in Brno, the second town of Czechoslovakia, particularly cruelly. Though she was a German-speaking Austrian Catholic, her late husband, Gustav, the longstanding secretary and deputy director of the local German theatre, had been Jewish. Not long after his death in May 1941, her only son, Willi, a homosexual, was executed in Auschwitz and between November 1941 and March 1942 her three daughters were sent with their families, either to Poland, where they were all exterminated, or to the concentration camp at Theresienstadt in northern Bohemia. The camp was liberated on 7 May, the day when her eldest daughter Hermine, known as Minna, died of typhus. By the end of May only one daughter, Julia, known as Ully, who had just learnt of her son's death in the last days of the war, and two granddaughters survived. One *had fled to Palestine in 1940; the other, her sister Helga, was still critically ill with typhus in Theresienstadt where Ully was nursing her.*

It was precisely in these days that anti-German measures were enacted. They were to culminate a few weeks later in a forced march of the German-speaking population, regardless of age and health, to the Austrian border in the course of which many hundreds were to die of hunger, brutality and disease. Marie would undoubtedly have been among them and, though she was saved from expulsion, until her death in 1952 she had to pretend to be a deaf mute whenever she left her flat.

The first letter was secretly sent to Ully, who was still in Theresienstadt, by Ernst and Stefanie Back, a mixed race, Aryan/Jewish couple who had befriended Marie Bondi during the long years when she had been left alone in Brno. The second is from Ully to her friend Willi Neubauer, a refugee in London.

1 June 1945

Dear Madam Ully

Conditions here are such that there is a danger that your mother could lose her flat and be subjected to all the measures affecting the Germans. We've done what we can to protect her from being sent to a concentration camp.

If you are to protect and spare your mother from the upset, you absolutely have to come to Brno at once with the documents proving that you were interned in Theresienstadt for so long. These documents open doors everywhere and of course the advantages extend to your mother.

You have to come at once: I can't conceal from you that your mother is distressed by all of these upsets and even thinks of committing suicide.

We are doing what we can but only you can sort these problems out once and for all – and you can get them officially sorted out at once.

We know perfectly well that Helgele is ill, but your presence in Brno is absolutely essential. Take a few days off and come here. After you have sorted things out you can rush back to Theresienstadt and Helga immediately and also get everything sorted out there.

I'm writing this without your mother's knowledge since, out of her great love and understanding for you, she accepts that you would rather stay with Helga. Please come!
With heartfelt greetings and respect

Ernest and Stefanie Back
[Brno, 25 August 1945]

Dear Willi

The first written information from me after a row of years, and the second letter that I have written in three and a half years. A human lifetime is too short to endure what we have been through – and are still going through. But the ending and coming home were the worst: [my niece] Helga and I alone, no brother, no sisters, no nephews and nieces and, most frightful of all, without my boy! No living male or female friends. It would have been much better if we had all been victims of the extermination, since we will, hopefully, not live long enough to become capable of leading normal lives again.

First and foremost, thank you for your act of friendship – the first I've had – but please, no more. You can be sure that if I need anything I shall turn to you, the only friend from old times who is left. But please, please write to me whenever you have time because at the moment that is the best help of all. We ought, after all, to slowly awaken to life. Perhaps that sounds a little exaggerated, but you know me. A lot of guts are needed to carry on and first of all I should support my poor mother and secondly we have no gas, which is as well .

Clockwise from top: Leo, Harry, Eschi, Sylvia. None survived the transportations out of Czechoslovakia.

In July 1939 [my husband] Bruno died and with that my calvary began. In March 1941 [my brother] Willi and I were imprisoned, charged with high treason for supporting the Communist Party. They released me but poor Willi was there until August and then he was gassed in Auschwitz. On 22 August, two days before my birthday, my mother got the telegram. On 11 May 1941 my father died from grief at Willi's imprisonment: he foresaw everything. I wasn't stuck in prison for long but my impressions of it were so bad that I had scarcely recovered before I was faced, uncomprehendingly, with the other happenings. [My younger sister] Eschi's family moved in with me and that was very good. [Her husband] Leo lost his job immediately because his partner fled to London and he was blamed for everything. At that time I still had all my male and female friends. [Your wife] Rega was with us almost the whole time. She was in excellent health. We lived together like a big family – we weren't allowed to go anywhere any more and so people met up in our place.

In 1942 began the transports. First Act of Kuhreigen. Eschi with Leo and the children [Sylvia and Harry] went on the first transport. You can imagine the parting. We knew it would be for a long, long time but nobody said it out loud. Sylvia hung to my neck; I could not separate myself from that child. Eschi, as ever,

very plucky and the backbone of the family. Our feelings on remaining behind are indescribable. In the meanwhile we had to prepare everything for the next transport. I was at work from dawn to dusk because the German [Aryan administrator of my business] would not let me out and I also had to earn money. Rega made gloves for everyone; we all had the same outfit. [My sister] Minna and [her daughter] Helga went in the second transport and Rega in the next. I was alone. Of course you knew Rega. She comforted me and somehow we were glad when we knew for certain that we would be going, since waiting, and not knowing when it would be our turn was very unsettling. At that time [my 17-year-old son] Karli was working as a volunteer at the Oslawan coalmine and because of that we were still protected from being sent on a transport. He had a frightful attack of *Formikulose* but after that he went on working. In March 1942 the team at

Oslawan – and so the boy and I – were deported. My mother was left quite, quite alone. She was standing at a street corner when she saw us for the last time, since, as an Aryan, she was forbidden to walk in the street with us.

I knew I would be going to Minna in Terezin [Theresienstadt] and hoped to see Rega, so I just let pass all the trickery surrounding the allocation of lodgings. All my acquaintances were on the same transport and they were all really nice to me. Immediately on my arrival in Terezin I learnt that Rega had been sent on to Poland eight days earlier. She had often been with Minna and was in splendid health and quite contented since at that time things were easier in Poland than in Terezin, where we were sleeping in stables. For the whole of the time until our liberation we did not know what happened in Poland later. The later transports were sent straight to Auschwitz and, if you were not immediately gassed, it

Top: Julia, on the right, with her mother Marie Bondi and her son Karli in 1942. Karli is wearing the compulsory Star of David.
Bottom: A family holiday near Brno, Czechoslovakia, in 1933, in easier times. Willi Neubauer and Julia Fleischer are on the right.

happened to you six months later. The ovens burnt day and night and no-one knew whether they would still see the evening. So I did not speak to Rega again. I often saw Ossi from a distance when we were led out to work. Then he too was sent on a transport with Neugasser and again many of our acquaintances. I often spoke to your mother. She came to me in the hospital when she needed anything: we had more soup and also bread, and Karli also worked in the kitchen. She really missed Rega, but we always comforted ourselves with the prospect of a speedy end to the war. In 1943 there were a few transports of old people and your mother was on one of them. She came to say goodbye to me and I gave her Sana bread and sugar. So you don't need to worry: she was not hungry on the journey. What happened afterwards you can well imagine. It was fortunate that the old people went into the gas chambers immediately: i.e. they were sent to the baths and had no idea: instead of water, gas came out of the pipes. It would certainly have been better for us if they had gassed us at once rather than letting our decent young people starve.

Skeletons arrived in Terezin in May – that is, at the end of the war. Skeletons with typhus, and perhaps I took my boy [Karli] off the train without recognising him any more. He went into hospital in Leitmeritz, two kilometres from Terezin, in the middle of March with typhus and that was it. No one knows whether he died in Leitmeritz or was brought to us at the beginning of May as a corpse. We nurses had orders to empty these transports. The living were so hungry that they guzzled the corpses so that we only carried off half-corpses. The stretcher men who helped us vomited at the sight of this – there were no humans left. Karli went with the general workers transport at the beginning of September to Kauffering near Munich via Auschwitz. At the end of December 1944 he [had] volunteered for Leitmeritz in order to be nearer to me and we had no idea that he was only two kilometres from the camp. If only he had lived three weeks longer, he would have been saved. And I have been kept back and am so unhappy that every evening I pray that I will not have to see the morning, despite mother and despite Helga. You know what the boy was to me and I cannot grasp that I must go on living without him.

In the end either when emptying the transports or while nursing the patients, Minna herself got infected with typhus and even though I sat with her day and night and was given leave to nurse her, she died eleven days later on the day the camp was liberated. We had nursed people side-by-side for three and a half years in the Hospital for Infectious Diseases. In that time we nursed people with all the illnesses that a man can have or could possibly catch and on the last day she was the first nurse, endangered by these transports, to be sacrificed – anyway the majority of the doctors and nurses believed this to be the case. And I who had lost everything did not die! I returned to the hospital from Minna's deathbed (Minna was in the isolation hospital outside the ghetto) and found Helga down with typhus the next day – so more nursing. Day and night in the hospital. Hope for Helga given up, then things went better again and after 14 days she was out of danger. In the meantime I was bitten twice by fleas, had a temperature of 38–39 degrees, a day in bed, no nurses and then I got up and went back to duty. But the Russian commandant was fabulous. We finally got food – we were frightfully starved.

After 14 days I received one telegram after the other saying that I must go home to help Mama. She was classified as a German. So I was taken in a military car to Prague and from there, after three and a half years, alone, back to Brno. Can you imagine my poor mother?! Three and a half years of bravery, quite, quite alone and now me, who is supposed, above all else, to comfort her without knowing what was to happen now. Absolutely no living friends. On top of that, two weeks ago I got further information about Eschi and her sufferings. Leo died immediately after the transport and Eschi was shot with both children in 1943. Can you remain normal when you think about it? They aimed at my Sylvia and shot her. Eschi and Harry would have been brave – but poor little, trembling Sylvia! At least my mother doesn't know about it, and I won't tell her and so she is still expecting Eschi and children to come back. And I let her believe it.

Tomorrow, Saturday 26 August, Minna's urn, which I fetched from Terezin, will be placed next to Papa. I'll be glad when the day has passed, because I am always glad when a day goes by again and I am nearer the end. I have lost 40 kilograms and I'll write to you about my achievements as a nurse next time. Enough for today. I'm writing in my office that should belong to me again.

Heartiest greetings

Your old

Ully

ERWIN GRUBBA

Erwin Grubba was born in 1925 in eastern Prussia. He ended the war in Guernsey before being taken prisoner by British forces.

My father never voted anything but the Centre Party. He never voted for the Nazis, in fact he wouldn't even have a picture of Hitler in the house. He once took me on a walk in the woods near Berlin where we rented a small cottage and said 'I tell you one thing, this is going to be the story of the apocalypse because this fellow is going to bring us to war and disaster.' In our house my mother bought from Jewish shops on principle and I had a Jewish dentist and a Jewish doctor.

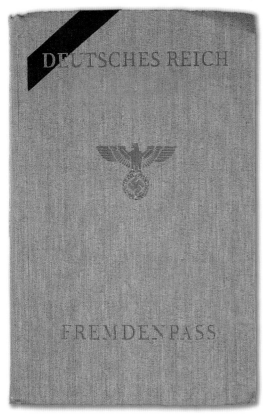

Channel Islanders were issued with German identity documents during the occupation between 1940 and 1945.

My school had no National Socialism. In fact, the teaching staff was like my father, all old Conservatives. We had no pictures of Hitler in the classroom, but there was one somewhere in the corridor near the assembly hall, just to go through the motions. I was with the Church Youth Movement and had good friends there. We always cracked all the anti-Hitler jokes that were circulating in Berlin; in a small town that would have been impossible. I used to stand up with a little comb to make a moustache, brush my hair down and imitate Adolf Hitler, because I was good at imitating voices.

The night before I was called up, the RAF paid us a visit and wiped us off the map in Berlin. We were in the cellar fortunately as the whole caboodle crashed on top of us. We had to tunnel our way out. We made it, and father had already made in the front garden a small trench like the First World War trenches – it was safer than the house actually – and we made a dash into there with what we were wearing. Singed shirts and smoky clothes, and that was it.

The next morning I had to report to the barracks. That was August 1943. Remember by that time they were taking almost anybody with two legs and two arms as cannon fodder for the Eastern Front. I think if I had four weeks that would be the maximum training, just enough to throw hand grenades, fire a rifle, learn how to cut barbed wire, and then we had to take an oath of loyalty to Hitler the day before we were shipped out - which I didn't, well, I mean I stood there as well but I didn't move my lips, I wasn't going to repeat that. I was lucky to be selected for duty in Guernsey. 'Yippee,' I thought, 'the Channel Islands are British, aren't they? Oh, it couldn't be better.'

Soon it became clear that the invasion was imminent. Everybody expected it. You could tell by the build-up of the bombing. They came over in hordes, like locusts, unloading stuff in northern France. When D-Day came, we had a first-class seat free of charge, like sitting on a balcony seat in a theatre, and by jove it was impressive. The sky was black with fliers for 72 hours non-stop and artillery from those battleships, you could see them with your glasses. I knew the British were not going to come and land here. What for? To kill their own and lose more lives? For what? They have us in the bag. As soon as they are on the mainland we are cut off. Very soon even the high-ups said 'well take your tin hats off and go back to normal duties but be more alert.'

In 1944 I remember when the fellow who read the news said 'An attempt has been made on the Fuhrer's life, but fortunately his life was saved,' whereupon a voice from the ranks said 'Oh shit'.

Three German soldiers lost hope after D-Day and committed suicide. For the following few months, we waited for the war to finish. There was a severe shortage of food. My ribs were showing like a key on an accordion. In fact, one day I was on duty with my steel helmet on and probably with the pressure of the helmet I keeled over. We organised concerts, we had literary readings, even a cabaret to take our minds off things and the hours of duty were cut. For instance there was a compulsory 40 winks period in the afternoon after our so-called lunch, which was nettles boiled in sea water. I mean these are all signs of decay aren't they, when an army has to do that?

We had a great celebration on VE Day. I had to be supported by the Sergeant Major on one side and another corporal on the other to get back to my billet and to my bed, because I had knocked back the wine a bit too much.

At the beginning of June 1945, six cyclists from the Royal Artillery in Portsmouth came near our barracks and stopped as they didn't quite trust us, so I stepped forward, cheeky me as usual and said 'How do you do, have you come to collect our weapons?' 'Oh no, we were just told to patrol and see you are behaving yourselves.' I asked one what he did in civvy street and he told me he was a taxi driver, and that was my first encounter with the British forces face to face.

Shortly afterwards we were taken as POWs to Haltwhistle in Northumberland. Some voluntary organisations were still working on the platforms issuing free tea to troops returning from Europe. They thought we were British and came up to us with cups of tea and when we started talking there was a mighty big scream, 'Ah, ah Germans!' and they scattered as if someone had thrown a bomb among them, which made us roar with laughter.

As we marched towards camp, the English countryside looked so beautiful – and this is the honest truth – that without a single word of command we burst out into song, and there were hundreds of German officers singing lustily as we walked down through the South Tyne valley until we stopped and saw the castle itself, and they had cleverly hidden behind it the Nissen huts, which were going to be our home for the next three years. Then I got my first decent meal. I remember going into the canteen barrack block and holding out my plate, and half a dozen bangers were put on it! That was too much actually because with our meagre diet up till then, it almost made me ill.

The interrogation officer, who was also responsible for our re-education, was a Frankfurt Jew, who had escaped before the outbreak of war. He had to screen us to find out our opinions and he spent a lot of time with ex-Nazis who were understandably very depressed. He would tell them 'Look, you were misled by an idiot, you thought he was going to save Germany but he ruined it. Now the future is what matters and we want people who have a sense of honesty, decency and a respect for humanity.'

We had a YMCA-organised visit to the Theatre Royal in Newcastle. I liked the music of *Coppelia* but I didn't care much for the bouncing ballet. Then the manager came down in the interval and said 'I have a reporter here who would like to interview you, any objection?' I said, 'No, not at all' and there was a woman, five feet two with a nice costume, a carnation in her buttonhole and a pencil and notebook, and that was the girl I married.

CLIVE DUNN

PRISONER OF WAR

Clive Dunn is best known for his portrayal of Lance-Corporal Jones in Dad's Army. *During the war he served in the 4th Hussars. He was captured fighting in Greece and sent to Austria as a prisoner of war before being liberated by US troops.*

I woke to the unfamiliar sound of a Yankee voice repeating over and over again, 'Get inside, get inside.' The owner of this voice had tommy guns up in the watchtower to prevent prisoners from leaving the camp through a hole that had been made in the barbed wire. We were now prisoners of the Americans. I scrambled out of the tent to take a good look at my new captors as a French prisoner went through the wire.

'Get inside!' yelled the Yank.

'He doesn't understand mate,' shouted a Cockney voice, 'he's French.'

'He'll be nothing if he don't get inside.'

Within a few days some lorries arrived and we lined up to have our smelly battledress blown up with DDT dust from hosepipes. Greatly refreshed from this odd experience, we then lined up for food, food, food. Great plates of mashed potatoes and spam and apple pie were rather bemusing to our shrunken stomachs, and a wander through the village in comparative freedom refreshed the spirits in anticipation of home. The villagers kept out of sight, but some released prisoners could not resist the temptation to use confiscated guns to bully females into bed. Others used issue cigarettes as barter. But there was little around the impoverished village that anyone might covet. Although after four years of enforced abstinence I was as keen as the next to jump into bed with a girl, I had more romantic ideas in my head than a quick bunk up with a vanquished foe.

After several days travelling we landed at an airfield, which turned out to be in Belgium. We checked in, and as I ran across the field for the final leg to England, the last Dakota of the day disappeared into the sunset while I stood wondering what to do.

Back in the hangar I signed for five pounds and was told to get on the next lorry going into Brussels and be back by nine in the morning to continue the trip home. I had now chummed up with an acquaintance from the Wolfsberg camp who had also missed the last plane out. We ambled about the centre of Brussels looking for a good time. The result was, as usual, booze: we both inflicted our unaccustomed insides to liberal doses of alcohol of all sorts and ended up in some central square. I remember fuzzily asking a very tall lady if she would come and have a drink with me. She agreed straight away and led me down a side street and up the stairs of a seedy hotel, where I handed over nearly all my remaining money. The room, designed specifically for one-night stands, was full of mirrors. I told this friendly girl that I must go back to England at eight o'clock in the morning, watched her strip in front of the mirrors, and then passed out – not from shock, but from wartime brandy. A nudge from the tall girl set me blinking about the room in the morning. I kissed her goodbye, vowed eternal friendship, and found my way back to the lorry. My mate was sitting on top with a satisfied grin lighting up his face.

'How was it?' he said.

'Great,' I lied, 'really great.'

We landed at Sompting in Sussex, where we went through more categorising and questioning. That same day, I was told that due to my age group my expected release from the army was still a long way off.

'How long?'

'It depends on the war against Japan.'

My heart sank into my new army boots. I had never thought for one second that after five years I would have to serve on now. I cheered myself up by drinking pints and pints of Guinness, which my body now seemed able to absorb effortlessly. Now every sinew waited for leave, a chance to get back to my family and my old haunts in Soho that I had dreamed about over the years.

The long years of waiting for peace ended for me with a groan of relief rather than a shout of triumph. The feeling of joy evaporated with Stalin's 'Now follows a period of peace' and Churchill's 'We can allow ourselves a brief period of rejoicing.' The two conquerors were now offering us ten minutes' break. Churchill might as well have said: 'Fall out for a smoke, and then we can get on with fighting the Japanese.'

WINIFRED BASHAM

HOME FRONT

Winifred Basham's wartime diary of her life with her husband Percy, a teacher, recorded Victory in Ipswich.

MONDAY 7 MAY – Tonight it was announced that the Germans had surrendered and tomorrow is to be VE Day and Wednesday is also a holiday. Flags are going up everywhere. I can't believe it's really over.

TUESDAY 8 MAY (VE DAY) – We went into the Park and through the town to see the decorations this morning. Crowds of people were everywhere, rather

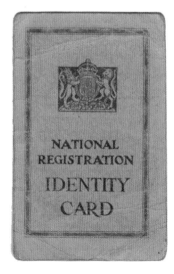

Compulsory registration of all citizens was introduced in Britain in September 1939. All civilians were issued with a National Registration Identity Card, which was carried at all times and showed the holder's name, registration number and address. The scheme lasted until Feburary 1952.

more subdued than I had expected but very happy. This afternoon we stayed in and listened to Mr Churchill and tonight to the King.

Tonight after dark everybody proceeded to go quite mad. A huge bonfire with an effigy of Hitler was lit at the bottom of the road and crowds of people danced and sang round it. Percy went but I didn't like to leave the children.

WEDNESDAY 9 MAY – There was some really good wireless this evening and we were able to indulge in baths without worrying about the siren. I still can't realise that it's over.

THURSDAY 10 MAY – Tonight came the joyful news that the basic petrol ration is to be restored. It will be lovely to be able to go places again.

TUESDAY 22 MAY – I bought myself a frock, but the prices – silk £6 to £9. I had to be content with cotton at 36/3 but plain and quite stylish.

WEDNESDAY 23 MAY – Mr Churchill has resigned and there is to be a General Election on 5 July.

FRIDAY 25 MAY – This afternoon I took Gillian to dancing, getting our basic petrol ration coupons on the way.

TUESDAY 5 JUNE – I went down before dinner and got our new ration books, having noticed that there is no queue at that time of day.

WEDNESDAY 6 JUNE – Percy went to a sale this afternoon and has bought four houses in Ranelagh Road for £920 as an investment.

TUESDAY 19 JUNE – This evening we all went to the Sports where I enjoyed meeting various old friends, including Mr Ford, just repatriated from a German POW Camp and looking very fit and manly.

TUESDAY 3 JULY – I was having a very busy morning when in walked Sonnie home on eleven days leave from near Hanover. He is looking amazingly fit.

SATURDAY 14 JULY – Japan was shelled by American warships today. The British flag flies over Berlin and tonight the street lamps are alight for the first time.

THURSDAY 26 JULY – Percy's last day as a class teacher was also the day for election results and we now have a Labour Government by a sweeping majority. Poor old Churchill. After all he has done. At school Percy was presented with a case for gramophone records with two records in it.

MONDAY 6 AUGUST – Tonight came the news of the invention of the atomic bomb and the dropping of the first one on Japan. Thank God it's our discovery.

WW2 People's War

Winston Churchill, mobbed by the huge crowds on his way to the House of Commons on VE Day.

3

'TODAY THE GUNS ARE SILENT'

GENERAL DOUGLAS MACARTHUR

By early summer, 1945, Japan's industry was virtually at a standstill. US bombers ranged almost unchallenged across her skies, her Merchant Navy lay at the bottom of the Pacific, and the few surviving units of the Imperial Navy were all but immobilised for lack of fuel. The sacrifice of the giant battleship *Yamato* on a suicide mission in April signalled the end of the fleet as an effective fighting force. American battleships bombarded targets along the Japanese coast as daily air raids pulverised the cities. Yet the Japanese continued to prepare to fight to the death in defence of their home territory.

It remains a hard truth, but the two atomic bombs dropped on Hiroshima and Nagasaki saved countless more lives than they took. The desperate resistance on Okinawa suggests what is likely to have happened had a conventional invasion taken place. Japanese die-hards remained in Burma and across many Pacific islands, the last not surrendering until 1972 on Guam. Only after the destruction of Nagasaki did the Emperor broadcast his order to 'endure the unendurable'.

In August 1945, the collapse of the Japanese Empire also signalled the end of European colonialism in Asia, although some of the powers concerned took another ten years to grasp the fact. Indian independence was on the cards long before the Indian Army won its greatest campaign in Burma, and the famous regiments that led the advance to Rangoon would soon be divided between Pakistan and India or pass into history. The advance across the Pacific had forced the US Navy to develop an ability to operate far beyond the support of shore-bases so that it ended the war with the global reach it has retained ever since.

Allied prisoners of war at Aomori near Yokohama, Japan, cheer approaching supply ships. 'The difference between being a POW in Japan and being a POW elsewhere was that there was clearly absolutely no hope of escape.' – John Brown.

WINSTON CHURCHILL, 8 MAY 1945
VICTORY BROADCAST

We may allow ourselves a brief period of rejoicing; but let us not forget for a moment the toil and efforts that lie ahead. Japan, with all her treachery and greed, remains unsubdued. The injury she has inflicted on Great Britain, the United States, and other countries, and her detestable cruelties, call for justice and retribution. We must now devote all our strength and resources to the completion of our task, both at home and abroad. Advance, Britannia! Long live the cause of freedom! God save the King!

JAMES PEMBERTON

FRONT LINE

James Pemberton was called up in March 1941 and served in the Royal Navy aboard HMS Victorious.

I JANUARY 1945 – Off to Sumatra for a month's raid. Just imagine, a month at sea and at action for most of the time. Absolutely fed up with Japs and heat and skin troubles, to say nothing of the homesickness.

6 FEBRUARY – Arrive at Freemantle, Australia. Lots of fresh fruit and presents come aboard. Very good of the Aussies.

11 FEBRUARY – Arrive Sydney and now changed from the Eastern Fleet to the new British Pacific Fleet. One thing about Britain, she is crafty, but it's hard on the men who have to stand for it. The whole world thinks this is a brand new fleet of fresh men from England. But no, it's the same men and ships who have been fighting this war from the start. Some of them aboard here were in the Battle of Jutland in the last war. If they had any thought for us they would send us home and get men out here who want to see the world and a bit of action. It's a long way from one's wife and family and it's not playing the game.

27 FEBRUARY – Sailed for God knows where.

8 MARCH – Arrive at Manus in the Admiralty Islands. A few days oiling, petrol, stores and ammo and off again steaming north.

12 MARCH – Arrive at Oulithi in the Caroline Islands. A few days, two to be exact, for oil and petrol again.

14 March – Off again, we don't know where but we know it's trouble for someone. Later Captain tells us we are going to bomb airfields in Okinawa and other Japanese islands. March, April and May we bomb and strafe airfields, oil dumps and various other things and we are pleased to know the war with Germany is coming to a close.

7 May – In again to Rhyku Islands between Japan and Formosa but weather too bad so we only get one strike off.

8 May – In again, weather better so we smacked him hard with little opposition. THANK GOD, THE WAR IS OVER.

9 May – In again to smack old yellow belly.

9 May – At 5.30 two suicide bombers hit the flight deck, one for'ard and one aft. Three dead and fourteen badly injured and burned terrible. All fires under control. Skipper makes hands put steel plates over hole in deck to try to keep aircraft flying. Doctors plead with him not to go in again tomorrow.

10 May – We go to oil and petrol for two days.

14 May – Back again. This is asking for trouble and I am frightened to death. More suicides, one just hit the fire hose with his tail and exploded in the water thank God.

14 June – Back again to oil etc. Nothing happened then until we arrived in Sydney on 6 June. Grand time in Sydney.

26 June – Left Sydney for Tokyo, this is going to be the real thing.

[Diary ends]

WW2 People's War

PRESIDENT HARRY S TRUMAN, 6 AUGUST 1945
WHITE HOUSE PRESS RELEASE

It is an atomic bomb. It is a harnessing of the basic power of the universe. The force from which the sun draws its power has been loosed against those who brought war to the Far East.

FRED NEALE

Fred Neale, of the RAF 36 Squadron bomber unit, was a British prisoner of war held by the Japanese in Nagasaki when the Americans dropped the atom bomb on the city on 9 August 1945. He had been a prisoner of war since spring 1942.

Fred Neale, on the right, with friend Joe Walker, in Singapore, 1940.

After the atom bomb we sort of regrouped on what was left of our camp. There were still guards and we had to sort of toe the line, otherwise you got beaten up anyway. The day after they dropped the bomb we went down and marched to the docks, what was left, and to see what would happen. We were severely left alone, there was nothing to work on, there was nothing left. We mooched around. I came across – and this has stuck in my mind – this woman with a baby. This poor woman, her baby was skinless and the flies... She was burnt and she was trying to feed it, and her fingers were sticking to it. What could I do? I picked up a piece of wood and fanned them to keep the flies off, until they keeled over.

During the morning we had nothing to eat or drink. Then a big black B29 flew slowly around. Under the wings were written, 'P.O.W. SUPPLIES'. We had to attract its attention. We took our rags off and spelt out, 'HELP P O W S'. They must have seen us as later a liberator came over and dropped a message using a field dressing. 'Hang on,' it read, 'We'll be back!' In the afternoon a flight came over and dropped lots of things, but we could not hold anything down. I was so sick, I rubbed some peach juice into my skin, but it attracted the flies. I had to wash it off so I jumped in the sea. One man, who was after boots, got squashed like a beetle under a parachute drop from the plane. We scraped him off the sack.

The next thing a little aircraft carrier, the *Chennang USA*, staggers in and tied up over what was left of the jetty on the other side. Then the invasion barges came across with the Marines in. To see those chaps! They must have been ten foot tall! Well I did not weigh six stone, and was all bones, gums all receded and teeth all rotten at the roots. We had no hair, left the whiskers though; I looked as if I had my head upside down. Amazingly, we suffered no radiation; Jesus must have been blowing the wind onto the land that day.

WW2 People's War

LORNA JOHNSTON

Lorna Johnston (née Whyte), an Australian army nurse stationed in Rabaul on the island of New Britain in the South Pacific, was taken to Japan as a prisoner of war when the Japanese invaded the island in 1942. She was held at Yokohama when the bomb was dropped.

We weren't close enough to see it or know anything about [the bomb]. Early next morning one of the guards came, yelling and screaming 'Parkersan, Parkersan!' (*san* was put on the end of everything) and [my friend] Kay Parker ran down and said, 'Now what do you want?' She was always just that jump ahead of the guards and they never got away with anything with Kay. She had her face slapped and she was kicked around but she would always be there on top. And she said, 'What now?' and the guard said, 'America no good, no good! One bomb, Hiroshima all gone, all gone!' And Kay said, 'I wouldn't worry about that, they've got plenty more of those up their sleeve.' And he went away disgusted.

Lorna Johnston, on the far left, in Rabaul before hostilities.

We had no war news but we figured it couldn't be long. Then the Japanese got us to enlarge one of the air raid shelters. They said 'For you, for you!' We had a very old guard, we called him Poppasan. He was really a kind old Japanese man, very good to us girls, the only kind guard we ever had. He'd been with us for a long time. He came, just after we'd dug this big air-raid shelter, and he said in broken Japanese and English: 'I have grown very fond of you girls. I am going to be asked to do something that I don't want to do. So I have decided that they will give me a position in Tokyo and I am going there.' We didn't know at the time that orders had been issued for all prisoners of war to be executed if the Allies landed. This 'air-raid shelter' was our own grave we'd been digging.

**WINSTON CHURCHILL, 6 AUGUST 1945
STATEMENT ON THE ATOMIC BOMB**

By God's mercy, British and American science outpaced all German efforts. These were on a considerable scale but far behind. The possession of these powers by the Germans at any time might have altered the result of the war...

It is now for Japan to realise in the glare of the first atomic bomb which has smitten her what the consequence will be of an indefinite continuance of this terrible means of maintaining a rule of law in the world.

This revelation of the secrets of nature long mercifully withheld from man should arouse the most solemn reflections in the mind and conscience of every human being capable of comprehension.

DR TAKASHI NAGAI

HOME FRONT

Dr Takashi Nagai was in his office at Nagasaki Medical College, only 700 metres from the centre of the atomic explosion.

The explosion of the atomic bomb came altogether unexpectedly. I saw the flash of light in the radium laboratory. Not only my present but also my past and future were blown away in the blast. My beloved students burned together in a ball of fire right before my eyes. Then I collected my wife, whom I had asked to take care of the children after my death but who now had become a bucket-full of soft ashes, from the burnt-out ruins of our house. She had died in the kitchen.

NOËL COWARD

ARMED FORCES

Noël Coward actor, singer and writer, entertained Allied troops all over the world throughout the war. He was in Liverpool when the bomb was dropped.

WEDNESDAY 8 AUGUST – The papers are full of the atomic bomb which is going to revolutionise everything and blow us all to buggery.

Not a bad idea.

FRIDAY 10 AUGUST – News that Japan has surrendered. If this is so then war is now over. I wonder how many years of *soi-disant* peace lie ahead of us. Here in Liverpool people are preparing for a little gaiety. I wish I had more feeling about it. My mind seems unable to take it all in. It has been too long and too stupid and cruel.

We shall see how sweet the face of peace looks. I cannot help visualising an inane, vacuous grin.

ROGER STANDSTEDT

FRONT LINE

Roger Stanstedt was an American NCO gunner who served with the 58th Bombardment Wing, US Army Air Force in India, China and the Pacific, 1944–45.

There were a lot of rumours that the war was going to be over pretty soon. We were wiping out the Japanese cities pretty fast. Usually what we'd do is get a briefing in the afternoon, then we'd go to eat and then we'd go to the movies. We had an outdoor movie theatre and I remember it rained every night. You'd watch war films of area battles in Europe and then as you're all primed up you'd go out on your own raid. At about eleven o'clock you'd go out to the line, get your stuff ready and take off.

We were supposed to go out to Haikeri naval arsenal when our radio man came in and said he'd heard over the radio that the war was over. Everybody in the squadron stood down.

The next morning we were called up in the briefing room and Colonel R gave us the dickens but the next night almost the same thing happened. Then he said,

Following pages: Dr Takashi Nagai in Nagasaki one month after the atomic bomb destroyed the city. This, the second bomb, was the final blow to Japan.

'You're going out regardless tonight and if there's anybody not out there, I'm gonna court-marshal them.'

We got anti-aircraft fire and bombed the target. It was a good hit and we pulled away. Major Mills radios in, 'We got no opposition!' About an hour later we got a radio call on our way home to say that the war was over. Back at base they asked people if they wanted to stay and do food drops on Japan. There was a big platform full of canned goods in the bomb bags of the B-29s. There was so much. We stole some peaches – we hadn't had peaches for ages.

EMPEROR HIROHITO, 15 AUGUST 1945
BROADCAST TO THE JAPANESE NATION

To our good and loyal subjects:

After pondering deeply the general trends of the world and the actual conditions obtaining in our Empire today, we have decided to effect a settlement of the present situation by resorting to an extraordinary measure.

We have ordered our Government to communicate to the Governments of the United States, Great Britain, China and the Soviet Union that our Empire accepts the provisions of their joint declaration.

... The enemy has begun to employ a new and most cruel bomb, the power of which to do damage is, indeed, incalculable, taking the toll of many innocent lives. Should we continue to fight, it would not only result in an ultimate collapse and obliteration of the Japanese nation, but also it would lead to the total extinction of human civilisation.

SADAO OBA

FRONT LINE

Sadao Oba was stationed in Java as part of the Japanese Army when surrender was declared.

The 15th of August was a hot day. In the afternoon, Major-General Mabuchi Itsuo, Brigade Commander, delivered his speech in a mournful voice, to all officers and soldiers of the HQ, that the Emperor Showa had just broadcast and ordered to surrender to the Allied Forces. He added that, 'Although we have been defeated we

No. 14,101 Lighting-up: 9.24 pm to 4.46 am

DAILY EXPRESS

WEDNESDAY AUGUST 15 1945 Weather: Fair, rain later One Penny

Attlee, at midnight, gives news that it is all over

PEACE ON EARTH

JAPS REPLY: We have the honour to surrender. Mikado orders all his Forces to cease fire

TERMS ACCEPTED—AND NO CONDITIONS

MacArthur gets ready to move in

JAPAN HAS SURRENDERED UNCONDITIONALLY. TODAY, AUGUST 15, 1945, BRINGS PEACE ON EARTH AND THE FINAL TRIUMPH OF ALLIED ARMS. THE NEWS THAT "THE LAST OF OUR ENEMIES IS LAID LOW" WAS ANNOUNCED BY RADIO TO BRITAIN AND THE EMPIRE AT MIDNIGHT BY MR. ATTLEE, THE PRIME MINISTER.

Mr. Attlee read Japan's reply, which had been awaited for four days since first Tokyo broadcast that the Emperor was prepared to consider capitulation if his prerogatives were preserved.

Now there are no reservations. Hirohito submits utterly. Here is the text of the historic surrender:—

With reference to the announcement of August 10 regarding the acceptance of the provisions of the Potsdam declaration and the reply of the Governments of the U.S.A., Great Britain, the Soviet Union and China sent by Secretary of State Byrnes on the date of August 11, the Japanese Government has the honour to communicate to the Governments of the four Powers as follows:—

1 His Majesty the Emperor has issued an Imperial rescript regarding Japan's acceptance of the provisions of the Potsdam declaration.

2 His Majesty the Emperor is prepared to authorise and ensure the signature by his Government and the Imperial General Headquarters of the necessary terms for carrying out the provisions of the Potsdam declaration.

3 His Majesty is also prepared to issue his commands to all the military, naval and air authorities of Japan and all the forces under their control wherever located to cease active operations and to surrender arms and issue such other orders as may be required by the Supreme Commander of the Allied Forces for the execution of the above-mentioned terms.

(Signed) Togo, Foreign Minister.

Mr. Attlee "scooped the world" by announcing the news just before President Truman. But within a few minutes it was issued from the White House and by Moscow radio.

Tokyo radio announced that the Emperor would broadcast the surrender conditions to Japan and Occupied Asia at mid-day (4 a.m. British Summer Time).

The Allied armed forces have been ordered to suspend all offensive action. It is the last "cease fire."

The terms will probably be signed in a U.S. battleship in Tokyo Bay or on Okinawa, which was to have been the springboard for invasion.

General MacArthur, as Allied commander, will accept the formal surrender. British, Russian and Chinese officers will be at the signing.

FIRST VICTORY ORDERS

President Truman at once sent his victory orders to Tokyo. He instructed Mr. Byrnes, the Secretary of State, to transmit to Japan through Switzerland an order for the prompt halting of fighting by Japanese forces on all fronts.

The Japanese are directed to send emissaries at once to General MacArthur with information of the disposition of the Japanese forces and commanders.

The Jap emissaries are directed to be fully empowered to make any arrangements ordered by General MacArthur to enable him to arrive at a place designated by him to receive the formal surrender.

This was how the news reached the Allies. At 8.5 last night the Jap Minister in Berne called at the Swiss Foreign Office. He stayed only two minutes.

Then the U.S. Minister arrived. And at 8.10, it is officially announced, he was handed Japan's reply. It had been radioed in 160 coded words from Tokyo.

The U.S. Minister telephoned Washington and the Jap surrender was in President Truman's hands at 11.16.

While the people of Japan waited for the announcement that war is over—they had been warned to stand by for it—their cities still burned after raids by 800 Super-Forts. As peace day dawned big fleets of the giant bombers were making the last raid of the war.

TODAY AND TOMORROW ARE VJ HOLIDAYS

TODAY and tomorrow are the VJ holidays.

Mr. Attlee stated this in his broadcast after detailing the surrender terms. He went on:—

Let us recall that on December 7, 1941, Japan, whose onslaught China had already resisted for over four years, fell upon the United States of America who were then not at war and upon ourselves who were sore pressed in our death struggle with Germany and Italy.

Taking full advantage of surprise and treachery, the Japanese forces quickly overran the territories of ourselves and allies in the Far East and at one time it appeared they might even invade the mainland of Australia and advance far into India.

But the tide turned, first slowly, then with ever-increasing speed and violence as the mighty forces of the United States and the British Commonwealth and Empire and of our Allies and, finally, of Russia were brought to bear.

Their resistance has now everywhere been broken.

At this time we should pay tribute to the men from this country, from the Dominions, from India and the Colonies, to our fleets, armies and air forces that have fought so well in the arduous campaign against Japan.

Splendid Allies

Our gratitude goes out to all our splendid allies and above all to the U.S.A., without whose prodigious efforts this war in the east would still have many years to run.

We also think especially at this time of the prisoners in Jap hands, of our friends in the Dominions of Australia and New Zealand, in India, in Burma and in those colonial territories upon whom the brunt of the Jap attack fell.

We rejoice that their sufferings will soon be at an end.

These territories will soon be purged of the Japanese invader.

Here at home you have a short rest from the unceasing exertions which you have all borne without flinching or complaint for so many dark years.

I have no doubt that throughout industry generally the Government's lead in the matter of victory holidays will be followed and that tomorrow, Wednesday and Thursday will everywhere be treated as days of holiday.

There are some who must necessarily remain at work on these days to maintain essential services. And I am sure they can be relied upon to carry on.

When we return to work on Friday morning we must turn again with energy to the great tasks which challenge us, but for the moment let those who can relax and enjoy themselves in the knowledge of work well done.

Peace has once again come to the world.

Let us thank God for this great deliverance and His mercies.

Long live the King.

As Big Ben struck

Guy Eden writes:—

Allied leaders are satisfied that the armistice terms will be carried out and that the Mikado's orders will be obeyed.

As soon as possible Japanese war criminals will be rounded up and the trials will probably take place publicly in Tokyo.

Mr. Attlee's broadcast was the climax to a night of great activity in Downing-street.

Leading Ministers were in almost constant conference all day.

So that they should not have to interrupt their work they had drinks and sandwiches taken in to them.

The draft of the Prime Minister's speech was completed just as Big Ben, heard faintly through the open windows of the Cabinet room, announced that he was due on the air.

Microphones were on the purple-baized table round which the Cabinet meets.

Truman: THE Day

Express Staff Reporter: Washington, Tuesday

JUST before midnight, London time, Japan's answer ended its long journey around the world. It came by an ordinary telegraph boy to the Swiss Embassy in Washington.

From there it was rushed to America's Foreign Office. James F. Byrnes, Foreign Secretary, stuffed it into his coat pocket and made a run for the White House next door.

President Truman and his Cabinet pondered Japan's dying words. Consultations among the victors then began. While they went on there was no hint of the contents of the telegram. Then Truman called in the reporters.

He told us Japan had accepted the Allied terms, without qualification, and he added:—

"Arrangements are now being made for the formal signing of the surrender terms at the earliest possible moment.

"General MacArthur has been appointed Supreme Allied Commander to receive the Japanese surrender. Britain, Russia and China will be represented by high

BACK PAGE, COL. EIGHT

PASTE THIS ON YOUR WINDOW!

日本降伏

This means *JAPAN SURRENDERS!*

250,000 TO CHEER THE KING TODAY

London's first victory drive

By GUY EDEN

LONDON'S first Victory Procession will be the King and Queen driving today to the House of Lords for the opening of Parliament.

Police expect that a quarter of a million people will gather for it in Whitehall and St. James's Park.

Today, too, Field-Marshal Montgomery drives to Lambeth, his birthplace, to receive the freedom of the borough.

Time-table of the royal procession is:—

10.40 a.m.—Leave Buckingham Palace and drive along the Mall.

10.45. — Cross Horse Guards Parade.

10.47.—Horse Guards Arch and Whitehall.

10.50.—Parliament-square and House of Lords.

The King and Queen will leave the House at **11.15 a.m.**, returning by the same route.

2,000 audience

From the House of Lords it is only a matter of yards to Westminster Bridge. There at **1.45 p.m.** Field-Marshal Montgomery will arrive, to be met outside the bombed St. Thomas's Hospital by the Mayor of Lambeth (Alderman W. Lockyer).

He will drive to the town hall in an open landau via Westminster Bridge-road, Kennington-road, Kennington-gate and Brixton-road, arriving at **2.20 p.m.**

At **2.30 p.m.** he will drive to the Empress Theatre, Brixton, to speak to an audience of **2,000.**

From the Throne in the Lords the King will read the Victory Speech.

Last night even the Cabinet was so uncertain of the exact position that Mr. Attlee had to send alternative drafts.

One—which the King will now use—expresses the "humble and solemn thanks" of the nation for the coming of peace. The other regretted that "the war continues."

Go to church

Today both Houses will go to special services at Westminster Abbey and St. Margaret's, Westminster, when they have heard the Speech and then return to pass a vote of congratulation.

The King and Queen plan to go to Parliament next Tuesday to receive these congratulations personally, and the King will make another speech in the presence of both Lords and Commons.

In this he will thank the whole nation.

Belgian Regent here

Prince Charles, Regent of Belgium, visited Buckingham Palace yesterday, and had lunch with the King and Queen.

This is the meaning of—

RESCRIPT

THE word rescript, used in the Japanese surrender, is from the Latin "rescribere" and means a written statement.

It is used to describe a written pronouncement by the Pope, such as an epistle in reply to a question.

It is also used invariably in Japan to name an official written document issued by the Emperor, an Imperial Rescript.

In ancient Rome a rescript was a reply sent by a Roman emperor to a magistrate consulting him on a point of law.

U.S. frees all labour

WASHINGTON, Tuesday.—The War Manpower Commission has abolished all manpower controls so that anyone can take what job he likes.

Plans have been issued to demobilise 5,000,000 men in 12 to 18 months.—Express News Service.

Extra grog—extra leave

An Admiralty general signal will be made to all ships and establishments today—"Splice the mainbrace."

This is the traditional naval method of ordering an extra tot of rum.

All personnel of the Navy, Army and Air Force now on leave from units in home commands, except for those on embarkation, sick or drafting leave, may add 48 hours to their leave.

The King tonight

The King will broadcast at nine o'clock tonight.

HARA-KIRI EVE IN JAPAN

Tears flow at Sublime Palace

From C. V. R. THOMPSON: New York, Tuesday

TOKYO'S last day of war, with crowds gathering at the Imperial Palace to weep, to wail, and to kow-tow, is described in a Tokyo despatch which will appear in all Japan's newspapers tomorrow.

The crowd has just heard the Emperor's decision. And this is the scene, as a reporter of the Japanese News Agency sees it:—

"The palace grounds are quiet beneath the dark clouds. Honoured with the Imperial edict, in the Sublime Palace grounds the mob of loyal people are bowed to the very ground in front of the Niju-Bashi (the bridge leading to the palace, and the nearest the public may go).

"Their tears flow unchecked. Alas, in their shame how can the people raise their heads? How shall the hundred million people, filled with trepidation, reply to the Emperor?

"His Majesty's subjects are moved to tears by his Majesty's boundless and infinite solicitude. With the words: 'Forgive us, our Emperor, our efforts were not enough': the heads bow lower and lower as the tears run unchecked."

"Ever since December 8, 1941, when we received the imperial rescript causing his majesty deep anxiety. . . ."

There the story broke off in transmissions in to the newspapers. The agency announced: "Editors, editors, hold that up."

Later the agency began broadcasting this statement by Lieut.-General Reikichi Tada, urging the Japanese to abandon hopes of revenge.

AND BLOOD

"The fact that the blood of our warriors was unable to set the world on a new path can be seen in the imperial message at this time as the revelation of God. I believe we should now divert all our efforts to the enhancement of culture through science."

Then editors were ordered to "kill" that.

After that, Tokyo's radio stood by. All musical programmes were abandoned. Most of the time there was silence.

1 a.m. bonfires all over BRITAIN

People get out of bed to celebrate

Express Staff Reporters

IN London, West End, East End, north of the Thames, and south of it news of the surrender fell flat at first.

Hardly anybody knew that Mr. Attlee was broadcasting at midnight. There were last trains to catch so people just went home.

At 12.15 in Piccadilly-circus there were a few hundreds—compared with thousands the night before—but they had not heard the announcement.

The hundreds of police on duty got the news over their flash system, but they did not bother to tell anybody.

At Buckingham Palace not more than 20 people were waiting for the stroke of Big Ben, while Downing-street and Whitehall were deserted except for 10 people who heard the Prime Minister's announcement from the radio of a car in the street.

But soon things began to warm up. The crowds began to gather again—not big crowds but crowds.

From the suburbs they began to hitch-hike to the West End. Lorries were commandeered, any and everything running on wheels carried a load of people.

Jeeps, klaxons on non-stop, led convoys through streets laden with smoke and glowing red with bonfires.

'AND ROCKETS

From the high point of Alexandra Palace London was ringed with the glow of victory fires.

The beacons began to light up in the mountains of Wales, and rockets soared into the sky at the war ports from Chatham to Bristol.

Bells, hooters, sirens, whistles, cheers, bands and laughter all the way from London to Londonderry.

Back in the capital city where the news came from the delayed action celebrations went on in style.

There are continuous cheers outside Buckingham Palace now. There are thousands in Piccadilly.

The G.I.s seem to have made the revelry their own property. How they dance! How they sing this war's, last war's songs!

Out to the suburbs: The lights are up. They're in their dressing-gowns, neighbours shaking hands in the streets. B.L.A. leave trains tearing through spare a little steam for a victory V toot.

Delayed action—but they made a night of it after all.

AND IN THE U.S.—

VICTORY TWICE IN A DAY

Express Staff Reporter

NEW YORK, Tuesday—America went wild. For the second time in a day—this time correctly—they celebrated total victory here with total pandemonium.

As if by magic, a crowd of a quarter of a million people assembled in Times-square, New York's Piccadilly-circus.

Someone started singing "Pistol Packin' Mama, Lay That Pistol Down," and it spread like a prairie fire until it became the theme song of the occasion.

To that tune, or if they did not hear it, to the tune of screeching motor horns and cheering crowds, the people danced. A girl could not move one foot in any direction without someone kissing her.

Within five minutes of the news coming out there were people on every New York rooftop, whether that roof was five storeys up or 50. And down came a deluge of scrap paper, telephone books, old bills, petrol coupons, ration books, anything throwable.

America had a premature wave of VJ jubilation earlier when the news—which was later cancelled—came through that the peace message had reached Berne.

Two hours after peace

WASHINGTON, Tuesday.—Two hours after the war ended Washington announced America's worst naval tragedy of the war.

After delivering a vital cargo of atomic bomb material to headquarters in Guam the cruiser Indianapolis (9,950 tons) was lost with all hands.

Her total personnel was 1,196 officers and men.—Express News Service.

Bomb talk

WASHINGTON, Tuesday.—The first international conference on the atomic bomb will take place in Canada next month.

PETAIN TO DIE

Sentence this morning

3 a.m. verdict: Petain guilty and sentenced to death.

From GORDON YOUNG

PARIS, Wednesday morning.—The jury is now considering whether Marshal Petain shall live—or die for treason.

Just after midnight Petain rose to hear Mass in his prison room.

"My conscience is clear," he said. "I do not mind what happens."

He told the jury as much when he spoke to them earlier. It was not a mercy plea, he emphasised—"just the last words of my defence."

He had written them on scraps of brown paper. Now, an old, tired man, he pulled them from his pocket and read in a faltering voice:—

"I stayed in France only to try to help the people and soften their sufferings. No matter what happens, the people will not forget that I defended them as I defended Verdun. Dispose of me as you like and according to your consciences. My own conscience is clear.

"In my long life, which at my age is in any case at death's door, I affirm that I have never had any other desire than to serve my country.

"You can take my life. My liberty is in your hands, but not my honour, for it is to my country that I confide that honour."

There was some cheering, but many women were in tears.

The court was deathly still as Petain entered for the last session.

He sat at his little desk, immaculate but haggard. His head sagged towards his folded hands. Once or twice he clenched his right fist as though trying to keep awake. All the colour was drained from his face.

Sometimes he ran his fingers restlessly along the carving on the desk. And sometimes he crossed two fingers of his left hand and clutched them nervously with his right fist.

His hands trembled no more than usual, but he would throw

BACK PAGE, COL. ONE

4.30 a.m. LATEST

REPRIEVE FOR PETAIN?

PARIS, Wednesday.—In addition to being sentenced to death Petain was also sentenced to loss of civil rights and confiscation of his property. The court expressed the wish that sentence of death should not be carried out on account of Petain's age.

It took the judge 18 minutes to read the findings of the jury.

Petain was found guilty of premeditation to change the form of government and of intelligence with the enemy.—Reuter.

Sadao Oba.

should not be desperate. In 30 years time, if we try our best, Japan will recover from the destruction and disgrace of the defeat of the War. We should recall the old story of 47 *Ronins* who united and avenged their lord's death. Be prudent in your behaviour.'

The surrender, which I hated even to imagine, was the greatest shock I have ever experienced. I felt as though a lump of lead had been put on my head. I felt shame at having failed to win the war for the Emperor, for the nation of Japan and for Indonesians and remorse towards friends and classmates who had been killed in action. I felt a growing fear for the future and sympathy for Indonesians who would be again under the yoke of Dutch colonialism. Together with those sentiments I noticed a vague new hope of returning home alive, something which had been impossible to imagine so long as the war lasted.

In the evening of the same day, fellow Lieutenant Murakami Mamoru, who hated to surrender, tried to persuade us young officers not to obey the Emperor's order but to appeal to young Southern Army officers to continue to fight for the final victory. By doing this, Mukakami said, patriots would join us. No one followed him.

The 'Surrender to the Enemy' had been unimaginable for Japanese. Some felt they had to apologise to the Emperor for the defeat by committing hara-kiri. In one or two weeks Lieutenant-Colonel Uesugi, Commander of Brigade's Artillery Battalion, together with a young lieutenant made hara-kiri. In Java 60 soldiers and civilians in total killed themselves. A Japanese man who had been living in Java for many years committed a double suicide with his Indonesian wife.

JOHN BROWN

PRISONER OF WAR

John Brown, an officer with the 5th Field Regiment, Royal Artillery, was captured in Singapore in February 1942 and held in Singapore, Formosa and Japan until August 1945.

The difference between being a POW in Japan and being a POW elsewhere was that there was clearly absolutely no hope of escape. It was just a matter of sitting back and waiting because, certainly as far as I and many others were concerned there was never any doubt in anyone's mind that in fact the war would end with the Allies winning and the Japanese being defeated. The only doubt in certain people's minds was whether they would survive to see this day.

At Fukuoka camp there was a wild rumour going around that the war was over. At five o'clock on 15 August on the train coming back from the farm, Frank turned to me and said it was all over. A rumour was always a stimulus in those days so we tried hard to read the faces of the civilians. They looked at us curiously with friendly smiles, but they had done that before. In the camp there was no confirmation at all, the guards gave us no indication. On the 18th, we were even warned there might be a fire practice down the mine, which was not something that anyone looked forward to. It wasn't until the 21st that we woke up and found that all the guards had really gone. At that point we decided that the war really was over and set about organising ourselves.

A number of us got out and went to Fukuoka where we found an aerodrome. An American Dakota came in and a senior officer started arranging the evacuation of the really sick. This went on for a couple of weeks or so. The rest of us were put on a train and taken down to Nagasaki, where we saw the results of the atom bomb, which really were absolutely horrifying. Because we didn't know about the atomic bomb, to arrive on the outskirts of Nagasaki just as dawn was breaking and to see this incredible scene of destruction was quite extraordinary.

EDWARD WADINGTON

FRONT LINE

Edward Wadington, stationed on the Missouri, was on deck for the signing ceremony of the Japanese surrender. In a letter to his parents, he expressed the feelings of many Second World War servicemen.

We are all proud that we have been able to help win this war. Let us all hope that this will be the last time that a war has to be won. Many of our friends have died with that hope. That hope has carried us through many a grinding, gruelling day. Let us pray that it carries those charged with formulating and preserving the peace to a successful accomplishment of their task.

GENERAL MACARTHUR, 2 SEPTEMBER 1945
SPEECH ON BOARD THE USS *MISSOURI*

Today the guns are silent. A great tragedy has ended. A great victory has been won. The skies no longer rain death, the seas bear only commerce, men everywhere walk upright in the sunlight. The entire world is quietly at peace. The holy mission has been completed. And in reporting this to you, the people, I speak for thousands of silent lips, forever stilled among the jungles and the beaches and in the deep waters of the Pacific which marked the way.

DAVID DOUGLAS DUNCAN

ARMED FORCES

David Douglas Duncan, First Lieutenant in the US Marines, was with the first American naval fleet to enter Tokyo Bay in August 1945.

The surrender terms demanded that every shore artillery position be marked by a white flag. Well, as the invasion fleet sailed – I should say crept – into Tokyo Bay, whose hilly slopes are heavily forested, it looked as though thousands of housewives had just hung out their laundry on the trees to dry. Everything from handkerchiefs to bedsheets seemed to be flapping all over the place in the morning breeze. But, as you already know, not one shot was fired. And as we steamed ever closer we didn't see a soul – just those spooky white flags.

Since I, personally, had waited a couple of years for that morning, I decided to document the historic moment of the final landing by shooting it in colour. Well, after clambering down the nets of the transport into my landing barge and bouncing merrily over the waters of Tokyo Bay – banging pictures left and right – suddenly, while still about a quarter-mile offshore, I started listening to my camera. It's something every professional does subconsciously. Historic morning it surely was! I was photographing the invasion with a pair of empty cameras.

It's true! After yanking the black and white rolls out of each of the two cameras being used, cleaning their lenses and gears, I had slapped them shut again to await the Big Moment – minus colour film – stark empty.

Luckily, I still had time before we hit the embankment of the naval base, so was functioning somewhat more sensibly when we went ashore.

Should anyone ever in the future ask whether I remember the morning the Marines landed in Japan, the answer is a curt, 'Damned right!'

Once ashore – with no one shooting at anyone – and the commanding officer of the Japanese Naval Base wandering off with the commanding officer of the American invasion force, for talks about the surrender, or the Yankees and the Dodgers, or to have a cup of tea – anyway, they disappeared very casually and I *knew* that the war was really over – at that moment I turned tourist. And toward Tokyo.

General MacArthur's orders to the invasion force had been explicit: no member of the first echelon naval assault troops was to enter Tokyo until permission came from his Supreme Headquarters. Well, I was there as a representative of the Headquarters, US Marine Corps, Washington, and had only the Commandant to answer to; besides, I was attached to the landing force only until I got to Japan. So I scrounged an ancient alcohol-burning motorcycle from a battered garage at the naval base and soon had it running. Not fast — maybe ten miles an hour — but faster that walking. Then I ran into two marvellous characters who didn't give a damn about MacArthur and his quarantine on Tokyo, or anything else. Sam Dietz is a huge Navy lieutenant who once played All-American football for Alabama, and Bernard Perlin is a slender, quiet, but good-natured *Life* magazine war artist. Sam had a Thompson machine-gun slung over one shoulder. Bernie had a rucksack filled with paints, and a sketchbook under his arm. I, of course, had my Colt .45 in my shoulder holster, my Fijian campaign hat on my noggin, and a side-car on my new motorcycle. So off we went — not having any idea where Tokyo was except to the north of us, about 30 miles up the road.

Outside the main gate of the Yokosuka Naval Base we were met by an extraordinary sight. A totally lifeless city. A lovely day, not much bomb damage among the low wooden buildings, and not a single civilian. But we weren't alone. Stretching along the road, in both directions as far as we could see, the way was studded with a line of black-uniformed policemen standing about 50 paces apart, with their backs to the street and us. We turned right, to the north, and chugged toward Tokyo, surely the first of the invades to pass that way. Not one man moved as much as a finger — or turned to watch us go.

And that moment our motorcycle exploded and died.

Bernie, who is extremely well-mannered and proper, saved the day. Turning to Sam and me as we pushed the smoking, lifeless motorcycle to the roadside, he said, 'Gentlemen, as we New Yorkers would say, "When lost or in doubt ask of the first gendarme the way". So let's ask that first black-booted b*****d.' We did. That is, Sam did, looking down from all of his six feet at that first policeman, who was about five feet four. Something like, 'Say, fella. Wheresa da way to a-Tokyo?' Bernie almost flipped. I came out with something like, 'For-Christ's-sake Sam make it so's he can understand — or at least so we can — we're not looking for Rome!' The little cop just stood looking up at Sam, as if he was trying to memorise what was before him so he could tell his wife all about what *he* had seen on the beat that sunny morning.

Funnily, really funnily, another cop then marched up, saluted, and wondered whether he might be of assistance — in perfect English. We explained, very seriously (as though we were accustomed to such situations just as much as he), that we were strangers in Yokosuka, that we had lost the way, that we were looking for the best way to get to Tokyo. 'But that is velly easy.' He looked at his wristwatch. 'Go back two stleets. Go light one stleet. You will find on the reft the station. Next expless to Tokyo — 17 minutes — on time.' And it was.

Roaring along to Yokohama, then Tokyo, we rode in a train not unlike a New York subway. Except all of the windows had either been blown out or removed to

prevent glass flying during our bombing raids. Each car was stuffed solid with Japanese – soldiers, more cops, children, parents, old, old, old folks, mothers nursing their babies, and three Americans. At the station stops more local people shoved their way inside, then, abruptly aware that they were confronting no ordinary barrier of kimonos and cotton suitcoats, some of them found their eyes climbing slowly up and over a vast barricade of Navy or Marine Corps khaki. To their credit and honour, each, upon finding himself, or herself, looking squarely into the eyes of an enemy soldier, simply bowed, ever so slightly, as though to excuse himself, and his countrymen, for having so inconvenienced us by providing such a crowded transport at a time like this.

From Yokosuka to Tokyo, none of us heard a single word spoken on that train. Tokyo... home of the Emperor... target of our devastating fire-raids... the end of the line in this war. Tokyo, that afternoon, was a place where three Americans got off the express train from the south – along with thousands of Japanese passengers – and walked down from the station ramp into the streets of a city that was no more. Or so it seemed at first.

We found what had been the main drag, the Ginza. Except for a couple of sagging, reinforced-steel-and-concrete buildings, gaunt and gutted, our view of the city centre was one of unadorned chaos. The place was burned flat. Only the abandoned, rusting safes of long-gone or dead shopkeepers, and the blackened scarecrows of jutting brick chimneys marked what had been the heart of Asia's greatest city.

Then, we wandered farther abroad in the desolation. We found that life still survived, rustling amid the ashes. Old couples were farming vegetables in bushel-basket-size plots of earth behind the fallen walls. Others lived in holes beneath the walls. Flotsam houseboats choked the canals that crisscross what had been Tokyo.

Just before sunset we found the Imperial Palace, apparently quite undamaged behind some ramparts and deep moats. It seemed forlorn and totally unrelated to the world war just ending, with its violence already faded into a long-gone yesterday.

Down the street, we walked into the lobby and across the polished floor of another also nearly intact, low, rambling palace – Frank Lloyd Wright's Imperial Hotel. We were met by the manager, in striped morning pants and cutaway – and with a bow. We explained that we were interested in the biggest, most comfortable room, or rooms – with beds to match our heights, and hot-water baths. The manager listened politely and imperceptibly raised a finger in response to which three bellboys shot out from nowhere. We had neither baggage nor gear, but they still led us to our rooms. However, just before the procession began into the plush innards of Mr Wright's masterpiece, we were presented with, and signed, the register of guests.

We each signed in the same way: rank or title, organisation. Then we each added the brief postscript: 'Present bill to Japanese Embassy, Washington, DC.'

And dinner? Three trays of soup and rice arrived while we were soaking.

For nearly two weeks of glorious sunny autumn weather I photographed the cinders of Hell – the charred hulk of Tokyo – in colour. Other photographers hurried down to Hiroshima, naturally, but I saw that as the final grisly equation on a remote physics blackboard. Tokyo, to me, symbolised the enemy – the fallen dragon – beaten in combat by mortal men.

During that period, General MacArthur flew in to one of the airfields, coming from the Philippines, and set up staff headquarters in Yokohama. Tokyo was still out of bounds to the occupation personnel, at least to the levels below Super-Brass. Sam Dietz headed back to wherever he came from, so Bernie Perlin and I had the place pretty much to ourselves, sharing it with only a handful of other guys in uniform who flitted through the Imperial, and, of course, some of the old professional news correspondents. The day General MacArthur made his first grand entry behind his 1st Cavalry Division MPs as escorts, Bernie and I wandered down to a good conspicuous street corner where we rested comfortably on the curbstone, on the tips of our spines watching the conquerors sweep past. I just sort of felt that a lot of other guys, staring back at Pearl Harbour and Corregidor and Guadalcanal, were sprawled out on that curbstone alongside me.

Of course, when the Brass poured into the Imperial I got booted out. Not by the really *simpatico* Japanese manager – he kept switching me from room to room for several days so nobody could at first catch me – hell no, I was tossed by a *full* colonel, the Army's new billeting officer. Anyway, by that time I didn't care because Bernie, as an accredited *Life* war artist, had been assigned a cabin, with two bunks, in the communication ship *Ancon*. He somehow fixed it so that I was given the other sack – and that's where I'm writing this letter right now. Then, through Bernie, I met two of the greatest guys in my profession, men whose work I have followed and admired and sort of aimed at for years: *Life* photographers Jay Eyerman and Carl Mydans. They're in the cabin across the corridor. Finally, halfway around the world from where I started, I have met two of the men who look at this old earth with my kind of vision – and a common challenge.

When Surrender Day was set for 2 September, Carl and Jay tried desperately to get a camera position assigned to me aboard the battleship *Missouri*, but it was hopeless. I had no press accreditation, and with Brass flying in from all over the Allied world, a crummy lieutenant photographer didn't have a prayer. Even as it was, there would be so many official representatives aboard that battle-wagon that only a miracle would keep it afloat or from capsizing in Tokyo Bay.

'Besides,' growled someone else who had no position, 'the whole show is locked up tight. Nobody is going to sneak aboard that ship. Everything is in the hands of one guy – the handsomest, toughest s.o.b. in the whole US Navy.'

Something started spinning forward through my memory... and I grabbed it. Turning to Jay, I asked just one question: 'By any chance is the officer in charge of this show a Navy captain named Fitzhugh Lee?'

Jay looked up from cleaning his cameras and nodded. 'Yeah, Dave. Only it's Commodore FitzHugh Lee. And he is really a tough guy. He's gotta be for this thing.'

I was already headed for the ladder and topside, toward the holy of holies, the commanding officer's quarters of the communication ship, so I only half heard Carl agreeing with Jay on the character of the commodore.

Commodore Fitzhugh Lee received me almost immediately, although for sure he did not place my name until we were again face to face. That's right! He was executive officer of their aircraft carrier Essex, aboard which I first shipped overseas, and whose portraits I shot and printed while we ran from San Francisco to Honolulu.

How could *anybody* have my luck?

He explained graciously and carefully that he was being besieged by the biggest guns from Washington to London to Paris and even Moscow, to get their representatives aboard. That was at the governmental level. At the press level he was being death-charged around the clock. While telling me this he kept right on working at his desk, writing. Then he stood up again and handed me a card, with a lean smile. 'Don't worry! You're aboard. Surely no man here deserves it more than a United States Marine.'

Or course, everyone has seen the newsreels taken aboard, and probably heard the radio broadcasts during the actual signing ceremony. I was upon a five-inch gun turret, back slightly from the deck where it took place. Just below me a catwalk connected the captain's quarters with the lower deck, where the surrender documents waited. There was a slight commotion atop one of the gigantic 16-inch gun turrets that had been converted into a press stand. One of the baggy-pantsed, leather-booted Russian cameramen tried to shove his way to the front, ignoring the place number marked on his card. Much to my joy, two lanky Marine Mps grabbed him by the scruff of the collar, and by the seat of those pants, and tossed him back to where he started from – and belonged.

A moment later, to my astonishment, General MacArthur and Admiral Halsey walked out on the catwalk right beneath me. Commodore Fitzhugh Lee really fixed me up royally! I certainly wasn't the person closest to the surrender signing table. But I did have one of greatest overall views in the momentous pageant taking place aboard that battleship.

That she should be the USS *Missouri*, of all the ships in the fleet, made that day an extraordinarily personal page in the old world's life story.

Yet for all of the glory and profound elation felt by all of us aboard, there was one sad and unnecessarily cruel aspect to the ceremony, which the movie cameras perhaps did not show. It was the moment when Mamoru Shigemitsu, the top-ranking Japanese civilian of their surrender signing group, came alongside the *Missouri* in his launch. The sea was calm but he had a terrible, humiliating, and probably painful time trying to climb the ship's stair-ladder to the main deck, and then get from there to the table where he was to sign the surrender document. He is a very old man. Like the other Japanese civilians aboard, he was dressed in formal morning clothes. But somewhere, either fighting as a youth against the Russians, or the Chinese, or the Koreans, someplace, he had been critically wounded. He could scarcely walk – for he had only one leg.

No one went forward to help him.

KENNETH WATERSON

ARMED FORCES

Kenneth Waterson was a telegraphist (trained operater) aboard the R Class destroyer
HMS Relentless, *anchored in Trincomalee Habour, Ceylon (now Sri Lanka).*

The end of the war came suddenly, date not recorded. I was on the middle watch and had read the last message, i.e. taken down the morse signal which then required decoding. First the message had to be decoded from the current 24-hour code in force and then decoded from the underlying six-monthly code. Up to then signals came through non-stop and were repeated immediately and at a few hours later. If reception was bad which was often during monsoon storms and electric storms one had the chance to re-read the message. Usually the second transmission came during someone else's watch. In one's own watch one got someone else's second transmisson. The messages were left for the two coders to decode who worked in shifts of forenoon and afternoon. If one was urgent in the night one sent for POTS (petty officer telegraphist) to allocate a coder.

At the start of the watch I read the first message, by reading I mean writing down a series of figures. Most transmissions from the Signal Station Trincomalee were machine-transmitted as numbers. Once that first message had cleared no other signals were sent. All that came through was the top priority grading - OU – which was repeated for the rest of the watch. I could not leave the WT (wireless telegraph) office in case the message, whatever it was, came through. No one came by so I had to wait until I was relieved before I had the Petty Officer Telegraphist wakened up to tell him of – OU – grading. I don't think he believed me; he told me to 'B' off. I think he did go down to the WT office on afterthought. The following forenoon he was in the office and said the Japs had asked for surrender terms. After some deliberation we were told terms had been offered. I think in fact we offered them terms and they had to have a second A-bomb dropped before they accepted.

That night Trincomalee had its celebrations. There were rocket (distress flares) displays, jumping jacks and concerts. The weather was cooler, the oppressive heat had subsided. VJ evening started just before sunset. Ships were dressed, every colour of flag was flown. There were lots of nationalities. The alphabet went down to the USA (America) and USSR (Russia). The latter flew the hammer and sickle. All the flags were hauled down at sunset but were then immediately re-hoisted. The dark night showed up illuminated Vs made up of coloured lightbulbs. Some of these were in many colours. When the last shadows had gone the ship next to us let loose with her siren. It was a horrible noise, worse than a air-raid siren. After an interval of about 15 minutes every ship in the harbour was blowing off a different note. The result was an awful din. In time various Vs could be distinguished on different sirens. Some put in a J after the V making VJ in morse code; rockets (distress flares) and Very lights (bright light flares) were being fired freely by now all over the harbour. Green, red, yellow and white ones. These offset the regular starboard and port navigation lights, green and red. Green and red lights shooting up into the sky and then down into the sea. Rustic VJs on hooters and much cheering completed an unreal atmosphere. Blackout was abandoned.

By 9 pm the fun increased in tempo. Many were drunk now, where they got spirits and beer from is a mystery. We had none. Earlier an attempt had been made to mount a concert but the hooters drowned out any attempt to sing. Shooting pretty lights into the air became tame after a while. Ships started firing rockets at each other. Then they all started firing at the aircraft lined up on the upper deck of the aircraft carrier. An urgent signal was sent round the harbour to stop firing rockets. Various petty officers went round their ships to put a stop to the practice. It says something for discipline that the rocket shooting stopped. How it started I know not as I thought all rockets were kept under lock and key.

Instead, jumping jacks were fired from rocket launchers. These were fearsome projectiles. They came in various colours and shot from left to right, from front

Ships in ports around the
globe celebrated the end of
the war with dazzling
displays.

to rear. Shooting down between deck awnings they scattered all and sundry. They
were powerful, much stronger than bonfire-night jumping jacks. They possibly
were Chinese ones, but who got them and from where is not known. The awnings
were burnt in various places and a fire arose on one of the gun covers.

This led to hoses being turned on to put out all the small fires that had started.
Generously ships put out each other's fires by hose. After that the hoses were
turned on the other ships' crews. Everybody was wet through. Chaps coming back
on board from shore leave were caught in this deluge.

After that, things died down; various concert parties were got up impromptu.
We were tied up alongside the *Woolwich*, the destoyer parent ship. We got up a
singing party and wheeled our piano out onto the quarter deck so that others
could see and hear us. The quarter deck was beautifully decorated with bunting.
Out came our players in their costumes and started to sing. The stokers on the
Woolwich did not seem to appreciate our singing, they turned a hose pipe on us.
The drums were soaked as was the piano, the bunting all bedraggled. They did
have the foresight to close the bulkhead that gave us access to their ship. Had we

made contact World War III would have broken out between us. By now a lot of people were drunk. Where they got their booze from is not known; we had none.

After all this excitement things quietened down, just Very lights now and then. A 'feel good factor' abounded. The only alcohol we had was from the splicing of the main brace (an extra tot of rum).

WW2 People's War

SALLY HITCHCOCK PULLMAN

ARMED FORCES

First Lieutenant Sally Hitchcock Pullman, US Army nurse in the 126th General Hospital Unit, was stationed in New Guinea and the Philippines. She wrote of her joy at the war's end in a letter to her parents on 14 August 1945.

... For the past few days I've been dying to write you – THAT IT'S ALL OVER, that this terrible war has ended and what it was like over here when word first came over the radio. My wards were bedlam. What a time! I wouldn't have missed it for anything, being on nights, that first night when the news of the surrender came over.

My four wards went wild. I have never been hugged or kissed or spun around so many times in my whole life. Even had a dance with a cute young guy who had been over here 28 months and states that this was his first dance in all that time! How wonderful it was to see such pure, unadulterated joy and bedlam, and real smiles and laughter!! Of course each night my ward men and I were sweating out the news, ready at the moment to switch on the lights and say it is all over. AN EVENT TO REMEMBER!

Just before I went on nights for the fourth time, I told the kids it was my luck in the Army to have something momentous happen. It did! There was the surrender. Then I went to bed, slept and did not know until late this afternoon. Plunged into bed this morning and slept all day, staggered into the tent at 4:30 pm from the night nurses' quarter.

'Anything happen today?' I asked.

'Oh, nothing new! Of course you knew the war was over!'

That's how I knew. What a momentous event!!

I think back to the news we got of the dropping of the atomic bomb. First we were ecstatic, then there was this reaction to the reality of its awesomeness. There were endless discussions about what had happened: joy, guilt, thoughtfulness. What a gamut of emotions. Above all was the relief we would not have to invade Japan. We all knew there would have been terrible casualties if we had to invade.

And so it's over. Now the talk is how and when we will get home. Maybe for Christmas – 'I'm Dreaming Of A White Christmas' and 'When The Lights Go On Again All Over The World'. How appropriate these song titles are now. Some homes will be so happy this year – not just because it's Christmas, but knowing there will not be a dreaded telegram at the door...

**ELEANOR ROOSEVELT, 2 SEPTEMBER 1945
SPEECH ON VICTORY OVER JAPAN**

Today we have a mixture of emotions, joy that our men are freed of constant danger, hope that those whom we love will soon be home among us, awe at what man's intelligence can compass, and a realisation that intelligence uncontrolled by great spiritual forces can be man's destruction instead of his salvation.

FATHER ZABELKA

ARMED FORCES

Father George Zabelka was a Catholic chaplain with the US Army Air Corps. After VE Day he was reassigned to the Pacific where he became the Catholic chaplain to the 509th Composite Group.

When the news of Hiroshima hit me, my reaction was a split one. Gosh, its horrible, but gosh, its going to end the war. Finally the boys will get home. This was going to save millions of lives. We would have lost a million soldiers invading Japan. But, as a priest, I should have considered: We're killing little kids, old men and old women, burning them to death. I don't recall any feeling of guilt at the time. I must say there was a little difference in my feelings when I found out Nagasaki was a Catholic city. The bomb was dropped right on Urakami, a suburb. It was dropped within a few hundred metres of the central church. It was an almost totally Catholic settlement. Saint Francis had come 400 years before and brought the faith into Japan. That's were the shoguns tried to eradicate the faith and thousands of Christians were martyred.

Here was Charles Sweeney, a good Boston Irish Catholic, piloting the plane, dropping the bomb, killing our fellow Catholics. Brothers and sisters killing fellow brothers and sisters.

I got acquainted with a Japanese priest who was in the prisoners' compound in Tininan. Some Irish Seabees told me about him. We built a chapel for him in the compound. We had a little choir. The Japanese priest said the mass and I said the mass with him. All of us went to communion, the GIs and the Japanese prisoners. A Quonset hut, I think it was.

On 15 August, the war ended. We had a big mass. It was the Holy Day of Assumption. It's the day we celebrate Mary's Assumption into heaven. The war started on 8 December – they're a day ahead of us – which was the Feast of the Immaculate Conception. We had the mass. We were all happy, but everybody was kinda quiet. There was no great yelling or shouting or anything. Everybody was just walking around. War's ended, we're gonna go home. No more kamikazes coming over, no more danger.

EUGENE ECKSTAM

FRONT LINE

Eugene Eckstam volunteered for active duty with the Navy in 1942. On 28 April 1944 – about six weeks before D-Day – his boat, LST (Landing Ship Tank) 507, was sunk by German torpedo boats during Operation Tiger, a pre-invasion exercise off the southern coast of England. He was then sent to the Pacific.

They said, 'You are going to go to the Pacific.' We knew that. We were going to stay Stateside for a little while and then go to the Pacific. That's all I needed after being sunk – more war. I didn't want any more part of it; I'd been sunk and I went through D-Day – that's enough. But, that wasn't enough...

We landed in Boston and then flew to Chicago and then went back up to Madison where we had a month survivor leave. I don't remember what I did; I think I just stayed home. I got used to civilian living again.

I thought, these people at home don't know what is really going on. There is zero appreciation for the war effort and what the GIs are going through and the British are going through in trying to save the United States. The people at home didn't appreciate the war effort at all. They were going out to parties and having a good time. Of course, we had a good time over there too, but these people were having a super good time. We didn't have a good time at all compared to the Stateside people. That bothered me for a long time.

So on 17 April we invaded the west side of the main body of Mindanao as a Victor 5 operation. Boy, the bombardment started at 5 am and I was just scared to death, coming in on an LST and just terrified. The Japs thought we were going to come in the other side of the island. The deception worked great and the Japs ran 35 miles that first day. The Army had a heck of a time trying to keep up with them.

The major problem on Mindanao was mental. Since the invasion was two weeks ahead of time, we didn't have our supplies; we didn't have our mail either and people need mail from home in order to avoid the blues.

It was very obvious after a week or ten days went by that the morale – not only of the Navy base, but the Army guys, too – was deteriorating. There was fights and everything else breaking out in the Navy itself, in the Army and between Army and Navy – fist fights. Lots of arguing, bitching and moaning and groaning around. Tommy, the old experienced Navy guy recognised this as what it was before I did. He said: 'Doc, we gotta do something. The Army Special Services has a bunch of musical instruments. Why don't we put on a variety show? And, why don't we build a baseball diamond?' I asked him where he was going to get all that stuff. He said the Army has it. They even had a baby piano. This is only a week after an invasion. A piano! A full set of band instruments. Well, now I know why they need it. So, it took a little bit of GI alcohol. I said, 'Tommy, I don't know what you're talking about; I don't know how much we got.' And he says, 'You don't want to know.' So, I don't know what he did, but by the next morning bulldozers were leveling out a field for a baseball diamond and we had horseshoe pits and a badminton court.

We had all the supplies to go with it and planning was going on between the Army and the Navy guys; just the planning effort helped everybody. In about two days we had a Bob Hope-type variety show, just Army and Navy guys. They did the most stupid kinds of entertainment; you wouldn't even listen to them at home – it was lousy, rank amateur. But for four hours in drizzling rain, they put on a hell of a show. Instantly the gloom went away. Everyone was happy. Then it was another week before the mail started coming. That didn't make any difference. ...

[When the Japanese surrendered] the base just erupted like a volcano. Work stopped and they broke out the beer and everybody got drunk. Everybody – the skipper on down. There was just no action that day. I think it was afternoon when the word came in –fortunately, because nightfall wasn't too far away. But it was one big party right on the base. No alcohol in Navy quarters, of course. Ha, ha! But that was a happy day! We took a deep breath and from there on we weren't really worried. I think that changed the morale of the whole situation from that point on.

We got in the medical jeep – my jeep – and we got permission to leave the base for that day. And we went up in the hills and talked our way past the Army. We knew the Army Commander, I guess, 'cause we had to see him about something for sick bay so I knew who he was. So I said, 'Colonel So-and-so gave us permission to come.' He said that we shouldn't be there and where were our papers? We didn't need any; just tell the guard and we went right through. We were lying through our teeth. But we drove right on through and we just stood at the edge of the perimeter watching the Japs come in.

There were sub-machine guns – this was an armed camp. And the Japs came in just as proud as they could be; their uniforms were tattered and patched but they were clean, they were neat, everyone was erect – and full discipline. They came in. The officers all laid their Samurai swords on the table in front of the American officers. The enlisted people all threw their guns on a pile in the middle of it and just lined up as neat as a pin. I talked with one of the Japanese doctors in the prisoner camp afterwards and he didn't want to be in the war – he was drafted just like most of us were. Most of the soldiers were drafted and they didn't want to be in the war. They were happy to see the end come. The Japs felt the same way we did. No different.

They were glad it was over. They were glad to be in our care. They were scared that we might do something to them – like the Germans were scared that we might do something to them on our ship, which didn't happen. As a result of our firmness but not picking on them, they shaped around and were smiling after a while and appreciated the care that they were given. They wouldn't have given us that care. We knew that, but that's beside the point.

SHUICHIRO YOSHINO

PRISONER OF WAR

Shuichiro Yoshino, a Lieutenant in the Japanese 11th Epidemic Prevention and Water Supply Unit, 18th Division, was taken prisoner by the British at Hukawng Valley, northern Burma.

The Hukawng Valley was known for its severe climatic conditions and as a breeding ground for cholera and malaria. When the supplies were cut off by General Orde Wingate, we Japanese had to retreat gradually. And food became scarce, so that we had to live on local yams and bamboo sprouts from the fields. This made me weak and I had to spend two months at a field hospital. Hearing that the unit was to retreat to the railhead, I left the hospital without the doctor's permission and rejoined my colleagues before the final withdrawal, leading a group of patients with ox-carts and eight horses to the base camp.

The war ended on 15 August 1945, and we were then disarmed, labelled 'Japanese Surrendered Personnel' (JSP) and put in a concentration camp. One day a brigade commander of 'The Black Cats' (17 Indian Division) came to our camp. We assembled and listened to him. He said: 'You have not become prisoners as you have been defeated in war. Don't hang your heads; you stopped fighting by order of the Emperor. I know from my experience of fighting with you that you Japanese have great ability. I believe that you are sure to make Japan a first-rate country after you have returned to your home country. Be confident and behave yourselves so that you can get home without trouble.'

What a splendid speech by a high-ranking officer of the victors! We were really moved. At that time we did not know when we would get home and what the situation was in Japan under the occupation of the Allied forces, so we were in a depressed mood. The speech was a great encouragement to us.

MASAO HIRAKUBO OBE

FRONT LINE

Masao Hirakubo was a young Japanese lieutenant fighting in Burma when news came through of Emperor Hirohito's unconditional surrender.

Every day in the war, when the day was finished, I said to myself, 'Today I am alive.' We were always between the borderline of death and life. And from my previous weight of 75 kilograms, I ended up weighing 40 because of disease, dysentery and malaria. We had little to eat, so I was sent to the army hospital and transferred here and there. Finally when I was cured of my disease I came back to the front line. I went to a training centre in my base and my weight increased ten kilograms a week, ten kilos, like a pig. And I returned to the front line; but soon we were defeated.

People in Britain ask me, 'When you heard news of the ceasefire were you happy?' I say, 'No I was not happy,' because we were fighting still. Then suddenly the Headquarters instructed me to finish fighting and act as the British officers instructed. The Emperor announced that the war was now finished, it was

Masao Hirakubo.

broadcast and then the news was transferred to our division by telephone. It was announced to us person to person. Nobody said anything, just shock, disappointment. Everyone in the division felt the same. And I then had to tell my men what happened, but from Headquarters to my regiment it took about ten hours' rowing by the local people. So I had ten hours alone on that boat, to think about what to tell my men, what we should do. Some people thought about ignoring the surrender. But I said to my men, 'We are Japanese, we cannot live alone like Robinson Crusoe. We can always fall back on our country. How the British Army will treat us we don't know – but good treatment or bad, whatever happens we must not forget we are Japanese.' Some wanted to escape to the mountains and await the next Japanese attack, whenever that would be, some wanted to marry locals and remain in Burma as they now had no attachment to Japan. I said we must go back to Japan fast to re-establish Japan itself. Japan is now debris from the American atom bomb, so we must go back.

We repatriated on an American ship, the *Liberty*. About two thousand people in one boat. It took about two weeks. Everybody went back to their homes, but many people were surprised that their homes no longer existed, because they had been bombed. My house was very good and comfortable, by the seaside, but all that area was bombed and a new house was established on the site and an American officer's family was living there.

Before I reached home I met my father. I went by train and at the platform I immediately acknowledged him but he didn't recognise me, I was so changed. My face was like the colour of soil, a muddy colour. He didn't recognise me, I said 'Father, I am here,' and then he understood it was me.

At the beginning of the war I was a very right-wing nationalist. Everybody was at that time. Everybody intended to give their lives for the nation. When Japan attacked Pearl Harbor I thought, Oh no! Japan could not win a war against America and Britain. I knew that the war had been started for colonial reasons, to push Europe out of south-east Asia. My father had always said that Japan was a trading nation, not a fighting nation. He said that we had no resources, coal or iron ore but that we were a trading nation, and that we could not survive a war with the British and Americans. When I saw him after the war, I told him that he was right. And we were all responsible for the restoration of the Burmese economy. My first thing was to reconcile with the British; that was my pledge.

CHARLES WHITEHEAD

PRISONER OF WAR

Charles Whitehead, of 48th/21st Regiment Royal Artillery, was taken prisoner by the Japanese in 1942 and held in Java until released by Lord Mountbatten in 1945.

The men were now coming back from the Burma Railroad. Few of these men lived to tell the world how they had suffered. We struggled against a hopeless task, but these men wanted to die, they knew they only had to stand and they would be sent off again. We had to dig a large communal grave for those who died. There is now a cemetery in Singapore in memory of those lads who died in the prison camps.

We are now in our second year. Our clothes are now just loin cloths, two per man. The rice diet has just about kept us alive. I suffered much dysentery, malaria, ulcers, but when I looked round at the mere skeletons of men around me, I realised I was thankful for my medical experience and for the help I was able to give.

Towards the end of the third year things got better. The Japs altered our diet. Buffalo meat appeared in our rice, with sweet potatoes. The guards were becoming friendly, we began to realise the end was near.

We had to wait a further six months before that was to happen. The great day arrived, for those of us who had survived. Lord and Lady Mountbatten, both in white naval uniform, came into the camp to announce the Japs had surrendered. The war was over.

WW2 People's War

ANTON BILEK

PRISONER OF WAR

Anton Bilek was a member of the US Air Corps. Captured after the surrender of the American–Filipino Army at Bataan in April 1942, he was a prisoner in Japan until the end of the war.

I guess it was 9 August when they dropped the A-bomb on Nagasaki. We were 25–30 miles away. They dropped it around ten o'clock. There was nothin' between us and them but the bay. I felt the windows vibrate. The whole barracks shook. But it always shook when there was heavy demolition on Nagasaki.

But this time we turned around and there's the big mushroom, way up in the air.

We didn't know much about Hiroshima. The guys said they must've hit an oil refinery for so much smoke to go up. We were due west of Nagasaki and prevailing winds usually come from the west. If there was any fallout whether it hurt anybody in camp, I don't know.

A day or two after that, the end of the war. [Sighs deeply.] We were talkin' about it: What you gonna do when the war's over? Well, I'm gonna get that son of a bitch, Fuji-san, that bastard beat me so many times. I'm gonna tear his toenails out or I'm gonna do this to him. Everybody had somethin' they were gonna do. [A half-laugh, half-cry.]

They got us all out on the parade ground. There were about nineteen hundred of us. About a thousand Americans, some Dutchmen, some Australians, some English. They lined us up and the Jap commander got up on his pedestal. And the interpreter, [cries silently, sighs] he says, 'Take care of yourself' [almost a whisper]. He told us the war was over, and he turned around and left. The nineteen hundred men, you could hear a pin drop. Nobody said anything. Finally, some of the boys turned round and [cries; a long pause] they all walked back to the barracks. Nobody said a damn word. It was quiet, quiet. Just the shufflin' of feet. I went behind the first barracks there and I bawled like a baby.

It took a couple of hours, and then the guys started yellin' and beatin' one another on the back. The day before that, they gave us a Red Cross parcel, with American food. They had these in camp for the past two years and they never gave us one of 'em. They had tons of food there brought in by the Red Cross ship. They also had medical supplies. And our doctors had been amputating legs without anaesthetic.

The Japs left. They all took off. We were the only ones in camp. We didn't know where to go or what to do. We got the radio and we kept it turned on. Finally, American broadcasts start comin' over. It says: 'All American prisoners, all prisoners of war, stay where you are. We're sending airplanes to look for you. Put a big POW on the barracks or on the parade ground, with sheets or paint or anything.'

The B-29s found us and started droppin' us food. They told us there was an airbase on the southern part of the island and told us they were sending in supplies from Okinawa, and from there to the Phillipines.

The only thing you talked about is, What're ya gonna do? Where you gonna eat as soon as you get back? Everybody was goin' to Frisco. They wanted to go to Fisherman's Wharf. Everybody wanted to get some fried oysters or a big steak.

REG RAINER

Private Reg Rainer, 4th Suffolks, 18th Division British Army was taken prisoner by the Japanese at the fall of Singapore on 15 February 1942 and worked on the infamous Thailand—Burma railway.

One of the more peaceful times as a POW was in the evening after you finished the shift. Laying down on your bed or the ground listening to the Pom Pom boats slogging up the river with supplies for those further up the railway, thinking about the folks back home. Wondering if they were alright and what they were doing, had the home changed and the niggling, torturous thought, would we ever get out of this alive. There were no books to read — even if there were, it was nearly always dark when we finished work. Most of the books had long gone, used in the early stages as toilet paper or fag paper. The thoughts in the mind was one thing the Japs couldn't get at but being worn out after the day's work it was not long before we dropped off to sleep. At some camps we used to sing the old songs. This helped to keep the spirits up and the odd joke was also an added bonus. Looking back it was amazing how anyone could survive in those conditions but the British and Australians are a tough old lot and want some knocking down when it comes to it. If it hadn't been for the disease and starvation many more would have made it out. It was our bad luck to be taken prisoner by a fanatical Army bent on destruction, power and greed to rule the eastern part of the world. I know this did not apply to all Japanese.

Reg Rainer, just visible at the end of the top row, left, at Kanasai. Red Cross food was laid out and prisoners were given uniforms by the Japanese just for this photo — many are clearly too small.

When the Burma Railway was finished I was sent with 150 Americans and 250 British to Kanasai in Japan. We sailed in a party of six ships most of which were sunk by US submarines. I was in a lucky ship, although battened down and in cramped condition; the height was only four feet. After this perilous journey we were in for another treat. We were to work in the hills near Kanasai, at a factory which made black gunpowder!!!

On getting to the camp we were sorted out after a kind of interrogation. I was a lathe hand and was ordered to work on one of their lathes — no other Englishman or American was present so I more or less became a Japanese. I took over from a young Jap who I found out was a kamikaze pilot and after about five days he went off to war and was killed some days later. We worked a 12-hour day with other duties when we got back to camp. I was lucky because when going to work the children were going to school and were always talking. I learned about the death of President Roosevelt and the landings in Italy, etc.

Many things were learnt, mainly by experimentation as we tried to survive; they didn't always succeed. Due to our low state of health, many of us suffered with boils, which were very painful to say the least. However, someone came up with the bright idea about milk being injected into the patient's backside. The thinking behind this was to draw all the poison out, away from other parts of the body like the neck and back where most boils seemed to appear. Unfortunately it didn't work very well, but it did create a large lump on the backside. This would not allow the patient to sit down for several days. On top of this nobody was keen to part with the precious milk.

Notification sent to his home that Reg Rainer was alive. A year before this arrived construction of the Death Railway had begun. Many had already perished within this first year of construction.

During the last months of the war I saw the first US plane come over and, being at the factory that made explosive material, I felt a little uncomfortable. One bomb or a few bullets could have set everything off and there would have been very few who would have survived. Those down near Tokyo were in a different situation and, as the air raids there were numerous, many died. Our camp, being up in the hills, was hard to find – so perhaps we were lucky in some ways.

There were rumours of a big bomb being dropped on Japan. Whenever there was a raid we were all taken out on the square and someone would be for it. Also I heard the men talking at work. The Jap on the next lathe told me we would soon die like everyone else because a bomb had been dropped and killed many people. If the guards had heard him he would have paid a heavy price.

It was midday when we were having a break and the guard who was always outside the door with his rifle went away. We opened the door expecting someone to shout to us to start work but nothing happened. The next morning we were told the Jap officer in charge was going to speak to everyone and so we went on parade as usual. A box was brought out for him to stand on, then he told us that he'd been informed that General MacArthur was going to make a speech and we might possibly be going home. In the meantime working at the factory would cease and during the next few days we were to do camp duties. He would give further instructions later. Perhaps this news took the Japs by surprise and may have accounted for their actions in making us work hard.

Unknown to us Japan had surrendered on 15 August 1945. The next thing

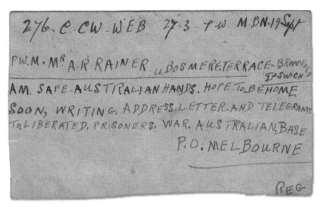

Reg's handwritten letter telling his parents he was safe and well, the first time they had heard from him for three and a half years.

we were told to do was get up on the roof and paint POW on it, so that a B-29 could drop us some food. The B-29 came but was much too high and he dropped his load of oil drums packed with food which missed us. We managed to get a few but in them were cigarettes and chewing gum. I don't think anyone did any chewing. We were so hungry we just ate the stuff. We found out afterwards the drums that missed us killed some of the local people.

Back in Blighty, my parents received a notification letter of my release from a Jap POW camp – handwritten on spare paper. Quite an informal letter for one being away three and a half years.

SHOGO IITOYO

PRISONER OF WAR

Before the war Shogo Iitoyo was an official in Japan's Ministry of Commerce and Industry. He volunteered for service as a front-line administrator.

I was feeling pretty important, having been appointed an Imperial official. But I feared I'd be called up as a common soldier, even though I was married and had been classified C in my army physical. So I volunteered to go to the very front line as an administrator. Because I made that choice I'm alive today.

When I was first in Jakarta, as a general administrator sent from the industrial division of the Ministry of Commerce and Industry, I really didn't need to know Malay. But in October 1944, I was transferred o the Bandung Industrial Lab. Malay was essential for that job, and the language studies I'd taken up after my arrival really paid off. There were about 120 workers from seven or eight different countries – Germans, Russians, Chinese, Dutch and native people from all over...

At home I had a chauffeur, a cook, a male servant, and a female servant. I had a grand residence in the best part of Bandung. It was just like when the American forces moved in to the finest neighbourhoods of Tokyo, in the occupation. I had a garage, a car, and bananas and papayas grew in my garden. I had a guestroom, dining room, three bedrooms and detached quarters for my servants. There I lived with Sakai, the head of the lab – just the two of us.

We needed to have documents available to us, so we were able to secure an exemption from the Army to use Dutch workers. We negotiated with the *Kempetai* [Japanese Military Police] to use Dutch from the POW camps. The Dutch working at our research site had all been at the camps. Their families were allowed to live normal lives outside. I went out of the camp by car at 10 am and picked up those we needed. They worked until 4 pm, and then I took them back. It was only human to develop a relationship with such people, even though they were prisoners. We let them meet their families behind the backs of the military police. They were very appreciative. Many of their families were making a living by selling what they owned to us. Some were even high-class call girls with Japanese partners.

One day the *Kempetai* came to pick up Tiessen. He was then chief of one of our most important technological areas. He was actually a spy. I was told he had hidden a shortwave radio in the ceiling at his home. That was June 1945.

On 14 August, we were told there would be an important announcement the next day. Reception was so poor that we couldn't really make out what was coming in on the radio. We couldn't understand what the Emperor was saying, so we called the headquarters of Field Marshal Terauchi, commander of the Southern Army, to ask what we should do. The Southern Army was going to fight until the last, they told us. We should continue our work as before. The next phone call we got informed us of Japan's defeat. Give up everything. Surrender to the British–Indian Army. Orders changed completely. Things were in total confusion. That day was truly painful. Everyone was staring at us. I sensed sharp, beast-like glares. After a while I couldn't take it any more. I closed my door. Sakai and I just thew ourselves down on the floor and cried out loud, uncontrollably, without regard for status, position or the consequences. Thus overseas, I experienced the collapse of our nation.

On 16 August, Tissen appeared before us. His form still floats before my eyes to this day. He was covered with grime and sweat. He had a strange smell. His beard was overgrown. He loomed in front of me like *Nio-sama* (one of the frightening gods at a temple gate). He slammed his fist down on my desk as if trying to break it. He shouted '*Nippon kara!*' meaning Japan's completely defeated. 'Do you know what that means? Do you repent what you have done?' He told me he'd been tortured by the *Kempetai*, but said, 'Look at me. I'm back now!'

We fell from heaven to hell overnight. Until that moment, I had reigned with impunity as an administrator in the midst of other races. Now, I was under the British–Indian Army command. The officers were all British. The sergeants were all Indians, mostly Gurkhas. We were taken to the camps where the Allied captives had been held. The next day we were stripped naked, except for our

shorts. Even our undershirts were taken. We were paraded down the main avenue of the town over which we had ruled, where the British were now ensconced in the high-class residencies where we used to live. We were told to clean the filth from stopped-up toilets. That was the beginning of our humiliating work. Naked, we cleaned the roads, in plain sight of onlookers of all sorts. If we relaxed even a little they kicked and beat us and called us shirkers or accused us of sabotage. It was really worse than dying. Everybody I knew in Indonesia was watching me.

The Indian soldiers were fairly good to us. Out of sight of their officers they'd let us slack off at their labour, and they discreetly gave us food. They told us they too had suffered under the British as a colony. We understand your station, they'd say. They were relatively generous to us Japanese from the yellow race. They were like gods of mercy. Between 700 and a 1000 people were in our camp. I'm ashamed of myself to admit that we sank to the depths. We fought among ourselves for scraps of foods. The overseas Chinese I'd use at my home, and Indonesians, too, brought me bread and fruit. For the first time, I myself had been degraded. In that forlorn state, I came to understand the warmth of the human spirit.

It was a terrible time. We were forced by the Allies to scrub the runways of airfields with wire brushes under the scorching sun. You got so thirsty you felt you would faint, but there was no water. It was two kilometres away. To get water you had to run there, drink, and run back. Many collapsed of sun stroke every day. Our skin blistered. We told them we weren't soldiers and asked to be excused from heavy labour. We were told 'Japanese are all the same. Civilian or not. If you don't do as we say, we'll kill you.' British Army policy seemed to be to imbue in us the consciousness of our defeat, physically, mentally, and even spiritually. We were there from August to February 1946.

Finally we were taken to Tanjon Priak, a harbour. There a British officer questioned us one by one. He spoke clear Tokyo dialect. He asked us the date of our arrival, our job, and our rank. He already had a complete list in front of him. There was no point in lying. We were given white, blue or red cards. I learned later that red was for war criminals, blue for those under suspicion, and white for those not guilty. I was given a white card. I got really excited, since those with white cards were going to board a ship. It was April and we would be going home. But the ship turned out to be only a 500 toner – much too small to get to Japan. After the ship started moving, we learned we were heading for Galan Island. There were two islands, Galan and Repan, about three hours from Singapore. Several tens of thousands of men from the armies in Malaya, Burma and Java were being shipped to those islands. On our arrival, I was appalled by the people who met us. They were hanging on to walking sticks. Their limbs were swathed in bandages. With their rotting flesh and oozing pus, I thought they were lepers, but it turned out they were suffering from tropical ulcers that come from extreme malnutrition and the breakdown of your circulatory system. Even if you only got a mosquito bite, the next thing you knew, you'd developed a running sore. Within five or six days I looked just like them; you don't ever really recover.

There was no natural source of water. The islands were less than ten kilometres in circumference, and located at the equator. People were dying. When I tried to wake my neighbour one morning, he didn't move. Dead. They had us make a road on that island. My guess is that there was no real purpose for it.

Near the end an observer team from Geneva came, after learning that such a horrible place existed. Then the food got better. We were issued combat rations. We were given only breakfast, but I thought I'd never eaten such delicious food in all my life. That tiny box contained tinned corned beef, butter, cheese, four or five cigarettes, and some sugar. It was really compact. We ate with tears streaming down our faces. When I saw those rations I realised Japan's defeat had been inevitable. I was on that island for 40 days until the former Japanese aircraft carrier *Hosho* came to pick us up on 25 May 1946.

PETER HADLOW

PRISONER OF WAR

Peter Hadlow was a Leading Aircraftsman in the RAF during the war. Captured in Java, he was a prisoner of war for three and a half years. He was held in various camps including Changi Jail in Singapore. He was 23 when he was liberated.

We thought the Japs wouldn't want two or three thousand blokes to feed, they would have gotten rid of us. But our officers were persuasive enough to convince them that we were a good task force and that we would be able to do jobs for them as long as they weren't military, which it turned out to be. We were split up and taken to various prison camps where we all did various jobs.

When we were at an aerodrome in Malang we met up with some decent Japs. I'd got a touch of malaria so I was allowed to do light work on the aerodrome. We were sat in a row against this hangar waiting to be fetched to do various duties. Then a high-ranking officer came and started going down the line asking where everyone was from. Most of the chaps were saying 'London', 'Manchester', 'Liverpool'. A lot of the Japs knew of these places and they were going 'oh yes', well I thought I'm buggered if I'm going to tell him that I come from Manchester or London. So when he came to me he said 'you live where?' I said, 'Grantham, Lincolnshire'. His whole face lit up he said 'Oh Grantham, Red Lion, The Angel Royal, The George'. Of course they were all high-class pubs then. It was my turn to look astonished. He said 'I worked in Cranwell, you come with me.' So he took me off to his office and I had a good day smoking and eating fruit. He said 'I see you another day and we talk.' He was dead against the war and he'd been in Lincolnshire for a year or so learning how to fly. Next time I went up there they'd made this plane work, a Boeing 29. They'd stuck it together and he had got to fly it back to Japan. They were going to copy it as a heavy bomber because they hadn't got anything as heavy as that at the time. I don't know what happened to him.

The last nine months of the war I spent in a camp in the Docklands area of Singapore. There were two or three hundred of us and we were actually working on the very edge of the docks. It was a very vulnerable position because if the Japs hadn't surrendered we would have got blasted to hell. Ours was such a secret camp that the spies and that hadn't found it. They knew about the other ones that were on the island but they didn't know about ours.

It was a few days before the end of the war, when we realised that something strange was happening, the Japs suddenly went from being very aggressive to being gentler and then everything went quiet. They stopped us going out to work and after two days we wondered what was going on and we got up this particular morning and there was no food. We all wanted to find out what was going on, especially when one of the chaps came back and said 'there's no guards in the guard room, no patrol'. We didn't know whether it was a trick. It was the kind of thing which they might have done – waited for you to come out and then start shooting at you. So we hung about and then this one Naval chap climbed a tree in our compound. He started using a bit of language and he said, 'There's HMS so and so,' and it was a British naval ship. We thought we'd better watch things because it seemed strange that it should be like this. Then a few hours later a scouting bi-plane took off from the deck and flew over the camp and I said, 'That's one of ours.' By that time we had got some food and we didn't know quite what to do. Then we heard some shouting; we were leaning against this barbed wire when an Indian regiment came down the road with rifles and bayonets. In the middle of them were all these Jap officers, and it was such a strange feeling we didn't say anything, we just stood there like twits. The British Embassy bloke came down and said to one of the soldiers, 'Get those bloody natives away from that wire.' We shouted back, 'We're not bloody natives, we're British.' He came down and started talking to us and we told him that we were ex-POWs. He thought we were natives because we only had on little G-strings and we were so tanned. As soon as he knew that we were British he told the blokes to pull the wire down. We still didn't try to get out, it was only a couple of days later that we started feeling our way out a bit more.

While we were hanging around waiting to be shipped home, the British Army blokes, for our entertainment, asked us what the Japs used to make us do. Then they started one little gang off digging a hole; it had to be so much by so much by so much, ever so precise. When they'd dug it they had to go on another few yards and start digging another one. Then another gang would come along and they had to fill it all in again. Also there were all these telegraph poles in the ground, and they made another lot get up these poles, five or six at a time. They each had a pot of paint and while one was painting near the top there was another under him painting and so on. Then they all had to come down and obviously they were lathered in paint. Of course it was humiliating for them, very humiliating but we thought it was funny. It's amazing how we didn't take it out on them more because they were really cruel. There was one time we were in camp and we were unravelling barbed wire and putting it on reels. This Jap came down and he could speak a little bit of English and he said, 'You eat food?' He had this bag of roasted peanuts and he gave us all a few in our hand. As soon as he'd gone we ate them but he waited around the corner and then he came back and asked what we were eating. We said, 'You gave us them.' He said, 'No, no, no,' and gave us a good thrashing. That was his way of amusing himself.

It wasn't very long before we got back to England but we had to take it gradually because they said our bodies couldn't stand the change in climate because we had been working in the tropical sun all that time with no shade, no medicine, and very little food. It was about ten days after we were released until the start of the journey home. We had to watch what we ate of course. One ship that we went on gave us a beautiful meal, you know, done ever so well, and what did they give us for afters? Rice pudding. That went over the side, the officer came down and said, 'What's the matter with it, ain't it cooked very well?' 'Cooked very well', we said, 'but we've been eating that for three and a half years, breakfast, dinner, tea and supper.' He said, 'Well, we gave you one of our luxury meals!' We stayed in Solon, now Sri Lanka, for four days and then went back home. Once we'd got back that was it, cheerio lads.

**PRIME MINISTER CLEMENT ATTLEE, 14 AUGUST 1945
BROADCAST ON SURRENDER OF JAPAN**

Japan has today surrendered. The last of our enemies is laid low. ... At this time we should pay tribute to the men from this country, from the Dominions and India and the colonies, to our fleets, armies and forces, that have fought so well in the arduous campaign against Japan. Our gratitude goes out to all our splendid Allies and, above all, to the United States, without whose prodigious efforts this war in the East would still have many years to run. ... Peace has once again come to the world. Let us thank God for this great deliverance and for His mercies. Long live the King!

WILLIAM WINTER

ARMED FORCES

William Winter was a British NCO serving in 38 General Hospital and 5 Field Ambulance in India and Burma, 1942–45.

I got back to Calcutta and travelled by train cross-country to Bombay. From there I was shipped back to England. When I got back in August, the homecoming was quite a hairy one for Betty. I'd managed to get a cable from Southampton to tell her that I was arriving at Waterloo at roughly such and such a time. She was there at the arranged time, but she was faced with about 500 fellas in bush hats, all yellow, all looking the same and she didn't know which one to look for. We were all yellow from Mecaprin and though I didn't suffer from malaria, Mecaprin was a very good suppressant. But eventually I spotted her in a red coat leaning against a pillar and we got together and hired a taxi to take us to St Pancras, which was the nearest station to get to St Albans. When the taxi driver saw that I was wearing my Burma hat he refused to accept a payment.

What struck me about the parade in London was that people were recognising the so-called forgotten army, those who had fought beyond the European theatre of war. I had never seen such crowds in my life and I was choked with emotion. The whole scene was very impressive.

I went to the King William IV pub in St Albans. It had been my regular haunt before going out to Burma, though there was a new proprietor. When VJ Day came along I was in there with a bush hat on and wanted a drink. The landlord had already put towels over all the pumps indicating there was no more drink available. I didn't create a fuss at all, then suddenly the door opened and two fellas walked in and said, 'Two pints please.' He took the towels off the pumps, poured them a pint each and put the towels back on again. I was a bit irate and asked, 'What's the idea?' He said, 'Those are my regulars, don't you know there's been a war on?' At which I blew my top, I could've throttled him. Fortunately I kept my temper and walked out but I felt very bad that he couldn't recognise that there was no way I could've been a regular at his pub.

DIANA LINDO

ARMED FORCES

Diana Lindo served as a driver with the WAAF in Great Britain, 1941–46.

I was quite determined, as I'd been on the sick list during VE Day, that I was going to enjoy VJ day, but we were actually astounded by the pictures of the devastation from the atom bombs. We could hardly believe it when it was made official that the war had come to an end, because quite frankly I wasn't too keen on celebrating VE day when there was still fighting going on in the Far East but now on VJ day it was really over and we could all go mad.

We all celebrated in the camp if we were on duty. But the next day one of the chaps and I decided we would go into town and really see what it was like, because in those days you didn't have television, so you couldn't see all the crowds. So we set off into London. We had quite a lot of money and were hoping for the best, and when we arrived in London and it was absolutely mind boggling, the amount of people. We tried to get out at Shaftesbury Avenue but we couldn't, so we got out at Piccadilly – and I've never seen so many people in my life. All cheering, shouting, singing, waving. We went and had a look around Piccadilly and stumbled along; the Americans were having a high old time throwing crackers out of their rainbow corner club windows. We finally decided it might be prudent to have a meal before we really got going so we pushed our way into the NAF clubs and stuffed ourselves, then we went into a pub and bought a bottle of whisky and a few hats and things and then we went off to Buckingham Palace. I don't think I'll ever forget, everybody was cheering and not a sign of any bad temper, everybody was laughing and climbing off the lampposts, the police were joining in. We spent a long time around Buckingham Palace, yelling for the King and he came out and then we wandered around a bit and came back again and it really was something. Everybody was singing 'Land Of Hope And Glory' and 'God Save The King'. We had flags, rattles, we waved hats. You've no idea how one managed to get these things, I think one probably found them. Eventually when it started to drizzle around ten o'clock we thought we'd better get home. How we got home I'm not quite sure. I had a terrible headache the next morning and my uniform was covered in red paint, but still.

LORD HESELTINE

Michael Heseltine was a child visiting London for the first time.

I can see it, hear it, now, as I write, as though I was watching the event itself.

I will never know what it was that encouraged my parents to take their young son to London for the first time. Perhaps my father had received leave from his posting in Europe where the war had ended three months earlier, or perhaps he had recently been demobilised.

It was a long time ago but my memory is crystal clear. The Regent Palace Hotel occupies a wedge-shaped site with the sharp front end commanding an exceptional view over Piccadilly Circus. I believe – though with no real evidence – that my room was on the twelfth floor. That does not matter but what certainly did matter was its position near the tip of the building and its perspective over the Circus.

It was the night of Wednesday 15 August 1945. That day the Second World War had ended. VJ night and there – a few hundred feet from my window – I saw an indelible snapshot of history.

To many in Europe the war, with its imminent presence and threat, had ended months before. But for the men and women of the Burma Star, thousands of miles away and their friends and relatives back home, the war had dragged on until Hiroshima and Nagasaki changed the world.

Now this really was the end. A kaleidoscope of colour, noise, laughter and tears etched itself on my memory. The pent-up fears and frustrations of those five years in one magic moment of history, overwhelmed by the rebirth of hope and confidence.

*Previous pages: Huge crowds
stop traffic in Piccadilly
Circus. The statue of Eros is
still boarded up.*

KING GEORGE VI, 15 AUGUST 1945
SPEECH TO THE NATION ON VJ DAY

The war is over. You know, I think that those four words have for the
Queen and myself the same significance, simple yet immense, that they
have for you. Our hearts are full to overflowing, as are your own. Yet there
is not one of us who has experienced this terrible war who does not realise
that we shall feel its inevitable consequences long after we have all
forgotten our rejoicings of today.

RUTH PARTINGTON

HOME FRONT

*Ruth Partington was born in 1921 in Manchester and grew up in west London and
Middlesex. During the war she wrote diaries and notes, which she has kept.*

On the evening of VJ, like a lot of people I felt utterly exhausted by the war, but
of course relieved that it had ended at last, though the impact of the atom bombs
was very sombre. I made a note on my VJ night walk: Walk though local streets
to Fulham Road, dirty battered tattered houses, bright with flags, noisy with
bonfires, festive processions in fancy dress, large numbers of children, one group
pathetic, almost symbolic, scrambling around rubble in bombed patch, only open
space in sight. Dressing up, making a bonfire, playing at victory among ruins.
Queues outside smelly pubs and at bus stops, weary faces too tired for much
spontaneous gaiety. Train to Victoria, out into a crowded street under a sky of
Prussian blue, faces and shops lit up. Tower of Westminster Cathedral silhouetted
attracted me. I was reminded by incense and candles of Bruges and Brussels that
I had visited as a school girl. Walked to Westminster, felt thrilled by the beauty of
the floodlight scene, theatrical almost fairylike, the Abbey presenting white stone
slabs to the light, receding into shadow, surrounded by yellow fluttering plane
leaves. Big Ben sharpened and brightened by light, a floodlit flag making a patch
of molten colour in the dark sky, crowds surging up Whitehall, patches of colour
in flags, flashes of colour in rockets, fireworks, a wonderful view from
Westminster Bridge, an oily swirling river, streaked with waving rods of light on
the Houses of Parliament bank, bordered by darker buildings on the opposite
bank, lit above by a clear bright half moon. Home through sober crowds, a bath,

bed, quiet in the flat, sudden noises without rockets, no longer guns or bombs. The news begins to sink into my numbed mind, fighting is finished, a war-weary world must be repaired, rehabilitation must begin, will disillusionment descend? I still live, some have died, many have suffered, we must build peace.

MASS-OBSERVATION ARCHIVE, 10 AUGUST 1945
CIVILIAN ON OXFORD STREET, LONDON

I can tell you where that paper [on the street] came from. My son came home early today, it couldn't have been much more than four o'clock – he works in the income tax office near here. Some of his paper is what he threw down, I expect. He told me that directly they heard the news they all stopped work and went up on the roof and threw down all the paper they could get hold of. Tore up the telephone directories and everything. He told me that they all went home at three o'clock. Oh, they did have a time.

American GIs and English girls dance the conga to celebrate Victory over Japan in Piccadilly Circus, London.

SIDNEY NUTTALL

Sidney Nuttall was serving as a private in the Special Air Service in north-west Europe in 1945. He was in Paris at the end of the war with Japan.

On VJ Day I was in Paris. We were off-duty, myself and three men. We were in a café and we were drinking. The driver and I were sat down drinking, the other two – Cockneys – were stood at the bar drinking Calvados. Very high-powered stuff, Calvados. They'd had quite a lot when the door came open and in came these two tall Texans, they must've been about six foot three apiece. They walked up to the bar and they'd had plenty to drink as well and they shouted, 'Cognac!'

Chappy brought a bottle to pour them a shot and they grabbed the bottle off him and just helped themselves. One of them turned to one of my two stood at the bar and said, 'Say, guy, what do you think about our atomic bomb?'

And our chappy said, 'Whose atomic bomb?'

'Our atomic bomb.'

'Whose atomic bomb?'

'Our atomic bomb.'

And it went on for about five minutes, they were both paralytic. Finally one of the other of our lads got fed up with this and he pushed our other guy aside and hit this American, flattened him. And he said, 'What do you think about *our* atomic bomb?'

So he's out cold on the floor and the other guy says to the Amercian's mate, 'Do you want some?' He says, 'No, I don't want some.' So they picked up the carafe of water they had on the bar and they poured it on him. He came around and he stood up, and he's rubbing his chin and he says, 'Say, you're the first guy that's hit me in five years.' My other blokey hit him and says 'I'm the second!' So they got him out and they disappeared.

Then about 20 minutes later the door opened and the cavalry came in, must've been a dozen Americans bursting in, after blood. They was going to do us deaf. Charlie and I were fairly sober, and you can't fight fair when there's so many, so I shouted for belt buckles. Now, a belt buckle, if you whirl it around your head, it clears a space. So you whirl it and no one wants to get in the way of it because it cuts, as it's got big buckles on. We advanced on them, lined up, whirling the things, and they gradually worked their way around until we'd got them behind us and we're stood in the door and we had a jeep outside. I said, 'Charlie, get that jeep going,' and he shouts, 'Ready!' So the next one goes, and the next one. Finally

I'm stood in this doorway whirling this belt and he says, 'Now!' So I ran out and made a jump for the back, and he set off before I was ready and I didn't make it. I'm hanging on the back and my feet are sliding on the floor, and I've got half the US Army beating me over the head. The lads are dragging me over into the jeep.

We got away, but they would've killed us, no doubt about it. When you look back on it it's funny, it wasn't really funny at the time.

**MASS-OBSERVATION ARCHIVE, 15 AUGUST 1945
HOUSEWIVES SHOPPING IN HAMPSTEAD, LONDON**

– What a miserable day for it. They might have chosen a better day for it if we got to line up like this all morning.
– There were fewer flags out in the streets – only about one house in three displayed flags this time, whereas well over half of them did on VE Day.

NORAH MCGREIG

FRONT LINE

Norah McGreig (née Harris), from south London, joined the ATS (Auxiliary Territorial Service) in 1941, aged 20. She was stationed in Italy from 1943 until 1946.

Norah Harris's ATS and VAD Release Book. She was released from service in May 1946.

My boyfriend was killed in the push for Kohima in the 14th Army and I decided that I wanted to go abroad. We were stationed in Italy. My father didn't agree with it but he didn't say anything because I was 21. He was a bit upset at the time because my brother was in the Royal Marines, so both of us were away at the same time, but it's just one of those things. We're not children tied to apron strings are we? And I'd do it again, if I was younger. I went in at 20 and I was 26 when I came out.

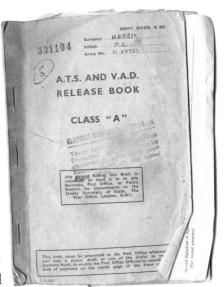

I was in the catering department. We trained with cooks from the London hotels, when we started off. It wasn't really difficult but we had to work hard. We had to be up at about 4.00 in the morning. We used

Nora McGreig, left, with a friend, in Italy, 1945.

to feed 500–600 troops. When we went to Italy we were looking after the people who were working at the Royal Palace in Caserta. I liked Italy but the southern part of Italy was very poor. The women that worked for us, they would take food instead of wages. We used to give them whatever was left to take home to their family, that's how poor they were. Most of the women that worked for us had to give up their money to the Church; they did it because they thought it was the right thing to do. They'd hardly got shoes on their feet.

On VJ Day we weren't allowed out – they kept us in. We had a bit of a party on our own. We were never allowed out on our own because a couple of times our girls got caught and had their hair shaved off by the Italians, because they thought we were taking their boyfriends. We all used to say if it was the Italian women who were fighting, the war would have gone on longer – the men, they were lazy. If we were out on the army lorries (this is in the south,) and we saw a woman carrying a huge bundle on her head and her husband riding behind on a donkey, we'd take him off the donkey and put the woman on it. When we went through Salerno the women were clearing all the rubble up and the men were just sitting there drinking vino.

HENRY PHILLIPS

FRONT LINE

Henry Phillips was a British Merchant Navy seaman who served aboard Royal Fleet Auxiliary tankers 1941–46.

When we arrived in Hong Kong we were still firing. Two days afterwards the surrender was completely signed. Life wasn't normal in Hong Kong, all the Hong Kong dollars were overstamped with the Japanese stamp. The bank that I used to deal with was a one-man operation. He would change any currency into Hong Kong overstamped dollars and the rate of exchange was fixed according to how he felt about it at that moment. On VJ night there were a lot of ships in and there was a large Irish contingent. We all congregated at a big hotel with a square and the party started about six o'clock in the evening. I remember about 2 am we were moving the grand piano from one floor to take it downstairs to put it in the square so we could have everybody dancing. The manager was a very nice man, he saw that we couldn't get it into the lift. So, he persuaded us to carry it and we carried it downstairs with this little man sitting on top of it.

One of our people was a very good pianist and, by the time he began to play, the hotel was seething with people and everybody was letting off fireworks. It was quite a do. I arrived back at the ship in time for my watch at six o'clock in the morning. While I was showering the quartermaster came to me and said, 'There's a rickshaw man asking for you, I think he wants some money.' So I gave the quartermaster some money and said 'Well give him this.' He went and came back and said that he wanted more. I said, 'No, no, that's more than enough.' He said, 'No, you bought the rickshaw last night!' So I was lumbered with this rickshaw for about a week.

TIMUEL BLACK

ARMED FORCES

Timuel Black was 23 when he was drafted into the US Army in 1943. He was in Belgium during the Battle of the Bulge.

VE Day had now occurred. I was in Marseilles. We were being processed for the invasion of Japan. I got word through *Stars and Stripes* that an instrument had been dropped on Japan such as boggled my mind. A city had been devastated with one instrument the size of a golf ball. Most of the soldiers were elated. I was saddened. I wish we had gone and taken our chances. I sensed a new world I had never dreamed of. I went back to my bed and lay there. What does this mean?

VJ Day was declared and we're on the journey back home. I still had a heavy heart. I had considered seriously staying for a while in Europe, but my affection for my family was tugging at me. My father, my mother and I were very close.

We're coming up the Hudson River. You could see the shore. The white soldiers upon deck said 'There she is!' They're talking about the Statue of Liberty. There's a great outburst. I'm down below and I'm sayin', 'Hell, I'm not goin' up there. Damn that.' All of a sudden, I found myself with tears, cryin' and saying the same thing they were saying. Glad to be home, proud of my country, as irregular as it is. Determined that it could be better. Just happy that I had survived and buoyed up by the enthusiasm of the moment. I could no longer push my loyalty back, even with all the bitterness I had.

GEORGE E SCHUPP

George E Schupp was aboard a US Navy minesweeper in the Pacific.

I will never ever forget VJ Day. It was one of, if not the happiest, day of my life! I was a crewman on a Navy minesweeper and we had 'lucked it' by staying alive through Okinawa, two landings in Borneo and then clean-up operations in the Phillipines. There our luck ran out. We snagged a Jap mine, which detonated before we could cut it loose, and it blew away our port screw and rudder. We were then towed back up to Subic Bay where we were waiting for our turn in drydock when the news came in that the Japs were surrendering. Guns were firing up into the air, sailors were jumping off ships into the water, ship's horns were blowing, and everyone was delirious with joy. The medical alcohol was broken out and we had a BIG party! The long bloody war was over and we didn't have to invade Japan. You cannot believe what a relief that was. Our ship was immediately ordered to be decommissioned, repairs were cancelled and most of the crew was scheduled to be sent back to the States. While it took several weeks for it to really sink in, it was like beginning a whole new life.

**PRESIDENT HARRY S TRUMAN, 1 SEPTEMBER 1945
SPEECH ON THE SIGNING OF THE SURRENDER BY JAPAN**

The thoughts and hopes of all America – indeed of all the civilised world – are centred tonight on the battleship *Missouri*. There on that small piece of American soil anchored in Tokyo Harbour the Japanese have just officially laid down their arms. They have signed terms of unconditional surrender.

Four years ago, the thoughts and fears of the whole civilised world were centred on another piece of American soil – Pearl Harbor. The mighty threat to civilisation which began there is now laid at rest. It was a long road to Tokyo – and a bloody one. ...

As President of the United States, I proclaim Sunday, September the second, 1945, to be VJ Day – the day of formal surrender by Japan. ... it is a day which we Americans shall always remember as a day of retribution – as we remember that other day, the day of infamy.

FAITH MCNULTY MARTIN

ARMED FORCES

Faith McNulty Martin, an American journalist, had been working at the Office of War Information in London since early 1944.

When the war ended in Japan, I was on a ship coming back from overseas. I was being returned by the US government and they had put me on a liberty ship that left from France. Everything was in French and it was an interminable voyage, it seemed to me. There were about ten passengers. They all were French and my French wasn't very good. As we approached the USA — we were going to dock in Portland, Maine — one of the French officers came to me and said, 'We heard this tremendous news over the radio.' He said it all in French, you know. 'The war is over! The war is over! You have eradicated Japan with one bomb.' Well, this sounded awfully insane to me, that we had eradicated Japan, that the war could end like that. I had no idea what he was talking about, that we had this enormous bomb. And in the next few hours, as we approached and I saw the shores of the USA, I began to believe that the war was really over, but I didn't understand about this weapon. As we came into the harbour in Portland, it was the moment that they decided to blow all the whistles to celebrate the end of the war with Japan. This enormous surge of sound welled up — every factory whistle, every boat whistle, every horn. It was the most extraordinary sort of orchestral sound, really thrilling. I was certainly moved to tears. It was so wonderful to think that it was over, and it was so dramatic.

DOROTHY GODDARD

HOME FRONT

Dorothy Goddard was a young girl living in Manhattan.

I remember the Italian section on Amsterdam and the big block party we all had together on VJ Day ... my girlfriends and I marched all over the neighbourhood singing patriotic songs until we couldn't do anything but croak. The adults were busy sampling the Italian wine, the Irish whiskey and the Jewish pastries that appeared on tables everywhere. What a grand day that was!

Following pages: US troops returning from Europe fill every porthole as the RMS Queen Elizabeth pulls into a pier in New York Harbour, 31 August 1945.

EDITH SHAIN

Edith Shain, a 27-year-old nurse, was in Times Square on VJ Day.

If you were a New Yorker, you knew exactly where you had to go to celebrate – Times Square. I grabbed one of the other nurses, and we jumped on the subway downtown. We got off at Times Square, and had walked only a short distance when this sailor grabbed me, spun me around, and kissed me. I let him. I thought this guy had been fighting for our country. He deserved a big kiss. It's amazing how long that kiss lasted. After he kissed me I told my friend we better get out of there, so we left. I went home and never told my parents or anyone else about it for years because I was so embarrassed. [But] I knew it was me because of the stockings. It's amazing how people still respond with awe to that photograph, especially when they find out I was the nurse. Even the kids today are enchanted by the romance of it.

YVONNE AND JUNE BRADLEY

Sisters Yvonne and June Bradley (originally Yvonne and June Nakamura) of Japanese and English parentage, were separated from their parents during the war.

We were born in Cardiff, our mother was English and our father was Japanese. Aged five and two, we were taken into 'care' in 1940. Our father was a shipping butcher and had been in this country for a number of years. During the war we don't know what happened and we never saw either our mother or father again.

We looked very Japanese with short black hair and the inevitable fringe. Punishment for our parentage was on a daily basis by way of beatings and several humiliations. On VJ day we were put in the middle of the floor whilst the other children were told to dance round us singing 'We won the war'. We had no idea what was happening to us except that it was a long cruel time before we were sent to Essex in 1948. The war years were ones of dread, fear and terror but for rather different reasons than usual.

WW2 People's War

Previous pages: Snapshots:
celebrations in New York
at the end of the war
with Japan.

SVEA HENDRY

HOME FRONT

*Svea Hendry lived in Midway, a small town in British Columbia, Canada, with her
husband and two small children.*

When the war ended in Europe, my husband, two daughters and I were living in
the village of Midway, British Columbia and we heard the news on the radio.

Svea Hendry with her
husband Ed, centre, in
Canada, 1944. The end of
the war had a dramatic
effect on the lives of
Japanese Canadians.

My own feelings were joy and relief as my brother in the
Canadian Army was still at Aldershot and would be in
the European part of the war at any moment. My
husband's brother and brother-in-law were in the
British Army in Italy. Another brother-in-law died at
Dunkirk leaving a wife and three small children. Just
over a week previously, I had consoled the family of a
lifelong school friend following his death in Europe
while serving in the Canadian Army. Many of the
people I knew were affected in some way by the war,
mostly by death it seemed. The happiness of that day in
early May was clouded knowing that in the Pacific the
war was not yet over. The Japanese did surrender in
August, following the devastation in Nagasaki and
Hiroshima; none of my family were involved in military
operations there. That particular day was a day of relief
as well as being sombre, knowing that many innocent
civilians had died.

The city of Greenwood, nine miles from Midway,
had become a major evacuation centre for people of
Japanese descent since the spring of 1942. Soon there were many families living
in Midway as well. Mostly the Japanese were from the coastal area and the
authorities had thought they were some sort of threat to our security. We were
now living next door to the perceived enemy – but the evacuees had become our
neighbours and our close friends. Some served in the Canadian Army and fought
for our country. This war changed our lives and the lives of the Japanese
Canadians who were victims in this, their homeland.

I remember when they came, thousands of them. In time the city itself became
a hive of activity, with its new residents bringing with them a whole new culture. I
had never seen a Japanese person before the day they arrived. Most families

consisted of old people, mothers and children, as the fathers were conscripted into work camps elsewhere. First thing you know we were introduced to new foods and Japanese dancing. The many talented people gave us dressmakers, plumbers, electricians, dentists, a doctor, a Catholic school, United Church missionaries, bakery, drycleaners and the list goes on. They are a stoic and proud people – at evacuation all their properties had been seized and they were not compensated. The war had personally changed their lives as well as ours. In a few years, my daughter, my brother and my husband's nephew married Japanese Canadians. My brother in England brought home his English wife and small son after the war.

Only when the war ended in the Pacific did we finally think, 'Thank God it's over'. People felt that there would be no more wars. After nearly 87 years on this earth, it seems that wars are still going on. But one thing is certain, we must all be grateful to those who sacrificed their lives for us in the Second World War. We are fortunate that the Allies won.

HIDEKO NAGAI

PRISONER OF WAR

Nurse Hideko Nagai, 490 Relief Squad, Japanese Red Cross, was 18 years old when she embarked for Burma, where she was captured by Burmese and British forces.

Next morning we woke up when the bright sun was shining on us. We followed four Japanese soldiers who happened to pass by. Those without shoes wrapped their soles with banana leaves but they were worn out in a short time. We walked quietly; nobody dared to speak. It started to rain, and when the sun set we lay down on the ground and slept.

Next morning it was not raining. We walked following the soldiers. I felt something strange, and looked around. I heard 'click, click' from down below and then 'click, click' from the opposite direction. When I looked ahead, I could see men with rifles. Suddenly four or five young Burmese came out from the bush. We ten ran into a bush, where a senior private was. We sat around him and asked, 'Please kill us with your grenade. Quick, quick!' Then I saw a young Burmese close by pointing his rifle towards us. The private looked at his grenade and said, 'Ten cannot die with one grenade.'

Chief Nurse sat down on the grass and loosened her belt saying, 'I will kill myself here. You over there!' As everybody looked at her, the private said,

'We could kill ourselves in the final five minutes.' He started to run. Everybody jumped up and left the place; eight of us slipped beneath a fallen trunk of a rotten tree, except Kiyomi and one other.

There horrible worms were slithering around, and as Sumie muttered, 'I don't like these worms,' a stray bullet hit Chief Nurse. I untied my belt, wrapped it around my neck and tried vainly to strangle myself, and then tried to bite my tongue with my teeth. Then I heard Japanese spoken, 'Girls, girls! Don't do the foolish thing.' Instantly I stood up and started to run. Chief Nurse said to me, 'Hideko, don't be captured!' She then gasped, 'Long live the Emperor!' and fell dead.

When I came to myself, I was taken, staggering in semi-consciousness to a small hut. I sat there in a daze. I thought without any anxiety that I would be killed. I was concerned that my hair was in a terrible mess. After a while Chiyoko arrived, painfully supported on the shoulders of the Burmese; she was shot through the right arm and right thigh. Then Sumiko was carried in as she was unable to move, being wounded in six places.

That evening I was told, 'Your friends will be buried.' I went and made sure five bodies of nurses were carefully buried in a deep hole with ritual services. I was given a finger of each of them, cremated and wrapped in paper. Chief Nurse and four nurses were killed in action and were buried on 21 May 1945. I did not know what happened to Kiyomi and Tadako.

In November we were transferred by train to the camp for Japanese located in central India. The camp was in the midst of a big desert and was surrounded by barbed-wire fences. After some time, we volunteered to work at the hospital in camp, and lived in the hospital building. A German doctor, Indian nurses and British nurses worked there and three Japanese ladies were in the kitchen. Soon after I moved to the hospital I attended a birth. When I touched the soft skin of the baby, I felt that now I was in a different world after having nursed only the soldiers.

We received a letter from the Victory Group of Japanese in the camp who believed that Japan had won the war and it was enemy propaganda that she was defeated. And another – the Defeated Group – wrote to us that Japan had surrendered unconditionally. Through lack of information we could not judge which was correct. One day the Victory Group attacked the Defeated Group with bamboo sticks and the situation in the camp became chaotic. In order to quell this riot, soldiers were brought into the camp and fired rifles recklessly; 24 men of the Victory Group were killed. Unfortunately many innocent women and children were shot by their bullets and were brought to the hospital for treatment, which made us very busy.

STANLEY JONES

Stanley Jones was a schoolboy in Trowbridge, Wiltshire.

Strange to say, my memories about the latter part of the war are vague compared to the days of 1944 and 1945 leading up to this time. I have often wondered why, and there could be a number of reasons why the celebration of the end of the war against Japan was not quite the same as VE Day.

Winston Churchill had of course been defeated and Clement Attlee was certainly a different character. VE Day had only been some three months earlier and it was difficult to again work up such enthusiasm and spontaneous excitement in such a short period. This war was not on our doorstep any more, and sadly the troops fighting in those far-off countries have often considered themselves the forgotten army.

As a result of the change of government we were already entering into what was to be a long period of post-war austerity, and many of the horrors of the German concentration camps were being made known. The war had been ended by the dropping of the atomic bombs on Japan.

At the beginning of the war I was just starting infants' school. In June I had left junior school and in two weeks time would be going to the big new world of secondary modern school. I certainly was not looking forward to this, and of course whereas in May we had the excitement of two days' holiday at very short notice, now it was the middle of August and we were not at school. In fact, many families may have been away on their first holiday after the war.

Many reasons, but nevertheless there were still celebrations in Trowbridge with our dear friend Albert Taylor once again organising the children's sports in the park. Again we had our street parties with the children of Union Street returning to Zion Chapel Schoolroom (still suffering from wartime use as a food depot) for their party.

This time, however, there were fireworks in the street, something we had not experienced for years. Boys will be boys! The next morning we collected up all the bits and pieces from spent fireworks, some of which contained gunpowder or whatever it was that made them go bang! All this was put in a pile on the roadside and lit. It's a good job the amount was only small – it could have been a disaster! We certainly had to jump back very quickly and we didn't try it again.

Trowbridge Park has always been the place where the townspeople meet on special occasions – be it sad or glad – and on the Sunday following VJ Day once again a service was held, led by dignitaries from the bandstand. I think, however, that this was rather curtailed by heavy rain and we spent a large part of the time sheltering under the trees.

So the war had ended, but my abiding memory is not of VJ Day but the night before. The surrender of Japan was announced very late on the radio and my dad came upstairs to my bedroom and said, 'It's all over.' I turned over and went to sleep – I could not remember a more peaceful night. No more fighting, interrupted nights, bombs. Peace had come.

WW2 People's War

NANCY ARNOT HARJAN

Nancy Arnot Harjan was a 17-year-old schoolgirl in San Francisco when the war ended.

I do remember VE Day. Oh, such a joyous thing! It was in early May. It was my younger brother's birthday and my oldest brother would be most likely coming home. And San Francisco was chosen for the first session of the UN. I was ecstatic. Stalin, Churchill and Roosevelt met, and somehow war never again would happen.

Hiroshima hadn't happened yet. They met in the June of '45 at the War Memorial Opera House. They needed ushers, so I signed up to do that. I was still in my little Miss Burke school uniform. Little middy and skirt. I remember ushering as Jan Smits of South Africa was taking the stand. I couldn't hear that very well. But I was thrilled to be there. I was excited. I was part of it. And so deeply proud.

My dad, my younger brother and I, and my mother went to the Sierras for a two-week vacation. In the middle of it came August 6, the bombing of Hiroshima. The war was over. He had everybody dancing the Virginia Reel, he was up there clappin' his hands. I was just so proud of him.

Within a week or two, bit by bit, it sank in. Seventy thousand or a hundred thousand or two hundred thousand civilians? It came as a shock after seeing so many war movies with the Japanese portrayed as militaristic brutes. To see women, children and old innocent civilians brutally burned. And Nagasaki! Two of them?

As the war came to an end, I was totally blown away by how quickly our former enemies became our friends and how quickly our former friends became our enemies. I couldn't understand that. I began to ask, What was it all about?

... When I was that young girl, I saw on the news films the Parisian people, with tears streaming down their faces, welcoming our GIs. They were doing what

I wanted them to do. When the Holocaust survivors came out, I felt we were liberating them. When the GIs and the Russian soldiers met, they were all knights in shining armour, saving humanity. I believed in that. It's not that simple. It's true, Nazism is evil. But Nazism is not totally gone. We still have the seeds of all those evils here.

CHARLES HLKADY

FRONT LINE

Charles Hlkady of the US Coast Guard was at Okinawa aboard a Mettawee Class Gasoline Tanker when he wrote this letter to his sister in Chicago on 10 September 1945.

Well the war is over now and they have lifted censorship. I'm sure glad this thing is over with as we have really seen hell out here. So don't ever let anyone kid you by telling you that the 'Coasties' didn't do their part in this damn war. And they have seen tougher times as our ships are all so damn small.

Well I suppose they really cut loose in Chicago on VJ Day. We were unable to do much celebrating out here but when we first received the news this place looked like all hell had broke loose. But all in all those yellow bellied Japs just can't be trusted. We received the word about 8 pm and at 10 pm we had an air raid and the battleship *Pennsylvania* was hit. She was only a few hundred yards from our tub. Those suicide planes were hell and they really threw plenty of them at this place. Those Japs sure did a lot of stupid things out here. There are still a lot of them hiding over on the island. I suppose they don't even know the war is over and our boys are still picking them off.

WW2 People's War

MASS-OBSERVATION ARCHIVE, 10 AUGUST 1945
LONDON CIVILIAN

I didn't know anything about it until my husband came home and he said they were putting out all the flags. He said it will be next Monday the public holiday. It ain't confirmed yet, is it? But I expect they give it on any terms. It's this new bomb. It's a terrible thing. My husband says it'll put an end to all wars but I don't know. I wish you could see into the future sometimes. But perhaps it's just as well you can't! Seems too good to be true, it all being over [continuing to peg out washing], still we don't get any holiday do we! We can't stop doing the bits and pieces just because the war's over.

VINCENT HARRISON

HOME FRONT

Vincent Harrison was a child living in a mining village in the north-east of England.

On VJ Night I was staying in Darlington with Aunty Collis and Uncle Harry, together with two of my cousins, Jack and Rita Downie. Jack and I were alone in the house for much of the evening of the announcement of the end of hostilities and I remember that we celebrated in a small way by going out for fish and chips and I think we also had a bottle of beer between us. We had only just finished eating this celebratory repast when Rita arrived back at the house (from I don't know where) and she too had decided that in the circumstances we ought to have some fish and chips and had bought some on the way home. We considered that the circumstances were exceptional and we managed to eat the second lot of fish and chips too.

Looking back on it, VE Day and VJ Day were both a terrible disappointment to me at the time. We didn't have any television to show us the jubilation in towns and cities around the country but I was well aware that people everywhere were celebrating, sometimes with a singular lack of reserve and, as at the declaration of war, the sense of importance felt by adults around me was strong enough to penetrate even my self-centred view of the world. I knew that it was enormously important but, no matter how much I tried, I couldn't make it feel any different.

And so the beginning of post-war times had arrived and I can now see that, from this time onwards, vast changes were going to come about in my lifetime but austerity was going to stay with us for a long time yet and in fact we still had 'bread rationing' to come. The only difference was that now we couldn't use as an excuse, 'Don't you know there's a war on?'

DAVID GENTLEMAN

David Gentleman was born in London in 1930 and spent his early years in Hertford.

When the war ended I was a boy of 15, living at home in the safety of a small town 20 miles from London. I'd gone to the local grammar school only a few days after the war itself had started: I remember as a nine-year-old sitting by our open French windows and listening with my parents to Chamberlain's mid-morning broadcast declaring that we were at war. There was nothing quite so momentous about the day it ended – all the dramatic things had happened already – but the evening in particular remains vivid in my memory.

During the previous weeks the pictures in the newspaper had made the end of the war seem not merely inevitable but imminent: the westward-heading Russian soldiers and the American troops heading east banging into one another and embracing; British soldiers aghast at the heaped bodies of Belsen and trying to help the naked, stumbling and skeletal survivors. Hitler was dead in the bunker; Admiral Doenitz had signed the surrender only the day before; I'd already heard VE Day announced the previous evening on the plastic Phillips wireless that had replaced our old wooden Pye, and I'd read about it in the morning's thin four-page *News Chronicle*. Victory was what we'd hoped and waited for and the grown-ups had fought for, and now here it was.

Victory as a confidently held idea had been in our minds all through the war, reassuring even if vague and distant, and victory as a word had been worked pretty hard. When fighter pilots who'd been at the school felt high-spirited, it was victory rolls they performed in the sky over the playing fields. The Spitfire that had been parked in the castle grounds had been there as part of Wings for Victory week. We'd eaten our good school dinners under a Dig For Victory poster of a big spade, and I'd walked home past other posters telling us to Save for Victory. (Another had read 'Your blood, your sweat, your toil will bring us Victory', the 'you's and the 'us' much mocked by my bolshie artist father.) We knew how to make our own victory or V-signs too, by sticking up our first two fingers splayed out into a V-shape – patriotic, Churchillian and innocent enough if the hand was palm-outwards but rude and sexual if you twisted it round the other way.

There was a V-sound too: at school we learned that despite Beethoven having been a German, the four beats at the opening of his fifth (V) symphony – three shorts and a long, like the Morse code V that people chalked on walls – now stood for victory. Even the poky little teashop which I passed on my way to school but never once went into was called the Victory Café. So one way and another the word had acquired a pretty familiar ring.

But now Victory had actually arrived. Yet after a shortish spell of elation, the day must have felt a bit flat, even something of an anti-climax, or I'd remember it better. It must have been made a school holiday, for I can't remember anything

David Gentleman.

happening at school that day. What I do remember is the sound we could hear from our own garden all that afternoon, drifting over from the direction of the town common, a big meadow half a mile away where fairs were held. It was the sound of a cheeky French tune which had become all the rage. It had an insistent rhythm, irritating but inescapable, that went *di*-DA *di*-DA *di*-DA; *diddly-da di*-DA; and it was called 'La Raspa'. It went intermittently on and on into the evening and it became for me the unforgettable sound of VE Day.

That evening I wandered over to the common with my brother and one or other of the evacuee boys who had lived with us throughout the war, curious to find out what was going on and eager to join in. The meadow was ringed by big trees and people were gathering there, drifting about and meeting friends and drinking beer and cider and fizzy drinks from glass bottles – cans were still hardly known and plastic bottles didn't yet exist. Everyone was enjoying the May evening – the daylight lasted an hour longer than it would now because of the wartime double summertime. Apart from a few of my schoolfriends larking about, most of the people there were strangers. One of them was a pretty girl of about my age from the shop where my father bought creosote and distemper and the turps and linseed oil he needed for his paintings. I'd occasionally seen her among the paint drums at the back of shop, or on the pavement outside, but had never spoken to her. That evening, keyed-up and excited like everyone else by the occasion, she looked friendly and desirable and I plucked up courage to talk with her for a while. I'd have liked to celebrate VE Day by holding her hand or asking her to dance, but I only knew the slow waltz which was no use with 'La Raspa' throbbing away on the loudspeakers, and unsurprisingly she soon melted away into a group of her own friends; and that was that. Even so, what I remember most vividly about that day, along with the tune, is how she looked: her smile, her mischievous face, her provocative figure and her free-and-easy approachability. She was the first girl I'd spoken to not as someone I already knew but just because I wanted to; and it had taken the adventurous and flirtatious air of VE Day to break down my shyness, or reserve, even this much. Afterwards I walked home past the maltings, across the brewery's sports field and over the river, with 'La Raspa' still dancing tirelessly on in the distance.

But the war was still only half over; now there was School Certificate (GCSEs) to take – the art exam was on polling day of the general election which ousted Churchill – and then came the school holidays and helping to get in the harvest (still with a horse) on a friend's farm. Then one day early in August, our neighbour – a surgeon – came round to our kitchen door (for the first time ever) to tell my parents that something staggering and awesome had happened. The Americans had not only found out how to make an atomic bomb but had dropped it on a city called Hiroshima, and everyone there – half a million people or so, he said – had died. I immediately felt relieved that now the Japs were finished and the war was finally over. At first, however, no one surrendered; then a few days later another bomb on Nagasaki did the trick, though making the point twice over struck me as a bit high-handed – even heartless. In the days that followed, playing tennis with friends on the asphalt courts at the now-empty school, we talked solemnly between sets about the changed situation: before very long, we thought, everybody might have their own bombs and would be able to drop them on us or maybe blow the world up.

In the meantime, though, London was now safe enough to visit again, and at the end of August I cycled to Kew to stay with another schoolfriend, the son of a Jewish couple from Bratislava in Czechoslovakia. The family had arrived here as refugees just before the war and my parents had in a modest way befriended them so that they would not feel wholly isolated and uprooted. At first the boy, who was my own age, had spoken no English, but he had come to the school all the same, put up with some initial teasing about being a German spy, and soon been accepted as one of us.

VJ Day was at the beginning of September. That evening, he and I took the tube, its windows still pasted over with anti-blast netting, from Richmond to Hyde Park Corner to see the second and final end-of-the-war celebrations. Constitution Hill and the Mall were full of people, many in uniforms – khaki, RAF blue-grey, navy blue. The American soldiers and airmen had ties and their uniforms were made of smoother cloth than ours. Everyone seemed more cosmopolitan and grown-up and surer of themselves than the people on the common at home. For what seemed a long time we milled around in the crowd, which meant either being squashed tightly together and lifted disconcertingly off one's feet, or able when the crush thinned to wander about, half-expecting something exciting to happen. People were crowded most densely round the Victoria Memorial in front of Buckingham Palace, the bold ones climbing onto the sculptures and up the lamp-posts to get a better view across to the long façade of the Palace. I can't remember if the King and Queen or Churchill appeared on its balcony while we were there; if not they would have done so later on, and probably by then everyone also got a bit more riotous and victorious and let their hair down. But after a while we got bored with watching all the fairly low-key grown-up revelry so far visible, and took the underground or the green-painted Southern Railway back to Kew; and that too was that. A few days later I cycled back round London to my own home 20 miles to its north. The war was over. It had been fought for a just cause and we'd won. End of story.

My home town carried a few scars: a V-1 doodlebug and a V-2 rocket (the Germans had worked the V-word hard too) and plenty of ordinary bombs had fallen on or near the town, but without causing much loss of life (or so at least my reassuring parents had told me). As a family too we'd got off lightly enough. Despite food rationing we'd always had enough to eat; throughout the war, even in the air raids, nothing even momentarily terrifying had happened to me because of it; none of my friends had been old enough to fight in it; no one I actually knew had been killed. Yet by the end of it I felt as though I'd grown up. But now victory with its triumphant certainties was over too, and we faced its unforeseeable fruits, though we didn't yet know what they'd be. Peace had begun. Yet out of it a new war soon took shape. In no time our old wartime friends and enemies confusingly switched places: we had to learn to think of the Germans and the Japanese as our friends and the Russians as our malevolent enemies in the Cold War that would stretch ahead for four uneasy decades.

W F DEEDES

ARMED FORCES

Bill Deedes spent the war commanding a company of the Queen's Westminsters and in 1944 was awarded the Military Cross for bravery.

Perversely, but in common with many others, I greeted the day the war ended with mixed emotions. It was good to be reunited to loved ones, but for five years, in return for placing my services at the Army's disposal, it had, through the offices of the battalion quartermaster and the padre, looked after me body and soul. The first had supplied my bodily wants, the second gave me a decent burial if I fell. Such useful services had ended. From now on I must stand on my own two feet, clad in a pair of thick and reliable demob shoes. Control over my life, which had been in the hands of others since September 1939, had been restored to me. Partly because those of us who had been fighting our way across Europe for a year were more tired than we realised, the responsibilities confronting me seemed formidable. I wondered where the nuclear power that had so abruptly ended the war with Japan would carry us. I pondered on the soldiers' letters I had been required to censor, and what they portended for their marriages. I sought in vain through an influential relative to see if we could get Queen Elizabeth to broadcast to their wives, 'Be patient, be understanding, it won't be easy...' The post-war divorce rate soared. Then, aiming to shorten the list of grieving families I felt obliged to visit, I wrote down the names of only sons who had been killed in action while under my command, six of them junior officers. When I could lay hands on it, I turned up a collection of Christina Rossetti's poems: 'Does the road wind up-hill all the way? Yes, to the very end.'

FRANCIS CAMMAERTS

FRONT LINE

Francis Cammaerts was born in 1916. A pacifist, he changed his mind about the war after the death of his brother who was in the RAF, and was recruited into the SOE in 1942. He became one of its most successful and legendary agents.

In May 1945 I was on Lüneberg Heath in a Jeep with my dear friend and radio operator Auguste Floras. We were in the organisation called SAARF (Special Allied Airborne Reconnaissance Force) having been sent in, too late, to try and prevent last-minute massacres in concentration camps and prisoner of war camps. My friend Auguste knew that his wife and 17-year-old daughter were in Ravensbrück and we were hoping Soviet troops would take us there to look for them – they did.

What were my thoughts in May and September 1945? Shame and horror. We had ruined the victory with the massacres of Hiroshima, Nagasaki, Dresden, Hamburg and Berlin. I had heard of the stupidity of non-fraternisation. I was to see officers of all four powers using their soldiers to exploit the poverty of crushed people. With a packet of cigarettes or half a pound of coffee you bought a woman or a car or a boat. The behaviour of the victors filled me with shame. The infection of Nazi sadism was to infect us all for another 60–70 years. Torture was to be used by all four powers in Kenya, Algeria, Indo-China and the Middle East – again the officers got the men to do the dirty work and yet my war (the

Resistance in south-east France) had been inspiring and necessary.

I registered as a conscientious objector in 1940. I have not really changed my views.

SIR TAM DALYELL

Tam Dalyell was born in Edinburgh in 1932 and was at Eton at the war's end.

On VE Day I was a new, very new indeed, boy at Eton, having arrived a few days earlier in the summer term. A holiday was declared. Many boys took off home. I couldn't because I was a far-away Scot. The whole place was like a cemetery.

My feeling was selfish, that our family had come through unscathed, in contrast to what had happened to my grandfather at Gallipolli, and others during the Great War. I was relieved that a doodlebug or a V-2 would not hit us.

I wondered how many new teachers would take the place of the 70 year olds who had helped Eton during the war, well past their well-earned retirement. Those who came back in October, having been through Alamein to the Rhine crossing would take no nonsense from any 12 to 17-year-old, and expected us to serve the country, in return for our privileged educational circumstances. Teachers generally treated us like undergraduates.

On VJ Day, my dad, then 58, having had a hard war, was taking his first holiday in seven years, fishing at Lochboisdale in South Uist. We heard of the Japanese surrender beside a loch called Upper Kildonan. Our thoughts were divided between the likely consequences of 'these new and shattering bombs', and the ferocity that August day of the West Highland midges.

Fifty-nine years later, in May 2004, my wife, Kathleen, of 41 years, and I went to Independence, Missouri, as the only identifiable European members of the family – we share a great-grandmother at five removes, Magdelene Daylell – of the 32nd President of the United States, Harry S Truman. The occasion was celebration of the 120th anniversary of Truman's birth. We wondered whether Truman had made the right decision to bomb Hiroshima and Nagasaki. In August 1945, after Singapore, the Soloman Islands... and Okinawa, my parents thought it justified. Sixty years later, I still think that Hiroshima, if not Nagasaki, was justified by the prospect of appalling losses involved in any attack on the Japanese mainland. Truman is a family hero!

JOHN KELLY

John Kelly, nine years old, lived in Tyneside.

The seemingly endless war did end as I approached the age of ten. It had made an enormous impression and memories remain vivid. Who could forget that barrage balloon which 'escaped' from time to time and went lurching over our heads, enough to terrify any German pilot? And there were all those notices asking if our journeys were really necessary or warning us to beware of the squander bug or to save our salvage. We knew that if we wasted food Lord Woolton of the Food Ministry would surely get us! And we had to be careful because 'walls had ears' and spies were 'everywhere' and we were convinced that at least one elderly man in the neighbourhood was a spy even though my mother assured us he was in truth a retired butcher and a 'very nice man'. We followed him from time to time to see what he was up to and we carefully watched his house at night to see if he was signalling skywards with his torch. We pestered soldiers from the local barracks calling out cheekily: 'any badges or buttons soldier?' And often we got some badges and occasionally some chocolate. We ate few sweets which like just about everything else were rationed but we learned to enjoy apples and raw carrots. We all carried our identity cards. We 'dug for victory' on our allotment and took money to school for the 'cot-fund'. Amazingly, like little refugees we sometimes got food parcels at school from America, and tins of sweetened cocoa. And we played endless war games like 'commandos', firing off our toy 'tommy-guns' at the 'Germans' whom we absolutely hated. We were not sure who the Germans were but we knew we lived on an island and they lived in Europe and were trying to get into our country, sending planes over to bomb us. Our soldiers were 'over there' somewhere fighting and, of course, we were winning! At the beginning of the war some of our children had been evacuated to the Lake District and I recall the long queue of youngsters at our local railway station though I was too young to go. Towards the end of the war, when the doodlebugs were dropping on London we actually got some evacuee 'cockney' kids into our northern school. They talked in a very funny way, and we could scarcely understand a word they said. When we were convinced that they were not actually Germans in disguise we became quite friendly towards them but they always seemed foreign.

The radio was all-important, especially 'Children's Hour' and 'Toy-town' and Uncle Mac, but we also listened to the News which always seemed to begin with something like: 'Here is the News and this is Alvar Liddell reading it: yesterday 100 allied bombers raided Germany, three are missing...' And there was 'Workers' Playtime' with Bill Gates and 'Music Hall' and funny comedians like Vic Oliver and Rob Wilton whose jokes always seemed to involve 'the foreman' or 'the sergeant'. And there were of course all those lovely sentimental wartime songs about bluebirds being over the white cliffs of Dover. Sometimes we had a good laugh listening to Lord Haw Haw.

We were very patriotic. England was best. And it was indeed England then, and certainly never Britain. We did not need the Test matches or the World Cup, we had the war! England was winning of course, helped by our friends in Scotland, Wales and America. And the sense of community was warm and palpable. Crime seemed non-existent despite the blackout.

Eventually VE day and VJ Day arrived and we enjoyed happy street parties and bonfires. It was all over. And we had definitely won as we always knew we would! In time the lights did come on and the black-out curtains came down and we all got back to 'normal' but in an odd sort of way, for people of my age who did not remember when there had not been a war, war had been 'normal'. It took a bit of time to learn to live with the abnormality of peace.

WW2 People's War

WINIFRED BASHAM

HOME FRONT

Winifred Basham's diary recorded daily life in Ipswich as the war drew to a close in August 1945.

WEDNESDAY 15 AUGUST – We were awakened soon after we got to bed by fireworks, guns and ships' sirens and when Roger looked out of the window this morning he could see a flag, so we were not surprised to hear that the Japs had really surrendered at last and the war is over.

Percy has a carbuncle or something on his nose so doesn't feel very festive but we drove round the town and saw the decorations. The ships in the docks were the most interesting.

THURSDAY 16 AUGUST – Percy was picking plums all morning. We have made nearly £1 selling to various people at 4d a pound.

This afternoon we went to Felixstowe. They have opened the beach at

Brackenbury though all the mines are not accounted for.

TUESDAY 21 AUGUST – We have had to let the boiler out for the first time since we were married. We simply can't manage on the little coke they send us. What we shall do in the winter heaven knows.

THURSDAY 23 AUGUST – We went to Felixstowe this afternoon. They have now opened the beach from Brackenbury to Cobbolds Point (a man with a red armlet wanders about the beach looking for 'suspicious objects' which is rather sinister).

FRIDAY 24 AUGUST – We have had an orgy of spending today. This morning we went to Footman's to buy me a coat and hat and had to pay £16.16s for the coat – quite an ordinary one at that. This afternoon we blew 40 coupons and over £8 on new curtains for the front of the house. Heartbreaking but necessary. What people with no children's coupons to purloin would do I don't know. It's lucky that I can cut down most of their clothes from our old ones. While Percy was at the Youth Centre I made the curtains and got them up before we went to bed.

THURSDAY 30 AUGUST – I haven't been able to do any washing for two days so tonight in desperation had to turn a lot of old nappies' sides into middle.

FRIDAY 31 AUGUST – I went out shopping while Mrs Scase was here but things are more difficult than ever since the war ended.

WW2 People's War

The aftermath. Refuse workers clean up the streets after VJ celebrations in London.

The publishers would like to thank the following individuals and institutions for permission to reproduce the texts and pictures listed below. Every effort has been made to trace the copyright holders. Weidenfeld & Nicolson apologise for any unintentional omissions and, if informed in such cases, will make corrections in any future editions.

TEXT CREDITS

AGAZARIAN, MARIE
Imperial War Museum (IWM) Sound Archive Interview ref 9579, reel 4

AMBROSE, KENNETH
IWM Sound Archive Interview ref 22682, reel 7

ARNOT HARJAN, NANCY
From Studs Turkel, *The Good War: An American Oral History Of World War II*, Phoenix Press, London, 1984

BBC BROADCASTS
Reproduced by kind permission of the BBC: pages 22, 26, 63, 78, 85, 95

BAILEY, CLIFFORD
IWM Sound Archive Interview ref 4647, reel 11

BARRACLOUGH, ARTHUR
The Second World War Experience Centre

BARTHEL, HEINZ
Courtesy of Tom Holloway, http://timewitnesses.org

BARTLE, JEAN
Interview with Jean Bartle 2005

BASHAM, WINIFRED
WW2 People's War

BAUMAN, JANINA
The Second World War Experience Centre. Taken from Janina Bauman, *Winter in the Morning: Young Girl's Life in the Warsaw Ghetto and Beyond, 1939–45*, Virago Press, London, 1991

BEAZLEY, SAM
Interview with Sam Beazley 2005

BENN, TONY
Courtesy of Tony Benn. Originally published in Tony Benn & Ruth Winstone (ed.) *Years of Hope: Diaries, Letters and Papers, 1940-62*, Hutchinson, London, 1994

BICHENKO, IVAN
The Voice Of Russia, www.vor.ru/world.html

BILEK, ANTON
From Terkel, *The Good War*, 1984

BLACK, TIMUEL
From Terkel, *The Good War*, 1984

BRADFORD, DAVID
IWM, Sound Archive Interview ref 9232, reel 2

BRADLEY, YVONNE & JUNE
WW2 People's War

BREITBURG, VICTOR
Originally published on www.newsday.com. Copyright Victor Breitburg

BROWN, ELSIE
Reproduced from from *Ten Days In May* by Russell Miller (Copyright © Russell Miller 1995) by permission of PFD on behalf of Russell Miller

BROWN, JOHN
IWM Sound Archive Interview ref 5355, reel 2

BUNGARD, KENNETH
IWM Sound Archive Interview ref 13040, reel 4

CAMMAERTS, FRANCIS
Courtesy of Francis Cammaerts

CARMICHAEL, IAN
Courtesy of Ian Carmichael. Originally published in Ian Carmichael, *Will the Real Ian Carmichael...*, Macmillan, London, 1979

CARRINGTON, LORD
Courtesy of Lord Carrington

CHAMPION, ELIZABETH
Courtesy of Elizabeth Champion

CHANNON, SIR HENRY
From Robert Rhodes James (ed.) *'Chips':*

The Diaries Of Sir Henry Channon, Phoenix Press, London 1996

CHURCHILL, WINSTON SIR
Reproduced with permission of Curtis Brown Ltd, London on behalf of The Estate Of Sir Winston S. Churchill. Copyright Winston S. Churchill

CHURCHILL, WINSTON (JR.)
Interview in Sunday Telegraph Magazine, 5 May 1985. Reproduced with kind permission of the Telegraph Group plc.

CLOSTERMANN, PIERRE
From Pierre Clostermann, *The Big Show: The Greatest Pilot's Story of World War II*, Weidenfeld & Nicolson, London, 2004

COOPER, DUFF
Courtesy John Julius Norwich. From the forthcoming publication John Julius Norwich (ed.) *The Duff Cooper Diaries*, © 2005 John Julius Norwich, to be published by Weidenfeld & Nicolson, London, autumn 2005

COWARD, NOËL
From Graham Payn & Sheridan Morley (eds.), *The Noël Coward Diaries*, Weidenfeld & Nicolson, London, 2000

DALE, STEPHEN
IWM Sound Archive Interview ref 14582, reel 8

DALYELL, TAM
Courtesy of Tam Dalyell

DAVIES, JOHN
Courtesy of John Davies

DAVIES, PATRICIA
Courtesy of Patricia Davies

DAVYDOVA, YELENA
The Voice Of Russia, www.vor.ru/world.html

DE ROTHSCHILD, EDMUND
Courtesy of Edmund De Rothschild. Originally published in Edmund de Rothschild, *A Gilt Edged Life*, John Murray, London, 1998

DEEDES, W. F.
Courtesy of W. F. Deedes

DELATTRE, HÉLÈNE
Courtesy of Tom Holloway http://timewitnesses.org

DIDDEN, MARGUERITE
Courtesy of Marguerite Didden

DIGHT, CARMELLA
Courtesy of Tom Holloway http://timewitnesses.org

DUNCAN, DAVID DOUGLAS
Courtesy of David Douglas Duncan. Originally published in David Douglas Duncan, *Photo Nomad*, W. W. Norton & Company, New York, 2003

DUNN, CLIVE
Courtesy of Clive Dunn. Originally published in Clive Dunn, *Permission to Speak*, Plane Tree Press, Powys, 1986

DUNN, WARREN
From Steven Spielberg, *The Last Days*, Weidenfeld & Nicolson, London, 1999

DYKE, FREDDY
WW2 People's War

ECKSTAM, EUGENE
Wisconson World War II Stories

EDWARDS, WYN
WW2 People's War

EISENHOWER, DWIGHT
Originally quoted in Rober Westall (ed.), *Children of the Blitz: Memories of Wartime Childhood*, Macmillan, London, 1995

EVANS, ED
Courtesy of Ed Evans

EVANS, JAMES
IWM Sound Archive Interview ref 14841, reel 4

FARRAND RADLEY, ARTHUR
From James Lucas, *The Last Days Of The Reich*, Cassell, London, 2000

FLEISCHER, JULIA
Courtesy of Peter Barber

FREE, HARRY
WW2 People's War

FREEMAN, ROGER
Courtesy of Roger Freeman

GAYLOR, SHEILA
WW2 People's War

GEDDES DA FILICIA, GIORGIO
Courtesy of Giorgio Geddes Da Filicia

GENTLEMAN, DAVID
Courtesy of David Gentleman

GEORGE VI, KING
From Sarah Bradford, *King George VI*, Weidenfeld & Nicolson, London, 1989

GIACCHI, PATSY
Courtesy of '9 Lives' Aaron Elson, Chi Chi Press

GLASER, WILLIE
Courtesy Susanne Reiger, Gerhard Jochem

GLUCK, BILL
Vancouver Holocaust Education Centre

GODDARD, DOROTHY
From www.heightsmemories.com

GOLDSTEIN ROY
WW2 People's War

GRIBOV, YURI
The Voice Of Russia, www.vor.ru/world.html

GRUBBA, ERWIN
The Second World War Experience Centre

GUTHRIE, MALCOM
IWM Sound Archive Interview ref 8153, reel 4

HADLOW, PETER
Interview with Peter Hadlow 2005

HALL-WILLIAMS, JOHN
IWM Sound Archive Interview ref 15323, reel 5

HARRISON, VINCENT
The Second World War Experience Centre

HELLER, JOSEPH
From 'New Yorkers Remember V-E Day' By DeQuendre Neeley and Michael Dorman. Published on www.newsday.com Copyright, 2005, Newsday. Distributed by Tribune Media Services. Reprinted with permission.

HENDRY, SVEA
Courtesy of Svea Hendry

HESELTINE, LORD
Courtesy of Lord Heseltine

HILARY, FATHER
Courtesy of Father Hilary

HILKADY, CHARLES
WW2 People's War

HINCHCLIFFE, KEITH
WW2 People's War

HIRAKUBO, MASAO
Interview with Masao Hirakubo 2005

HITCHCOCK PULLMAN, SALLY
From *Letters Home: Memoirs of One Army Nurse in the Southwest Pacific in World War II*, Sally Hitchcock Pullman, Author House, 2004

HOBBS, CHARLIE
IWM Sound Archive Interview ref 18423, reel 5

HOLNESS, CECIL
Courtesy of the Museum of London Oral History Project

HORGAN, NORA
Courtesy of Tom Graves

HUNTER, DAVID
WW2 People's War

HUT, LUCIEN
From C. Leroy Anderson, Joanne R. Anderson, Yundsuke Ohkura, Mike Mansfield (eds.), *No longer Silent: World Wide Memories of the Children of World War II*, Pictorial Histories Pub Co., 1995

HUTTON-FOX, DENNIS
Courtesy of Margaret Last

IITOYO, SHOGO
From Haruko Taya Cook & Theodore F.Cook, *Japan At War*, Phoenix Press, London, 1992

IVE, RUTH
Interview with Ruth Ive 2005

JASIEWICZ, JULIUS
Courtesy of the Jasiewicz family

JOHNSON, HUGH
Courtesy of Hugh Johnson

JOHNSON, ODELL
WW2 People's War

JOHNSTON, LORNA
Quotes from Lorna 'Whytie' Johnston appear by courtesy of Angell Productions Pty Limited, 130 Brooklyn Road, Brooklyn, NSW 2083, Australia, and can be found at www.angellpro.com.au/women.htm

JONES, STANLEY
WW2 People's War

KELLY, JOHN
WW2 People's War

KELLY, PHILIP
WW2 People's War

KIRSCH, HEIDI
Courtesy of Heidi Kirsch

KORZENIEWSKI, JANUSZ
IWM sound archive, ref 20065, reel 8

KUJAWINSKA, DANUTA
Courtesy of Danuta Kujawinska

LANGDON, DAVID
Courtesy of David Langdon

LAST, NELLA
From Richard Broad & Susie Flemming (eds.), *Nella Last's War: A Mother's Last Diary*, Falling Wall Press, Bristol, 1981

LEWIS, MICHAEL
IWM sound archive 4833, reels 8 and 9

LIEBERMAN, CELINA
Vancouver Holocaust Education Centre

LINDO, DIANA
IWM sound arhive, ref 23435, reels 4 and 5

LIPSON, MILTON
From 'New Yorkers Remember V-E Day' Copyright, 2005, Newsday. Distributed by Tribune Media Services. Reprinted with permission.

LOEWE, LOTHAR
From J. Steinhoff, P. Pechel & D. Showalter (eds.), *Voices From the Third Reich*, Da Capo Press, New York, 1994

LOFFMAN, PHIL
IWM sound archive, ref 21614, reel 14

LOWY, LEO
Vancouver Holocaust Education Center

LYDON, KATHLEEN
Interview with Kathleen Lydon 2005

LYNN, DAME VERA
Interview with Dame Vera Lynn 2005

MASS-OBSERVATION ARCHIVE
The Mass-Observation Society, a pioneering social research organisation, conducted an enormous investigation into all aspects of British social life, observing and recording the experiences and opinions of members of the public between 1937 and 1965. All material published by kind permission of the Trustees of the M-OA, University of Sussex: p.23 – Mass-Observation Archive, Victory Celebrations, TC49, 1A; p.59 – Mass-Observation Archive, Victory Celebrations, TC49, 1A; p.70 – Mass-Observation Archive, Victory Celebrations, TC49, 1A; p.79 – Mass-Observation Archive, Victory Celebrations, TC49, 1C; p.84 – Mass-Observation Archive, Victory Celebrations, TC49, 1C; p.85 – Mass-Observation Archive, Victory Celebrations, TC49, 1C; p.99 – Mass-Observation Archive, Victory Celebrations, TC49, 1C; p.110 – Mass-Observation Archive, Victory Celebrations, TC49, 1C; p.106 – Mass-Observation Archive, Victory Celebrations, TC49,1C; p.185 – Mass-Observation Archive, Victory Celebrations, TC49,1B; p.281 – Mass-Observation Archive, Victory Celebrations, TC49,1E; p.283 – Mass-Observation Archive, Victory Celebrations, TC49, 1E; p.299 – Mass-Observation Archive, Victory Celebrations, TC49, 1E

MCGREIG, NORAH
Interview with Norah McGreig 2005

MCNULTY, FAITH MARTIN
From L. Wood, J. Scott and Brown University's Scholarly Technology Group 1997: What Did You Do In The War Grandma?

MORISON, WALTER
WW2 People's War

MORROW, ALBERT
IWM Sound Archive ref 13650, reel 3
NAGAI, HIDEKO
From Kazuo Tamayama & John Nunnelly (eds.) *Tales by Japanese Soldiers*, Cassell, London, 2000
NAGAI, DR TAKASHI
From the website of the Nagasaki Atomic Bomb Museum
NEALE, FRED
WW2 People's War
NEL, ELIZABETH LAYTON
IWM sound archive ref 15119, reel 2
NICOLSON, HAROLD
From Nigel Nicolson (ed.) *The Harold Nicolson Diaries 1907–63*, Weidenfeld & Nicolson, London, 2004
NUTALL, SIDNEY
IWM sound archive ref 21116, reel 8
OBA, SADAO
Courtesy of Sadoa Oba
OLIVIER, EDITH
From Penelope Middleboe (ed.), *Edith Olivier: From Her Journals, 1924-48*, Weidenfeld & Nicolson, 1989
OWENS, ELSIE
From 'New Yorkers Remember V-E Day' Copyright, 2005, Newsday. Distributed by Tribune Media Services. Reprinted with permission.
PALMER, EDWARD
IWM Sound Archive ref 14800, reel 5
PARGETER, EDITH
Reproduced from from *Ten Days In May* by Russell Miller (Copyright © Russell Miller 1995) by permission of PFD on behalf of Russell Miller
PARKER, DAVID
Courtesy of Jim Parker
PARTINGTON, RUTH
Courtesy of the Museum of London Oral History Project
PARTRIDGE, FRANCES
From Rebecca Wilson (ed.), *The Diaries of Frances Partridge, 1939-72*, Phoenix Pres, London, 2001
PEMBERTON, JAMES
WW2 People's War
PETTIT, MARY
WW2 People's War
PHILLIPS, HENRY
IWM Sound Archive ref 14768, reel 5
POLIZZI, MARY
From 'New Yorkers Remember V-E Day' Copyright, 2005, Newsday. Distributed by Tribune Media Services. Reprinted with permission.
RAINER, REG
Courtesy of Reg Rainer and the FEPOW community: www.fepow-community.org.uk
RICKETTS, ALBERT
WW2 People's War
ROFFEY, JAMES
WW2 People's War
ROZEN, MARIETTE
Vancouver Holocaust Education Centre
SAMSON, SUZANNE
Courtesy of the Museum of London Oral History Project
SAWYER, MARY
IWM Sound Archive, ref 13742, reel 4
SCHMIDT, HUBERT
From *Hitler Youth to US Air Force*, a personal history by Hubert Schmidt, courtesy The History Place: www.historyplace.com
SCHUPP, GEORGE E
Courtesy of George E Schupp
SCOTT, LENN
WW2 People's War
SHAIN, EDITH
From the *Los Angeles Daily News*: www.dailynews.com
SHAW, TERRY
WW2 People's War
SMITH, TOM
WW2 People's War

SOMERHAUSEN, ANNE
From Anne Somerhausen, *Written In Darkness; A Belgian Woman's Record of the Occupation 1940-45*, Knopf
SOROKIN, GREGORY
The Voice Of Russia, www.vor.ru/world.html
SPIRO, LESLIE
Vancouver Holocaust Education Center
STAFFORD, EDNA
WW2 People's War
STANSTEDT, ROGER
IWM Sound Archive ref 14130, reel 4
STYAN, JOAN
WW2 People's War
UNKNOWN
From James Lucas, *The Last Days Of The Reich*, Cassell, London, 2000
VANDERHEYDEN, KEES
Courtesy of Tom Holloway
http://timewitnesses.org
VON SCHWANENFLUEGEL, DOROTHEA
From Dorothea von Schwanenfluegel, *Laughter Wasn't Rationed: A Personal Journey Through Germany's World Wars and Postwar Years*, Tricor Press, 2001
WADINGTON, EDWARD
Veterans History Day Project
WASSEM, VIOLETTE
Courtesy of Tom Holloway
http://timewitnesses.org
WATERSON, KEN
WW2 People's War
WEIDENFELD, LORD
Courtesy of Lord Weidenfeld
WEINBERG, ROLF
IWM Sound Archive ref 19912, reel 7
WHITEHEAD, CHARLES
WW2 People's War
WINKLER, EDUARD
IWM Sound Archive ref 18523, reel 4
WINTER, WILLIAM
IWM Sound Archive ref 16251, reel 3
YOSHINO, SHUICHIRO
From Tamayama & Nunnelly, *Tales by Japanese Soldiers*, 2000
ZABELKA, GEORGE
From Terkel, *The Good War*, 1984
ZBIROHOWSKA-KOSCIA, HANNAH
Interview with Hannah Zbirohowska-Koscia

PICTURE CREDITS

2   Bettmann/Corbis
8   Vera Lynn Archive
9   TopFoto.co.uk
    The ArenaPAL Picture Library
10 Vera Lynn Archive
11 Keystone /Getty Images
12 Mary Evans Picture Library
13 Vera Lynn Archive
14 Bettmann/Corbis
16 Courtesy of Wolf Suschitzky
18 Imperial War Museum Photograph Archive
21 Fox Photos/Getty Images
23 Courtesy of Dorothea von Schwanenfluegel and Tricor Press
25 Yevgeny Khaldei/Corbis
27 Novosti Photo Library
31 Associated Press, AP
33 Courtesy of Tom Holloway, http://timewitnesses.org
35 The Second World War Experience Centre
36 Fred Ramage/Keystone/Getty Images
40 From Walter Morison, *Flak and Ferrets*, Sentinel Publishing, 1995
41 From Walter Morison, *Flak and Ferrets*, Sentinel Publishing, 1995
42 Courtesy of Margaret Last
44 Courtesy of Margaret Last

45   Courtesy of Margaret Last
46   Courtesy of Giorgio Geddes Da Filiciaia
53   The National Archives (PRO): ref. CAB 120/559
56   Horace Abrahams/Keystone/Getty Images
59   Vancouver Holocaust Education Center
60   Vancouver Holocaust Education Center
61   Vancouver Holocaust Education Center
62   Vancouver Holocaust Education Center
65   From C. Leroy Anderson, Joanne R. Anderson, Yundsuke Ohkura, Mike Mansfield (eds.), *No longer Silent: World Wide Memories of the Children of World War II*, Pictorial Histories Pub Co., 1995
67   Courtesy of Jim Parker
68   Courtesy of Jim Parker
69   Courtesy of Jim Parker
73   Horace Abrahams/Keystone/Getty Images
77   Picture Post/Hulton Archive/Getty Images
78   The Trustees Of The Mass-Observation Archive, University Of Sussex
80   Courtesy of Tony Benn
87   Picture Post/Hulton Archive/Getty Images
90   Central Press/Getty Images
91   The British Film Institute
94   From Robert Rhodes James (ed.) *'Chips': The Diaries Of Sir Henry Channon*, Phoenix Press, London 1996
95   From Nigel Nicolson (ed.) *The Harold Nicolson Diaries 1907–63*, Weidenfeld & Nicolson, 2004
96   Bettmann/Corbis
100 ITN Stills Archive
104 WW2 People's War
105 Courtesy of Sam Beazley
106 Courtesy of Patricia Davies
107 Courtesy of Patricia Davies
108 Courtesy of Patricia Davies
110 From Rebecca Wilson (ed.), *The Diaries of Frances Partridge, 1939-72*, Phoenix Press, London, 2001
114 Courtesy of Kathleen Lydon
115 Courtesy of Ruth Ive
118 Bettmann/Corbis
122 Keystone/Getty Images
125 Keystone/Getty Images
130 Bettmann/Corbis
132 Courtesy of Lord Weidenfeld
136 Courtesy of Pierre Clostermann
138 Courtesy of Marguerite Didden
141 Courtesy of Tom Holloway: http://timewitnesses.org
141 Illustration by S. Gunther. The Bridgeman Art Library
142 Courtesy of David Langdon
143 Popperfoto.com
145 Archives Charmet, The Bridgeman Art Library
146 Keystone/Getty Images
149 Mander & Mitchenson Theatre Collection
154 The National Archives (PRO): ref.WO 204/6513
158 The National Archives (PRO): ref. FO 371/44647
158 The National Archives (PRO): ref. FO 371/44648
161 Courtesy of Roger Freeman
162 Popperfoto.com
164 WW2 People's War
166 Imperial War Museum, Department of Documents
170 Courtesy of Mary Edwards
171 Tom Holloway

http://timewitnesses.org
173 Courtesy of the Jasiewicz family
176 Alexander Ustinov/Slava Katamidze Collection/Getty Images
178 Ivan Shagin/Slava Katamidze Collection/Getty Images
183 Vancouver Holocaust Education Center
184 Vancouver Holocaust Education Center
187 WW2 People's War
189 Vancouver Holocaust Education Center
190 Vancouver Holocaust Education Center
192 Stevens/Topical Press Agency/Getty Images
195 Courtesy of Ed Evans
197 Courtesy of Heidi Kirsch
200 Willie Glaser www.home.t-online.de
201 Willie Glaser www.home.t-online.de
203 The National Archives (PRO): ref. FO 898/583
205 From the collection of the Polish Underground Movement Study Trust-London
206 Corbis
209 Vancouver Holocaust Education Center
210 Vancouver Holocaust Education Center
211 Vancouver Holocaust Education Center
212 Vancouver Holocaust Education Center
214 Courtesy of Danuta Kujawinska
218 Fred Ramage/Keystone/Getty Images
218 Courtesy of Peter Barber
220 Courtesy of Peter Barber
221 Courtesy of Peter Barber
224 The National Archives (PRO): ref. FO 96/222
230 W&N Archive
233 Keystone/Getty Images
236 WW2 People's War
237 From 'Brave Women', Angell Productions: www.angellpro.com.au/rabaul.html
240 The Washington National Archive, 342-FH-3A-49434-K-KE
243 Express/Express/Getty Images
244 Courtesy of Sadao Oba
246 Three Lions/Getty Images
249 Courtesy of David Douglas Duncan
255 US Naval Historical Center
262 Courtesy of Masao Hirakubo
265 Popperfoto.com
266 Courtesy of Reg Rainer and the FEPOW community
267 Courtesy of Reg Rainer and the FEPOW community
268 Courtesy of Reg Rainer and the FEPOW community
270 Keystone/Getty Images
278 Keystone/Getty Images
281 Popperfoto.com
283 Courtesy of Norah McGreig
284 Courtesy of Norah McGreig
288 Associated Press Archive,AP
291 Lt. Victor Jorgensen/US Navy/Time Life Pictures/Getty Images
292 ITN Stills Archive
294 Courtesy of Svea Hendry
302 Courtesy of David Gentleman
305 Courtesy of Special Forces Club. From Patrick Howarth, *Undercover: The Men and Women of the SOE*, Weidenfeld & Nicolson, London, 2000
309 Popperfoto.com
312 Courtesy of Ronnie Clelland
Front endpaper: W&N Archive
Back endpaper: Hulton-Deutsch Collection/Corbis

Able Seaman Clelland returns from the war with a box of exotic fruits for his mother.

Page 3:   *Wall Street, 7 May 1945.*
Page 14:   *The giant liner* Queen Mary *bringing over 15,000 troops back to the United States.*
Pages 16–19:   *Contrasting reactions to the end of the war: Piccadilly Circus in London on VE Day 1945.*

Front endpaper: *Piccadilly Circus, VJ Day.*
Back endpaper: *One of the many bonfires lit in Britain on VE Night.*

Front jacket: Victory party for children in south London
© Hulton-Deutsch Collection/Corbis

Back jacket: US 9th Army link up with Russians near Griebo
© Fred Ramage/Keystone/Getty Images

Front flap: A returning soldier greets his family
© Jack Esten/Getty Images

Back flap: Servicemen celebrate peace, August 1945
© Hulton Archive/Getty Images

First published in Great Britain in 2005
by Weidenfeld & Nicolson

Text copyright resides with either the writer
or the estate of each piece.
Design and layout copyright © Weidenfeld & Nicolson
2005

A CIP catalogue record for this book
is available from the British Library.

ISBN 0 297 84417 2

Design director: David Rowley
Designed by DW Design
Design assistance by Justin Hunt
Edited by Jennie Condell
Research by Katie Anderson and Tom Graves
Editorial by Brónagh Woods, Bea Hemming and
Rosie Anderson
Chapter introductions by Ian Drury

Printed and bound in Italy by Printer Trento srl

Weidenfeld & Nicolson
The Orion Publishing Group Ltd
Wellington House
125 Strand
London WC2R 0BB

www.orionbooks.co.uk